# Folk Travelers
## Ballads, Tales, and Talk

*Edited by*

Mody C. Boatright,
Wilson M. Hudson, Allen Maxwell

Publications of The Texas Folklore Society Number XXV

University of North Texas Press
Denton, Texas

Copyright © 2000 by The Texas Folklore Society

All rights Reserved

Copyright © 1953 by The Texas Folklore Society
Southern Methodist University Press

Printed in the United States of America

Permissions:
University of North Texas Press
P. O. Box 311336
Denton, Texas 76203
(940) 565-2142 FAX (940) 565-4590

ISBN 1-57441-109-8

# Contents

The Traveling Anecdote . . . . . . . . . . . . . 1
   J. Frank Dobie

Folklore in Natural History . . . . . . . . . . . 18
   Roy Bedichek

The Names of Western Wild Animals . . . . . . . . 40
   George D. Hendricks

Bonny Barbara Allen . . . . . . . . . . . . . . 47
   Joseph W. Hendren

Aunt Cordie's Ax and Other Motifs in Oil . . . . . . . 75
   Mody C. Boatright

The Western Ballad and the Russian *Ballada* . . . . . . 86
   Robert C. Stephenson

Signature in Ballad and Story . . . . . . . . . . . 97
   Robert C. Stephenson

The Love Tragedy in Texas-Mexican Balladry . . . . . . 110
   Américo Paredes

Come Buy, Come Buy . . . . . . . . . . . . . 115
   Elizabeth Hurley

Folkways on Bear Creek . . . . . . . . . . . . . 139
   E. J. Rissmann

Emerson and the Language of the Folk . . . . . . . . 152
   John Q. Anderson

Tales of Neiman-Marcus . . . . . . . . . . . . . 160
   James Howard

Origins of Uvalde County Cattle Brands . . . . . . . . 171
   Orlan L. Sawey

I Want My Golden Arm . . . . . . . . . . . . . 183
   Wilson M. Hudson

Black and White Magic on the Texas-Mexican Border . . . 195
    GABRIEL CÓRDOVA

Weather Talk from the Cap Rock . . . . . . . . . . 200
    EVERETT A. GILLIS

The Devil in the Big Bend . . . . . . . . . . . 205
    ELTON R. MILES

Wham, Jam, Jenny-Mo-Wham . . . . . . . . . . 217
    PEGGY HENDRICKS

Richard's Tales . . . . . . . . . . . . . . . 220
    RICHARD SMITH

Contributors . . . . . . . . . . . . . . . . 254

Index . . . . . . . . . . . . . . . . . . 259

# Folk Travelers
## Ballads, Tales, and Talk

J. FRANK DOBIE

# The Traveling Anecdote

WHEN TWO JET PLANES become a commonplace in family garages over the earth, hardly a traveler even then will be as much at home in as many lands of varying languages and latitudes as many tales and anecdotes have been for centuries. Any good story travels and keeps on traveling. As it travels, it both adds and loses, but keeps its shape. If it brings out the characteristic of some individual, it will before long find itself attached to another individual, illustrating a similar characteristic in him. Its point, like that of a proverb, a poem, or a text from the Bible, has universal applicability. Many a lifeless and pointless story gets into print, but that is no indication of its potency. Unless it have potency it cannot travel. After a potent traveler becomes familiar to nearly everybody it will stop for a while and rest, but it will not die. It will set out again when there are fresh hearers. The test of a story is not whether it is old, but whether it has vitality enough to keep from wearing out. Eddie Foy said he'd stick to the jokes proven by time and let somebody else test out the new ones.

A quarter of a century or more ago a friend of mine named Gates Thomas, whose people settled in Texas soon after Texas became a republic, who was a professor of English in a college and who collected folklore and knew what folklore is, told me a family story that for more than a hundred years has been considered historical.

Colonel Mason Thomas, grandfather to Gates Thomas, was a great admirer of Sam Houston. He had a plantation down the Colorado River (for Texas has its own Colorado) and was a member of the Texas Congress. One election year Sam Houston sent word that he would be at the Thomas plantation on a certain date. He was running for the presidency of the republic and had three opponents.

Colonel Mason Thomas spread the word up and down the country. Aided by other adherents of Houston, he killed several fatted calves and barbecued them.

On the appointed day Houston was on hand, hearty and ample. He was to address the crowd after dinner — eaten in the middle of the day, of course — but that did not prevent his delivering himself on the main issues, as well as on side issues, beforehand. He sat in a big cowhide-bottomed chair devouring barbecued beef, fried chicken, potato salad, with plenty of vinegar, onions and pickles in it, a special dish of turnip greens for his table, cornbread and biscuits, and other solids. He was a man of tigerish energy. His eating never interfered with his talking and his talking never interfered with his eating. During the meal he disposed of his opponents in a summary order. One, he said, had left Georgia for stabbing a man in the back; the second was a common hog thief, and the third was "nothing but a damned vegetarian."

At about this point, the talk having shifted to vegetarianism on principle, dessert was brought on. Most of the crowd helped themselves to food, but President Houston naturally received special service. Dessert was hot rice pudding, than which nothing this side of melted lead can be hotter. An ample bowl of it, topped by egg custard toasted a golden brown, was placed before old Sam.

Intent on pursuing the damnability of vegetarianism, he took an ample spoonful of the hot rice pudding and put it into his ample mouth. Immediately he ejected it back into the bowl and surrounding territory. Then pausing, with spoon held high, he interjected, "Many a damn fool would have swallered that."

Several years after I heard this Sam Houston story, during which time I had told it several times — and this isn't the first time I have put it into print — I spent a summer teaching in the University of North Carolina at Chapel Hill. My wife and I took our meals in a stately old home too superior in food, cheer and talk to be called a boarding house. In memory I associate it with the setting for Doctor Oliver Wendell Holmes's *The Autocrat of the Breakfast-Table* — though dinner is far more conducive to talk than breakfast. The autocrat at our table was one of the last leaves of Southern aristocracy. Major Cane was his name. He was full of stories about local characters of other days, and one of these characters was Zeb Vance,

Civil War governor of North Carolina and later United States Senator.

Zeb Vance was as much an individualist as Sam Houston. He was the kind of man to whom stories that ought to be true, whether they are or not, attach themselves. One time, Major Cane told, there was a big public dinner in honor of Zeb Vance. He was voluble by nature and he was feeling especially voluble that evening. Engrossed in telling a story and hardly noticing what he was doing, he transported a great tablespoon of soup to his mouth without first testing its temperature. But he was too quick for it to scald him. He spewed it back towards the soup plate and, holding his spoon up, snorted, "Many a damn fool would have swallered that."

I wonder how many other characters, over how long a time, have been credited with that remark epitomizing individualism.

During one of his administrations, Andrew Jackson met Henry Clay, his bitterest antagonist, on a narrow boardwalk along a muddy street in Philadelphia. Both stopped, glaring at each other.

Old Hickory drew himself up to his full six feet plus and said sternly, "I never step aside for a scoundrel."

Bowing low and stepping off into the mud, Clay replied, "I do."

Sam Houston was a great admirer of Jackson — though that may have nothing to do with the story, and nobody could, I judge, document it. As it goes, Houston came face to face with one of his political enemies in the then modest capitol at Austin.

"Howdy do, sir," he said with cold formality.

"I never knowingly speak to scoundrels," came the reply.

"You perceive that I do," and Houston walked on.

His retort to a challenge to duel, "Tell him I never fight downhill," has been attributed to a dozen men.

Frank Wardlaw, a South Carolinian now Director of the University of Texas Press, tells this story. Several years after the Civil War ended, General Jubal Early of the Confederacy was in Washington during a reunion of the G. A. R. A soldier in blue, with both arms and both legs gone, struck his attention. After looking at him some time, he stepped up to the wheel chair and put a ten dollar bill into the veteran's pocket. A reporter who happened to be on the spot and who was no doubt grateful for the item said to him, "General Early, that is the finest example of brotherly love I have ever seen."

"Brotherly love, hell!" General Early rebutted. "That's the only example I ever saw of a Yankee carved up enough to suit me."

When yellow fever broke out in Houston, Texas, in 1867, it struck Yankee soldiers stationed there to enforce Reconstruction. They died by the score. A native sexton named H. G. Pannell had charge of burying them. He and his crew were so overworked that they could not dig graves fast enough to keep up with the dead. Word reached the commandant of the Yankees that bodies of his men were being held over for burial while citizens received priority.

He hunted up the sexton and said, "Mr. Pannell, they tell me you dislike to bury my soldiers."

"General," the sexton replied with enthusiasm, "that is a damned lie. It is the pleasantest work I have had in all my life. I can't bury enough of them. I hope to God I'll have the chance to bury every one of you."

Recurring wars make war stories recur. Not long ago I heard a lady tell how during the Battle of the Bulge in Germany (World War II) a sergeant called out to his men, "Come on, you loafers, you want to live forever?" Has the name of the sergeant of World War I, at Belleau Wood, ever been established? He yelled out as he went over the top, "Come on, you bastards! Do you want to live forever?" I can't prove it, but I would wager that some such devil-dare was ascribed to some French or British subaltern during the Napoleonic wars.

One time, a story goes, Bigfoot Wallace, from Virginia, who became the rollickiest Indian fighter in the Texas ranger tradition, took a young journalist under his wing on a scout after Comanches. The first night out he gave the tenderfoot a stick of wood for a pillow, at the same time saying, "Tomorrow night we'll be on the prairie away from natural pillows and you'll have to rough it."

I have always set this down as one of Bigfoot's jokes, but something like it might have happened on the frontier. Charlie Goodnight, cowman and trail-breaker, used to tell of an old rawhide who lived in a dugout and made many a meal on raw dried beef. One evening a horseman who was a stranger to the country rode up to his dugout and asked shelter for the night. He was made welcome.

After a supper that was pretty much "Spanish," which means tighten up your belt a notch, the dugout man yanked down onto the dirt floor a dried cowhide. "Here, you sleep on this," he said to his guest. "I'll rough it."

Maybe it happened in Scotland four or five hundred years ago. I've read a book in which the incident is told this way. One of the Camerons took along his young son on a border raid. They camped in the snow, and after supper the father watched the boy roll up a snowball and arrange it as a pillow for his pallet. He arose and kicked the snowball down the mountain.

"No effiminacy, my son!" he said in his sternest manner.

Maybe it didn't happen anywhere. It could have happened wherever men with the bark on have exulted against nature in the rough. The winds have carried the story over the oceans.

This kind of variation is closely akin to variations in sayings — or ascribed sayings. It would be easy to deal with Lloyd George, Stanley Baldwin is reputed to have said, "if he merely thought he was Napoleon, but he insists that he is the Twelve Apostles." At Teheran F. D. Roosevelt is supposed to have said to General De Gaulle, "Yesterday you were Napoleon; today you are Joan of Arc. It would help us to get along if you'd let us know definitely which you are."

Here we are in the realm of sophisticated wit. Mother wit abounds in folk talk, but sophistication is often a handicap to the traveling of tales. The folkier an anecdote is, the handier it is for passing on. All we writer fellows can possibly do with a story is to retell it, supplying an occasional variation. As Lloyd Lewis retells in *Captain Sam Grant,* one night before the Civil War was to bring Grant back into the army from which he had resigned, he walked into a tavern in Galena, Illinois, wearing his old long, blue overcoat. It was court time, and lawyers were sitting in a tight circle around the stove talking about a case.

Grant stood outside the circle for a while listening until, in a lull of the conversation, one lawyer noticed him and asked, "Stranger here?"

"Yes."

"Traveled far?"

"Far enough.'

"Looks as though you might have traveled through hell," the lawyer went on.

"I have."

"Well, how did you find things down there?"

"Just about like this place — lawyers all closest to the fire."

One winter night in the year 1912, in Marshall, Texas, where a conference of Methodist preachers was going on, I was in a hotel lobby. All the chairs were drawn up near a big stove and every chair seemed to be occupied by a preacher. Presently I heard one of them ask in a jolly voice, "How does this place resemble hell?"

Another who knew the gag cracked out, "All the preachers close to the fire."

No doubt the application has been made to bankers and doctors.

The first of the next pair of yarns comes from West Virginia; its mate, from the plains of west Texas. They are both old.

One day whittlers on the board sidewalk of Hominy Falls saw Jake Harkey striding down the street carrying his long-barrelled, muzzle-loading rifle. It was the kind carried by Daniel Boone. When it was not in Jake Harkey's hands, on his shoulder, across his knees, or beside him, it rested on the prongs of two buck antlers over his fireplace up the mountain. He called it "Stop Running," and many a deer, many a wild turkey, and many a varmint had stopped at its word. As Jake Harkey carried it now, his eyes were as steely and his mouth was as fixed as Stop Running's muzzle.

The whittlers on the board walk had an idea where and why Jake Harkey was going. They knew that his daughter Sally had been acting mighty lively at square dances and that Wiley Poe had been seeing her home. They saw Jake head into the town's only pool hall and in a remarkably short time come out behind Wiley Poe.

The two went directly to the preacher's house. The preacher joined them, and all three walked up the mountain. Then, in short order, standing before Sally and Wiley in the Harkey cabin, the preacher said, "I pronounce you man and wife." With great labor, his rifle leaning on the table beside him, Jake made an entry in the family Bible. Then, and not till then, did his features relax. They became positively genial.

Holding "Stop Running" by the muzzle, he extended it towards his new son-in-law.

"Here, Wiley," he said, "she's yourn. Take good care of her. She's been handed down from father to son-in-law for five generations. Until you pass her on she'll help keep meat in the pot."

Well, one fall three city men from the East hired a kind of ex-cowboy and ex-several other things to guide them on a hunt. The first night in camp they got to talking about their common hobby, the collecting of firearms. One Easterner said he had Billy the Kid's six-shooter with twenty-one notches filed on the barrel; the second told how he had run down Jesse James's rifle with five nicks in the butt. The third bragged about owning a machine gun used by Al Capone.

After the talk had gone on for a good while, one of the Easterners confided that he was hot on the trail of a Sharp's buffalo gun used by Buffalo Bill. He was always looking for gun trails. Suddenly he turned to the guide.

"Say," he said, "you've been out here in the West all your life and seen a lot of action. I bet you've got a gun that's made history."

"No, no; all I got," the ex-cowboy guide answered, "is that old single-barrel shotgun standing behind the front door at home. It ain't got no notches on it and it ain't never took part in any famous shooting, but I'll tell you what. It has got four of my daughters married off."

When I was a child, my father used to tell us about a man riding along a boggy road in Arkansas. I know now that this man has ridden over about all the boggy roads in all the states of the Union and was probably riding in England in the time of Robin Hood. Anyhow, riding along a boggy road in Arkansas, he saw a hat right down on the mud in front of him. He stopped his horse, knee deep in the mud, and leaned over to pick up the hat. As he was raising it, a smothered voice called out, "Hi, there, leave my hat alone!"

"Why," the stranger exclaimed, "is somebody actually down there under this hat?"

"Yes, and that ain't all," the muddied voice came up. "I'm standing on my mule."

My father's imitation of two voices, the stranger's clear and high and the other dim, dull, and struggling, turned this ancient story into a drama that we children enjoyed immensely. A Leadville, Colorado, version has a freighter, as cross at his stalled oxen as a sore-headed bear, almost step on the hat before he saw it and then kick it, whereupon the subterranean voice said, "Hey, I don't mind you busting that new hat of mine, but watch out fer this race horse under me."

Joe Evans of El Paso hangs the story on Captain James B. Gillett of the Texas rangers. He wasn't really a captain, but everybody called him Captain, and his *Six Years with the Texas Rangers* is at the top of all ranger narratives. Captain Gillett was in El Paso to make a talk to a gathering of Masons from distant parts. The wind was blowing dust and sand, as it habitually does out there during certain seasons. The president of the El Paso Chamber of Commerce in introducing the speaker apologized for the dust storm. It wasn't at all typical of El Paso weather, he said.

"I came to El Paso in 1879," Captain Gillett began. "The country was having a dust storm that you couldn't see through, and it has been having dust storms ever since. That time the wind blew for three days and three nights and the sand had covered up the mesquite bushes. As another ranger and I rode through the sand hills between Alamogordo and El Paso, we saw the top of a hat on a sand dome. It was nearly covered up. We got down to pick it up and found a man's head in it. We scratched the sand out of his eyes and ears and mouth with our fingers. After he got a good breath he said, 'Get a shovel. I'm horseback.'"

Anthropologists and scientific folklorists, mining through the most ancient records, both Oriental and Occidental, and comparing folk tales in all languages, have endeavored to trace some to their sources. They always come to the curtain of remote antiquity beyond which all is speculation. Treatises on the Tar Baby story, immortalized in Joel Chandler Harris's Uncle Remus, conclude that it was told in India thousands of years ago and that it has traveled to every continent and many islands. They say that Spaniards brought it to America. At the same time, there is evidence that Negroes brought it from Africa. Also, at the same time, there is evidence that it was current among Indians on the Atlantic seaboard before Columbus sailed.

One night at a camp on a mule trail hundreds of years old, across the Sierra Madre of Mexico, a peon in sandals told me the story of a coyote and a heron. The coyote invited the heron to have dinner with him. The heron found the table spread with a white cloth.

The coyote's wife came out and sprinkled *pinole* (sweetened meal of parched corn) over it.

"Eat, eat, my friend," the coyote kept saying, while with his broad tongue he lapped the cloth. The heron could peck up only a few particles. After the coyote's wife had replenished the *pinole* several times, the heron gave thanks for the hospitality, invited the coyote to his house for a fish dinner the next day, and flew away.

The coyote found the table spread in the open and the heron's wife setting out long-necked bottles containing little fishes.

"Come, Señor Coyote, and let us eat," the heron said.

The coyote put his mouth to a bottle. All he could get was a smell. His tongue could not get down to the delicious little fishes. The heron billed them out as fast as he could swallow.

Aesop lived in Greece five hundred years before Christ. You'll find this story in his Fables, attributed to a fox and a crane. It was no doubt hoary in Egypt and elsewhere centuries before the Greeks had a literature. To native Mexicans and to other Indians of western North America, the coyote is what Reynard the Fox has been to the people of Europe and Asia. When the story traveled to them, they simply substituted coyote for fox.

Nothing is simpler than hanging an old story on a new peg. *Fifteen Thousand Miles by Stage*, by Carrie Adell Strahorn, is now chiefly remembered, when it is remembered at all, for its eighty-odd illustrations from the brush and pencil of Charles M. Russell. Yet it contains many a good anecdote. One day, the author relates, while she was sitting on the deck of a steamer plying between Puget Sound and San Francisco, she overheard a sailor telling his mates about a service he had attended at Mission Church in Frisco. The anthems had impressed him most of all. He was sentimental about them.

"I say, Pete, what's a hanthem anyway?" one of the sailors broke in.

"And you don't know what a hanthem is?" Pete replied scornfully. "I'll tell you. If I was to say to you, 'Here, Jack, hand me that anchor line,' that wouldn't be no hanthem. But if I was to sing out, 'Jack, Jack, Jack, hand, hand, hand, O hand me that anchor, hand me that anchor, Jack, hand, O hand me that anchor line, anchor line, anchor line, line, line, line, O Jack, ah men,' that would be a hanthem."

A long time after I read this sailor yarn in *Fifteen Thousand Miles by Stage* I heard an account of a camp meeting in Texas. "We sung hymns and spiritual songs but did not sing anthems," the describer said. He seemed to feel that a definition of anthem was necessary for his audience. He went on.

One time a farmer who was a deacon in the church was summoned to serve on a Federal grand jury in a city. He was gone two weeks. First thing when he got back home his wife asked him if he had attended church services in the big city. Of course he had. "Did you know any of the songs they sang?" his wife wanted to know.

"No, I didn't," the farmer replied. "They didn't sing songs. All they sung was anthems."

"Anthems! what on earth is anthems?"

"Well, it's like this, " the deacon answered. "Now, if I was to say to you, 'Ma, the cows is in the corn,' that would not be any anthem."

"Of course it wouldn't," Ma put in.

"Wait a minute," the deacon went on. "If I'd say in a long quavering-out, dying up-and-down voice, 'Ma, Ma, Ma, the cows—the cows—the Holstein cow, the muley cow, the Jersey cow, the old brindle cow, and old Spec too—all them cows—the co-o-o-w-s—is in—is in—the cow-ow-ows is in—is in—the corn, the corn, the co-oo-rr-n, ah men, men, men,' that would be an anthem."

I may be wrong, for I have never become a part of the machine age and, therefore, am not modern, but it seems to me that stories about simple times and simple people have more endurance and are more protean than the others. The best ones involve elemental humanity, and their point is never patronizing.

"Have you heard this one?" If it is a real story and not a jokebook gag, and if the teller is an artist, we want his variations just as we go to see *Hamlet* played by every actor who acts in it. The fact that we've seen *Hamlet* makes the new actor more interesting — provided he is not a butcher. There are just three essentials to a good story: humanity, a point, and the storyteller, and here are three ways of softening bad news.

Teddy Roosevelt used to tell about some cowboys who, while hunting a horse thief, found a man they judged to be guilty, hanged him, and then discovered that he had been innocent. They discovered also that his name was Jack Smith. They felt obligated to convey the news to the victim's wife. One cowboy declared he had a gift for always saying the right thing at the right time. There was no opposition to his acting as spokesman. The posse rode to the home of the late Jack Smith.

"Are you the wife of Jack Smith?" the tactful cowboy began.

"Yes, I am," the woman replied, apparently a little huffed.

"No you ain't," the news-breaker came back. "You're jest his widder. We got his body out there in the waggin, and it's dressed up mighty nice. We hung him for a horse thief, but please don't feel bad about that. He was plumb innocent. After we strung him up we found out he wasn't the guy we was looking for at all. We're all ready to swear he was innocent."

John McGinnis of Dallas credits his story to Mark Twain, though I don't recall having seen it in Mark Twain's writings. According to John McGinnis, Mark Twain used the story to illustrate how near tragedy and pathos the best humor often skims. McGinnis himself uses the story to enforce his theory that the farther west you go, the drier the humor grows.

Joe Toole was a rancher living way out in the Rocky Mountain sage lands. One day he told his wife that he was simply beat out with staying so long in the bushes and never seeing anybody and that he was going to town to celebrate. So he saddled old Paint and struck out for Cheyenne.

When he got there, he found the town as quiet as a funeral procession. It kinder riled him and made him more determined to celebrate. He raised up in his stirrups and gave a yell, and when he drew his horse to a sudden stop in front of The Cowboy's Delight, instead of getting down and hitching him to the hitching rail, where there wasn't a single horse to keep him company, he socked his spurs into him and rode right through the open door.

The barkeep was sitting on a stool behind the bar with his head down on his arms taking a nap. When he raised up, anybody could have seen his eyes were bloodshot. Cheyenne had had its celebration running two days and nights and now was sleeping it off. But Joe Toole was looking for nothing but life and not noticing signs.

"I'm a thirsting like the Prodigal Son," he yells out. "Pour me a straight and smell one yourself."

"If you want to drink any liquor in here," the barkeep growls back, "prodigal yourself off that horse and tie him outside. This ain't no livery stable."

"Livery stable be damned," Joe Toole answers. "What's good enough fer me is good enough fer my horse. Put a little Jamaica rum in a glass and pour him one, too."

The barkeep, without getting off his stool, reached like he was going to get the glasses, but what he got was a sixshooter and he raised up with it a-blazing. The bullet hit Joe Toole such a plumb center that his brains spilled out on the horn of his saddle while he was a-falling over.

The noise waked up some of the citizens, and the first thing they did was hold an inquest and preliminary trial. The barkeep pled self-defense and was immediately acquitted.

Then the question came up as to what to do with the body. The barkeep paid for a good coffin. It was put on a wagon and a committee of three was selected to accompany the corpse and convey the news to Joe Toole's widder. Before they got in sight of the ranch, they galloped ahead of the wagon. A man with the reputation of being tactful had agreed to do the talking.

"Hello," he yells at the front yard gate.

"Git down," Mrs. Joe Toole answers.

All three of the committee got down. When they were inside the gate, the chairman cleared his throat and says, "Does Joe Toole live here?"

"Yes," the widder says.

"Bet he don't," the chairman comes back.

Then he gave a sweep with his hand towards the coffin wagon that was coming up.

They say the widow caught on right away.

George C. Taylor, of the University of North Carolina, has the news-softening go this way. One time Governor Jackson of Mississippi was going up to Louisville to attend the horse races. On the way his train ran off a bridge, killing many of the passengers. The governor's secretary survived, however, and his first thought was the governor's wife. As soon as telegraphic communications were established, he sent her this telegram:

"Train wreck on L. and N. Railroad fatal to Governor Jackson of Mississippi. Two legs broken, two arms, one neck, one back, nine ribs. Corpse following by train."

An hour later more careful examination prompted the secretary to tone down his report. Accordingly he wired: "Train wreck on L. and N. not so bad as previously reported. Only one of Governor Jackson's legs broken, only one arm, only three ribs. Also neck and back. Corpse following by train."

Take the increasingly rare combination of silence and taciturnity. Harry Oliver, who publishes the *Desert Rat Scrap Book* at Thousand Palms, California, avers that a sheepherder told him the story as a personal happening. It is also related of a driller and a tool dresser in an Oklahoma oil field. I take my version from Carl Sandburg, who has a "constructive memory" on such things — and I don't claim not to have it.

Out in Montana two line-riders (cowboys) stayed alone in the same camp. Every morning one rode east and the other rode west. They usually got back to camp late in the evening. Each had said nothing all day, as there was nobody to say it to, and at night they kept on saying nothing. But one night while they were getting under their tarpaulins, the silence was broken by a deep bellowing from down the canyon.

"Bull," one said.

"Sounds like an old steer to me," the other said.

That was as far as the conversation went. The next morning after breakfast of coffee, fried salt bacon, and warmed-over biscuits, the cowboy who had said "bull" the night before caught his pack horse and went to tying up his bedroll.

"Riding?" the other queried.

"Yes. Too damned much argu-ment."

Chess players are usually a long way off the range. One night two of them sat down at their board right after supper. For hours they moved their pieces in absolute silence, after intense planning and with utter deliberation. Finally, the board almost clean, one said, "Check—mate."

"Well," the other surrendered, "you needn't make so much noise about it."

Some men just don't like to waste words or hear anybody else waste them. Grey Owl of Canada tells of a hunter of the far north who one late afternoon put up his tent on a particularly pleasant point of ground overlooking a lake. The smoke of his fire was curling up and he was smoking his pipe in peace when he saw a canoe heading his way.

Presently the canoe halted at the point, and a lone man, evidently hungry for company, got out, at the same time saying in the heartiest of voices, "Fine camping place."

"Yeah," the old hunter assented.

"Wonderful weather too."

"Uh-huh."

The newcomer, not to be deprived of company, began unloading his canoe, at the same time trying to make the atmosphere more cheerful. "There's a war in China. Hear about it?" he asked.

Getting no reply, he looked up to see the old hunter pulling down his tent and evidently preparing to leave.

"What in the hell's wrong?" he asked. "Not going to pull out are you?"

"Yes, I'm a-pulling out. Discussion never did suit my fancy."

John Dunn will long be remembered as one of the characters of Taos, New Mexico. He used to run a stage over the mountain road to Taos Junction and back. On this route he drove the first automobile of the country. One time he took on three passengers at the Junction — two men and a woman. The woman rode in front, exclaimed at the scenery, ejaculated at the perilous brinks along the road, asked questions, and chattered all the way. When the journey ended, the men descended with alacrity.

"How much?" one asked.

"Two and a half," Dunn replied.

He paid. "Can you change a five?" the second asked.

"Here's your change."

"What did you say the fare was?" the woman now chirped, offering a bill.

"Five dollars."

"Why, Mr. Dunn, I just heard you tell those men it was two and a half," she protested.

"Madam, they did not talk."

And John Dunn kept the talker's five dollars.

Some stories about Bourbon and Scotch mellow with age like whiskey itself. Brander Matthews knew the world's drama and dramaturgy, but all I recollect of his lectures at Columbia University are anecdotes lacing them. He used to tell one about Colonel Henry Watterson of Kentucky, who lived long enough to see the chief manufactured product of his state outlawed by the National Prohibition Act.

While sentiment in the South was boiling against all intoxicating drinks, Marse Henry accepted an invitation to speak to a convention of women in Nashville — where he had a particularly solicitous friend.

"Look here," this friend said to the chairman of arrangements for the lecture, "Marse Henry is old and getting feeble. He's going to have a cold and a cough from the train ride when he gets here. Not long after he gets up to talk he's going to need something to clear his throat and kind of stimulate him. I wish you'd let me provide the speaker's stand with a silver pitcher of refreshment and a silver goblet."

"You mean, of course," the chairman replied coldly, "that you want to place whiskey and water on our stand?"

"Well, yes. The Colonel has drunk it all his life, and he needs it now. Water won't do, I tell you."

"Then you can fill your silver pitcher with milk."

The chairman seemed happy at the thought. The solicitous friend was suddenly happy also.

Just before Marse Henry was to appear, he brought the pitcher of milk to the stand, making sure that the chairman saw it but did not smell it. Milk had turned the whiskey whitish. Sure enough, the old colonel's throat soon went to giving him trouble. He paused, reached for the pitcher, poured some of its contents into the goblet. The look he gave it was disdainful, but he had to moisten that throat. He raised the goblet to his lips. His eyes brightened. He took a swallow. His countenance beamed. As he drained the goblet, his whole frame seemed to take on vigor. "What a cow!" he exclaimed — and made everybody feel good with his speech.

I don't know where Henning Larsen, professor of English and Dean of the College of Arts at the University of Illinois, picked up his story, but this, more or less, is the way he tells it. After a cold day of travel and preaching, a Scotch minister went home with a hearty old farmer and his wife to spend the night. They were all solicitude for his welfare and before bedtime pressed him to take "something relaxing to the system." No, the most he would take was a glass of hot milk. The old woman felt that the minister did not know what was good for himself, and back in the kitchen she spiked the hot milk into a strong punch.

The minister took it wearily but after the first sip began to revive. At the end of the second glass he said in heartfelt tones, "The Lord be thanket for sic a coo!"

Who can be blamed for appropriating to himself or to somebody related by blood, marriage, friendship, geography, or otherwise an extraordinary experience? I am a kind of authority on panther stories — though the diction of pretense has translated the panther into mountain lion. I don't know how many times I have heard of how many pioneer women who, each alone in the woods with a baby, heard a panther scream, saw it coming, started for shelter, threw away a sunbonnet to detain the fierce panther, threw away a shawl, then a handkerchief, then a surplus petticoat and finally, having cast away everything but the minimum cover of modesty, got inside the house just ahead of the panther. Maybe the experience was one woman's somewhere. Maybe. It could hardly have been repeated. The tale about it has been a wonderful traveler.

I don't know how many times I have heard and read of a hunter on the plains overtaken by a blizzard who managed to kill a buffalo, skin him and wrap up in the hide, the hair side next to his body. He slept as snug as a bug in a rug, but woke up next morning to find himself cased by the green hide frozen as hard as iron and as binding as the swathing wrapped around a mummy in an Egyptian tomb. Thus bound, the hunter heard a pack of ravenous wolves. Soon he could hear and feel them gnawing on the frozen buffalo hide. The only opening in it was above his head, to let air in. Finally he managed to work a hand to this slit. Some wolf by accident got the tip of his tail into it. The hand closed on the tail. Presently the wolf moved, felt the pull on his tail, and jerked. The jerk loosed the frozen hide from the drift of snow. The hand still held and the wolf still pulled. He had a downhill pull and went so fast that friction warmed the hide and thawed it sufficiently for the imprisoned hunter to get free. He found his way to camp and told a story yet told by his great-grandchildren. It is told not as a tall tale but as a true happening. Maybe it was. Maybe to a single individual. Maybe.

I heard a drummer in a smoker on a Pullman car tell a story about a lady who was jealous of her husband and a Negro maid. It has an O. Henry surprise ending that involves darkness, a bed in the maid's room, the jealous lady in the bed, and a Negro man entering in response to an invitation in a disguised voice to "come in." I had just read the story, so far as plot goes, in Margaret of Navarre's *Heptameron,* of which the drummer had never heard and which I enjoy above the more famous *Decameron.* Don't ask me where the drummer got his story. The *Heptameron* was written towards four and a half centuries ago. Don't ask me where the liberal-minded Margaret of Navarre got her story.

People don't find traveling stories. The stories find them. They lie in wait for hosts to attach themselves to, like ticks in weeds and grass waiting for some hot-blooded mammal to come along. He cannot choose but be bitten. But instead of being phlebotomized like hosts for ticks, the hosts for traveling stories are made more sanguine. In the words of Falstaff's Nym, "There's the humour of it."

ROY BEDICHEK

# Folklore in Natural History

WHEN A TEXAS SUNFLOWER gets good awake of a morning, it stretches itself a bit and forthwith bends its neck around to face the sun. Using its neck as an axis, it continues to face the sun all day long.

But in Lapland it's different. There the sun wheels around in the southern sky and stays aloft for months, so the sunflower of that latitude instead of simply bending over from east to west for a matter of twelve hours and then getting a good night's rest — instead of this humane Texas schedule, the Lapland sunflower's neck must twist itself around for months without any letup.

So it comes about that the traveler standing in a field of Lapland sunflowers at sunset is startled by the murmur of multitudinous little snapping, cracking, and swishing noises all about him. But be reassured, stranger from the South, there are no spooks nibbling at your ankles: it's only the sunflowers untwisting their necks for a long snooze in the coolish polar night.

I had this little legend from a botanist, Dr. William G. Whaley, on his return from a summer's stay in northern Sweden a year or so ago. If this is not genuine folklore, it is at least folksy and naturalistic enough to bring into focus points that are common to much of the folklore that appears in the field of natural history.

The fancy-factor in this idyl is more easily separated from its factual base than is the rule in most natural-history folklore. It is a fact that the common sunflower follows the sun, as certain other members of the great thistle family do, but folk generally reserve the name *"sun*flower" for only that species which most obviously exhibits this curious fondness for the sun. It is a habit of the folk mind to let its fancy dwell chiefly upon the more obvious features of natural phenomena, irrespective of whether or not the obvious is the essential. It is also a fact that in our temperate zone the sun holds a course across the sky, whereas in the polar regions it describes more or less of a circle based on the horizon.

Upon these botanical and astronomical data folk fancy goes to work somewhat as follows:

1. If the temperate-zone sunflower follows the sun willy-nilly, facing eastward in the morning, straight up at noon, and westward as the sun moves down from the meridian, then what happens when the same sun-fascinated flower finds itself up towards the north pole where the sun simply circles around indecisively for a few months in the southern sky? What, indeed, could happen except that this sun-crazy plant must twist its neck throughout the months-long day to make the accommodation. That's what a man must do when he turns his face without altering the position of his body — he simply twists his neck. Twisting the neck in the same direction for any considerable period is a tedious and finally a painful process.

So, besides seizing upon the most obvious aspects of a natural occurrence, the folk mind here makes its interpretation upon an anthropocentric basis. It loves the pathetic fallacy quite as dearly as the formal rhetorician abominates it.

2. Now a human neck twisted steadily without letup all day leaves its owner in no condition at nightfall to enjoy his repose. Hence, when the sun sinks below the horizon and the hypnotic tension is released, the plant quickly untwists its neck just as a human being would.

3. At the end we find the touch of humor which makes the whole world of folklore kin. Accustomed all his life to the silent, deliberate behavior of the normal sunflower, the observer is placed by the legend in a whole field of Lapland sunflowers just at the moment when the last rays of the polar sun disappear. Presto! There ensue tiny snapping and swishing noises all about him, so he "jumps out of his skin," only to find that it's nothing but innocent sunflowers untwisting their necks, as anyone who knows anything about sunflowers would expect them to do. Poor dub, to be frightened at that! It's funny.

Maybe the "little noises" the Lapland sunflowers make are derived from the "growing" noises of corn, with which all rural folk in our

Midwest are familiar. Transpositions or analogies of this sort often bob up in folk interpretations of natural phenomena. It will be noted that a sustained neck-twisting is also the mainspring of the well-worn folklore "Western" about the burrowing owl. The burrowing owl, by the way, doesn't burrow, but merely avails himself of the burrowing activities of his roommate. This is another instance of the careless, don't-give-a-damn acceptance of the obvious, and of the *non sequitur*. The bird dives into a burrow, doesn't he? Ergo, he is a burrowing bird.

However, all your analyses of folk-thinking, your condescending exposure of its innocent tricks, its naive assumptions, its faulty observations, and its jumping at conclusions, fail to wean us away from it. Fact is, we're not ready to be weaned. The pap is pleasant and often nourishing to the very sciences which repudiate it. Particularly, as the machine more and more dominates our lives and an all-pervasive technology forces our thinking into stern mathematical patterns, do we find pleasant relief in the wild freedom of the old brain-tracks, grooved long, long ago, a heritage from the primitive — from the Neanderthal or Java man, for that matter — who in turn took his thought-patterns from animal progenitors. "For we are indeed one with Nature; her genetic fibres run through all our being; our physical organs connect us with millions of years of her history; our minds are full of immemorial paths of pre-human existence."[1]

The superhighways, motorcars, jet planes, and prospects of space travel really intensify the pleasure of winding along neighborhood roads, or of following footpaths or even animals trails in the, alas, too few wilderness areas now left our sadly devastated domain. Just so the mind likes to follow along the old trails of primitive thinking, coursed on still dimmer ones of animal thinking. Especially in natural-history folklore do we like the diversity, the *non sequiturs,* the aimless meanderings, the dallyings, and those sudden juxtapositions of incongruous ideas which constitute the soul of much of its humor. It's like parking the car at last to get out of the dizzy traffic and away from the glare of an undeviating highway, in order to wander off into the woods with nowhere to go and no set time to return.

With this trail-theory in mind we shall examine other instances of how folklore tends to deal with natural phenomena. We find it incurably anthropocentric. I cannot vouch for the truth of Voltaire's statement that man created God in his own image, but there is little doubt in the mind of any naturalist that man does create animals in his own image. Science, however, has invented a terrible word for this: *anthropopsychizing*. For instance, the anthropopsychist believes that birds sing generally because they are happy, as we ourselves whistle and sing because we are happy, or (in reverse) pour out our dismalist feelings into song as a necessary purgation.

The ancient Greeks, keen nature-observers and the most downright and practical people of whom there is any record — these unsentimental folk heard from the throat of a nightingale no warning to other nightingales to stay out of his territory, as the ornithologist of today interprets his song, but instead the most musical of mourning. In Greek legend the bird is a "bewildered mourner, bird divinely taught, for 'Itys,' 'Itys,' ever heard to pine."

Nowadays the really scientific ornithologist says "bosh" to all this. The song of the mocker or of the thrush, especially in the spring, is an expression of "territorialism"; that is to say, the sweetest and most seductive songs of these birds are only a warning to others of their own species to stay away, keep out, private property, posted, officer on guard. Twenty-five years ago it was "scientific" to attribute all spring bird songs to love, to the pretty little anthropocentric fiction of the male's serenading his faithful mate as she sits patiently hovering their eggs, a modest, home-loving little creature as all females in the world are or should be. And after this Victorian exposition, it was the fashion of the scientific person to get really profound and point out the importance of bird songs as a factor in sexual selection. Debunk, however, as much as you please, folk will continue to anthropopsychize bird songs and even fit words of human speech into the various rhythms of them; and I'm not so sure that they are not getting nearer a vital truth than the scientists are.

Seriously, there is sometimes truth in folklore of higher quality and of greater importance than the mere facts-is-facts of science. In nature lore and especially in folklore about animals, our ancient kinship in mind and body with all animate nature is revealed; and the folk mind, wisely following the old trails here, refuses to exchange a sympathetic and therefore emotional for a purely intellectual apprehension of nature.

We are conditioned from childhood to doubt folk tales about animals. As we grow up we find there was never such a bird as the roc, no such animal as the unicorn, no mermaids, no centaurs. Science delights in debunking these folk creations and substituting, quite properly, "the fairy tales of science and the long result of time." We naturally become incredulous. Our first reaction is to discount any tale of mysterious occurrences in nature, and especially any behavior-story in which the lower animal exhibits human intelligence. Science is especially suspicious of such stories, since it has virtually assumed the role of defense attorney for *Homo sapiens* against any presumptuous animal coming into court to claim any part or parcel of that sacred psychological area known as human reason. Loyal to the human race, it is determined that we shall not be dragged down to the bestial level without a fight. Man may become bestial, but animals can't become rational.

It is, however, a mistake to become too skeptical. I have often pooh-poohed a folk story only to be compelled later to eat my own words. I rejected forthwith the account of a praying mantis capturing and biting into the throat of a hummingbird, but found that this does sometimes happen. And I didn't believe it when a friend told me he had seen a grackle fly two hundred yards with a crust of toast in his bill, dunk it in water and eat it just as some of us dunk our toast in coffee. But it's so. On the other hand, I accepted at once a story from an old woodsman explaining why the folk name for pileated woodpecker is "Lord God" or "Good God." Says he, "When a feller who ain't never seen one before sees a woodpecker as big as a crow, he just naturally says 'Lord God!' and that's the way the critter got its name." I published this as a probable origin of the East Texas name for this enormous woodpecker, and presently there came through the mails the following explanation from Dr. Irving McNeil, of El Paso:

> One suggestion [he begins with disarming diffidence] that I think if I could have got to you before you published, you would have been glad to include about the folk name of the pileated woodpecker. The origin of the name "Good God" might be traced back a step further, to the section

where I was brought up in northern Mississippi and West Tennessee. The Negroes there called the bird "Lord God." As a boy I thought it was awfully funny but it was not until I was grown and learned that another name for the bird was "log cock" (see Webster's *New International Dictionary*) that the explanation came to me. There it is: Repeat the two names out loud to yourself, and see how much alike they sound and see how easily the name "log cock" could be mistaken by the illiterate for the other. All that is needed to complete the gap is to consider that East Texas was settled by Tennesseeans.

I don't like to give up the old forester's explanation, but I am driven by "preponderance of evidence" to accept Dr. McNeil's, at least, provisionally.

The bullfrog's mouth and his hind legs are his most striking somatic characters; and, true to its genius for enlarging plausibly upon the obvious, folk fancy has developed a whole cycle of tall tales about this batrachian's capacity for swallowing and jumping. The surprising thing is that science comes along and proves that none of them is an exaggeration. Indeed, folk fancy seems for once a bit sluggish.

An old fisherman told me when I was a boy that he had seen a bullfrog swallow things "twict" his own size — apparently a self-contradictory exaggeration. We have all heard trotline stories of a fish swallowing a baited hook, of a larger fish swallowing him and then of a frog swallowing the larger fish, and so on until the fifty-two-pound yellow cat that was the final swallower was made to disgorge more pounds of fish and frog than the swallower himself weighed — *on the same scales.*

So when I heard that a bullfrog had swallowed one of Dr. M. R. Gutsch's ducks, I put it at once in the tall-tale class, of value only as illustrating folk disposition to exaggerate the function of an organ of abnormal appearance. I confronted Dr. Gutsch with the story, expecting an instant repudiation, but instead he told me that one day he saw a duckling disappear suddenly from the surface of his duck pond. When it failed to come up in a reasonable time, he seined the pond and found his missing duckling with its head in the belly of a bullfrog. True it was a duckling, not a duck, and the frog hadn't yet swallowed the whole of it, but the facts certainly furnish a good, sound basis for the story.

L. T. S. Norris-Elye writes to A. C. Bent: "We have had instances of frogs capturing and swallowing ruby-throats [humming birds], one at Gull Harbor and one at Gimli, Lake Winnipeg. The Gimli case was observed by my friend Hugh Moncrieff, who captured the frog (leopard) and had some boys cut it open and recover the bird, while he took some good motion pictures of the operation."[2] Think of this gross Caliban having the agility of leg and the expansiveness of mouth and gullet to engulf our little Ariel while he is hovering over the water on iridescent wings vibrating 200 strokes per second![3] Folk-fancy never invented an unlikelier story, and still competent scientific observers, eyewitnesses, assure us 'tis so!

Dr. Osmond P. Breland in his excellent book *Animal Facts and Fancies*[4] records a swallowing reported to him by Dr. W. Frank Blair, Associate Professor of Zoology, University of Texas, who had an eleven-inch alligator confined in the same cage with a five-inch toad. One morning he missed the alligator and noticed that the toad was rather distended and appeared unusually drowsy. He felt the toad's belly and there, sure enough, coiled neatly inside was his alligator.

And the dark, unfathomed caves of ocean bear some curious instances of the swallowing capacity of certain of its denizens. There is a dragonlike creature whose immense mouth and elastic body make it possible for him to swallow a fish actually larger than he is.[5]

So the old fisherman who repeated folklore about the swallowing capacity of frogs and fishes was really nearer the truth than he thought.

For more than a century science has found folk belief in the hibernation of birds harder to kill than a cat with its nine lives. Since the days of good old Gilbert White, and before, it kept bobbing up here and there in spite of scientific proof to the contrary. Science has told us repeatedly that birds migrate, and that the ignorant, not being familiar with the facts of migration, attribute the disappearance of birds in the fall to hibernation. Possums, bears, bats, and other animals hibernate for the winter, so why not birds? — such is typical folklore reasoning. The learned world for a long time has dismissed belief in the hibernation of birds as completely without foundation. Even as late as 1948 Dr. Breland says, ". . . a recently compiled list of books and articles dealing with the hibernation of swallows contained no less than 175 titles. Despite these early beliefs and the learned published articles, however, so far as is known there are no types of birds that hibernate."[6]

Yet facts were coming to light here and there which rather supported the folk belief. In the coast country of Texas there is record of a cold snap in late spring which reduced hummingbirds to a state of suspended animation. People picked them up in great numbers, and it was found that many of them recovered when brought into a warm room. There was for a long time a question about the Carolina parakeet, colonies of which were found holed up in hollow trees during cold weather, but no reputable authority was willing to declare that it was a case of hibernation. Since this bird is now extinct, we shall never know whether or not his holing-up was hibernation or merely a case of temporary refuge. I read a year or more ago in the very reliable *London Illustrated News* an account by a scientist of a bird which nests in the far north of Europe and, after hatching its brood, is occasionally driven south by a late blizzard, leaving thinly clad nestlings unprotected for as much as a week at a time. Well, the nestlings are alive when the parent birds return! How is that possible? The scientist reports that he examined such a brood every day while the parent birds were gone and found that the little fellows were apparently asleep. Their blood temperature went down with the temperature of the air about them, which is a symptom of hibernation.

But the first actual proof of the hibernation of an adult bird generally accepted by the scientific world was recorded by Edmund C. Jaeger only this year (1953) in the February issue of the *National Geographic*. He found a poorwill sleeping away the winter in the hollow of a tree out in California, gave it all the hibernation tests, and solemnly pronounced it the real thing. So that's that: folklore right, science wrong, at least insofar as the poorwill is concerned. It is interesting to note that the poorwill belongs to the same order as the hummingbird, which we found exhibiting an inclination toward hibernation on the Texas coast.

Natural-history folklore is strong on function. Every organ of an animal is endowed, whether or no, with a function, and the more striking the organ the more functions are invented for it. Generally speaking, this is right: nature doesn't create an organ just for fun, and nature's disposition to economize makes her delight in multiple uses.

What, for instance, is the function of a rat's tail? It furnishes the sitting rat a prop for which a far shorter tail would serve, modeled, say, on that of the prairie dog, certainly the premier sitter of the rodent world. While climbing, the cautious creature sometimes takes a stabilizing twist with the pliable member around a small limb or other protection, but this very occasional convenience would seem to be more than offset by getting its owner caught in a snap-trap, although this is not always a fatal casualty. Many a time I have found about half or even two-thirds of the tail firmly clasped in the jaws of my trap, left there apparently as an insulting suggestion that the tail-owner had more intelligence than the trap-setter.

Some say that when a colony of rats in migration reaches a stretch of water lying across its route, a wise old bewhiskered member wades in while the next in line takes the tip of the leader's tail in his teeth. The second rat extends the same courtesy to the third rat, and so on in turn until the whole colony is strung chainwise across the water. Thus, it is said, many a weak one gets across a river who otherwise would be swept away in the current. I don't know whether this is science or folklore. Its picturesqueness suggests folklore, while the survival value would point to scientific speculation.

Dr. Gustav Eckstein, Professor of Medicine in the University of Cincinnati, quotes "a man from Guernsey" to the effect that he noticed the daily diminution of olive oil in a tall thin bottle on his pantry shelf.[7] Determined to solve the mystery, he watched through a hole in the door. About nightfall he saw a rat climb to the shelf above the bottle, settle herself at just the right point, lower her tail into the bottle, withdraw it and lick it clean.

Since this is reported anonymously, I thought maybe Dr. Eckstein was just telling a story. But the incident in the next paragraph I could not dismiss so easily, for he saw it "with his own eyes." A great gray rat entered his kitchen. "One spring to the back of a chair. One spring to the middle of the table. And there, set there every afternoon to cool, stood a flat dish of milk. Carefully she swung her stern, carefully she fitted it to the rim, and, in a single sweep, the job was done." One may ask why she didn't take the cream direct instead of skimming it off with her tail. The only answer which occurs to me at the moment is that the fastidious creature didn't want to mess up her whiskers.

But these Eckstein instances, purely anecdotal (not folklore), are included here only as a possible suggestion of how folklore may get started from the observation of a unique event. My own experience with a praying pig, who, by the way, kept a prayer-cushion, falls into this class, a seed of a possible folk tale which I shall now proceed to sterilize by publishing it. I quote it verbatim from an entry in my camp diary dated several years ago:

There's a pig running loose around my camp who gets all the table scraps from a neighboring farmstead, as much milk as he can drink, the constant attention of two boys who consider him a pet, and as much purslane and succulent roots as he can stuff in. I have never seen a rounder, cleaner, more self-possessed, or friendlier pig in all my life.

A talkative fisherman who drops by for a cup of coffee now and then tells me that this is a religious pig, that he prays almost daily and keeps a cushion to kneel down on. I tried to laugh this off as a "pig with a prayer cushion" but the man was serious. He told me about this praying act several times, and finally I decided to keep watch on the pig and see what activity of his justified my fisherman's conclusion. It took me about a week, for his praying habit proved to be irregular. I find these to be the facts:

This pig has attacks of bellyache from stuffing in too many table scraps and guzzling too much milk. His sides become bloated, and his grunts indicate discomfort. During such periods, he tries sinking down on his belly. That hurts, so he turns over on his side. That hurts, too, so he turns over on the other side. Still his belly hurts. Then he rests his great weight on the knees of his forelegs, but the place is littered all over with sharp oystershell, and the edges of it cut his knees, so he squeals a little, and rises, but his internal pain drives him to his knees again, which is apparently the only comfortable position he can assume. Again the cruel shell cuts him. Then he discovers an old castaway auto cushion in the corner of an open garage. He mounts this cushion, kneels down, and gives what I take to be a grunt of relief. He stays there kneeling on the soft cushion until the inner pain is over, and then with gratified grunts he goes his way again seeking what he may devour. This routine comes irregularly and I think only after gorging himself on some delightful dish, usually table scraps soaked in milk.

Animal folklore still adheres in its richest expression to two New World animals: the vampire bat and the opossum. Both were unfamiliar to Europeans when early explorers returned laden with marvels collected during their wanderings in lands beyond the seas. People were wonder-hungry and conditioned to believe anything. Rational processes were anesthetized and folk fancy was liberated to show what it could do. In the area of natural history it seized avidly upon these two animals concerning which there were no realistic inhibitions in the popular mind. As a result, the tales still current involving the form and behavior of the vampire bat and of the opossum would each fill a good-sized volume: the one, an enormous flying mammal which sucks the blood of its victim while he sleeps; and the other, a curious, fumbling, ambling, fuzzy, death-feigning quadruped equipped to nourish and bring forth at frequent intervals her litters of incubator babies.

When the bat lore of South American explorers met and married the vampire legend of the Slavonic countries of Eastern Europe, a union occurred, prolific of some of the weirdest conceptions the human mind has ever seriously entertained in the folklore of natural history. It was not a great while before the enormous frugivorous bat with wingspread of twenty-eight inches became the "bloodsucking" bat, perhaps to make it fit into the fanning-to-sleep feature of vampire legend. However, he is quite harmless. Bloodsucking is actually confined to two rather tiny species with wings too small for effective use as fans, so the innocent fruit-eater of the Amazon Valley, of wide wing and horrendous physiognomy, harmonized more closely with vampire folklore. His upright ears, fierce black eyes, savage teeth along with a spearlike projection sticking straight up from the tip of his nose, give this creature a really diabolical expression.[8] Nothing in the whole world of nature except the facial features of certain small insects under proper magnification can compare with the nightmarish horror of the face of this big bat. No wonder the vampire legend embraced it at first sight.

The bat's nocturnal habits and "supernatural" powers, such as accurate night-flight (although "blind as a bat"), created a climate hospitable to belief. Moreover, the creature prefers darkness rather than light because its deeds are evil, just like the bloodsucking ghost. "The ghost of a human being, preferably a suicide or sorcerer, was supposed to leave the body at night and suck the blood of living persons. When the grave was opened, the corpse was declared to be fresh. Such a vampire could be kept at home by driving a stake through the body of the corpse."[9] The freshness and rosiness of the corpse, by the way, when the grave was opened were due to the fact that the nefarious ghost had returned to its corpse gorged with blood sucked from its hapless victims during the night's maraudings. Other devices for making the vampire stay put were to cut off the head of the corpse, or tear the heart out and burn it, or scald the grave thoroughly with boiling water or vinegar. One or more of these remedies were applied with due ceremonies whenever any grave was known to be giving up its dead.

The build-up of bat folklore, hybrid offspring of the vampire legend mated with the marvel-stories of early South American explorers, went on for about two centuries, until the great era of scientific exploration of South America began, carried on by Humboldt (1799), W. H. Hudson in the mid-nineteenth century, and on to and including William Beebe (1918-25), with in-betweeners of such distinction as Charles Waterton, Richard Schomburgk, the great Alfred Russell Wallace, and the still greater Charles Darwin, Richard Spruce, Henry Walter Bates, and others.

These great travelers and scientists proceeded to unravel two centuries of European bat lore and, in so doing, came up with truth far stranger than fiction as follows:[10]

1. The bloodsucking bat doesn't suck, but laps blood as a cat his milk.

2. The vampire bat doesn't fan his victim to sleep, but his approach is as stealthy as that of the most cat-footed porch-climber. William Beebe, lying wide awake and purposely exposing himself, felt only a light tap on the breast as his blood-lapper alighted. The creature went from breast to wrist and on up the arm so softly that Beebe said if he had been asleep none of these movements would have been sufficient to wake him. And Alfred Russell Wallace, tapped for blood once on the tip of his nose and at another time

on the end of his great toe, reports that he slept through both phlebotomies like a babe in arms.

3. Our own Cabeza de Vaca contributed his mite to a flourishing folklore by the tale of bloodsucking bats as "big as turtle doves," which was "confirmed" three centuries later by Richard F. Burton's account: "It must be like a Vision of Judgment to awake suddenly and to find on the tip of one's nose, in the act of drawing one's life blood, that demoniacal face with deformed nose, satyrlike ears, and staring fixed saucer eyes, backed by a body measuring two feet from wing-end to wing-end."[11]

4. Darwin himself put an end to such imaginative exaggerations by being the first European to capture in the act and identify the real blood-lapper. Along in the same paragraph with mention of "wonderful and beautiful flowering parasites" and "enormous colonial ants' nests, which were nearly twelve feet high," occurs this passage:

> The vampire bat is often the cause of much trouble, by biting horses on their withers. The injury is not so much owing to loss of blood, as to the inflammation which the pressure of the saddle afterwards produces. The whole circumstance has been lately doubted in England; I was therefore fortunate in being present when one *(Desmodus d'orbignyi,* Wat.) was actually caught on a horse's back. We were bivouacking late one evening near Coquimbo, in Chile, when my servant, noticing that one of the horses was very restive, went to see what was the matter, and fancying he could distinguish something, suddenly put his hand on the beast's withers, and secured the vampire. In the morning the spot where the bite had been inflicted was easily distinguished from being slightly swollen and bloody.[12]

5. The great naturalist's eye here noted a circumstance that later put to rest another mystery of which folklore had made much to-do, viz., the stealing of blood without awakening the sleeper. R. L. Ditmars, the great snake-venom authority, noted the same things, and declared "something abnormal has happened to the tissue besides the opening of a mere wound by specialized lancing incisor teeth." The bat's saliva thus became suspect. It must contain an anesthetic agent. That it does contain an anticoagulant not present in the saliva of other bats was definitely proved by the investigations of O. G. Bier.[13] The presence of an anticoagulant is necessary to explain the profuse and continued bleeding from so small a wound

as the vampire bat makes. Otherwise, especially in human beings, the blood would quickly thicken and prevent the blood-lapper from storing in a hurry a week-or-so's supply of the nourishing fluid in his reserve- or storage-stomach with which nature has conveniently endowed the enterprising little creature.

Certainly, in the case of the vampire bat, the fictions of folklore are put to shame by that creative agency in nature which sets up, as if in mockery of man's flimsy effort, the incredible wonder of a tiny flying mammal, equipped with incisor teeth edged for both surgical shaving and lancing, with saliva which serves the double purpose of an anticoagulant and a local anesthetic, with a reservoir into which a generous supply of thin blood may be lapped up without disturbing the peaceful slumbers of the anesthetized donor, be it man or beast!

But folklore is never discouraged by being outdistanced. Let's take a look at the opossum. In 1717, Madam Merian published her drawing of a mother opossum carrying young on her back with their little tails coiled loosely around hers. A century or more later another creation appeared representing an "improved" folklore, showing the mother's tail arched grandly over her back and ending in a fine Spencerian flourish just over her head, while the babies, partially suspended by their tails, are strung along the mother's back from shoulder to rump. Another forty years of expanding folklore brought forth an "improvement" which transforms our sluggish, sleepy, dreamy marsupial into a really fearsome beast, tail more sharply arched over the back with the babies' tails twisted tightly around it and the whole litter holding on for dear life as the mother ranges madly like an enraged boar over the bumpy landscape.

Now this fictitious baby-carrying mechanism took such firm hold on the imagination of the people that it has not been loosened yet. The same type of illustration appeared in the schoolbooks and dictionaries of the last century, and may still be found in current editions of the Larousse foreign-language dictionaries.

A complete representation of evolving opossum folklore from 1516 on down may be found in a remarkable series of pictures reproduced in chapters 18 and 19 of Dr. Carl G. Hartman's fine work, *Possums*.[14] Dr. Hartman assures me, by the way, that it is an anatomical impossibility for the opossum to arch its tail over the back in the manner shown in his four-century album of opossum pictures.

Hartman also tries to put to rest a tenacious bit of folk biology about how opossums breed and bring forth their young.[15] Many people still believe this egregious folklore version of the breeding and birth of this very common animal. Again, it is the folk imagination bent on assigning a function to match the peculiarity of form observed in the organs involved.

But the folk have never discovered one gruesome function of this marsupial's tail. It is used as a reserve food supply. When the going gets really rough — no paw-paws, no haws, no Mexican persimmons, no chicks, no eggs, no insects (the animal is omnivorous) — when just about to starve, the resourceful creature sometimes curls up and chews off his own tail right to the root. Science scores here over folklore in the account of Dr. Harold C. Reynolds, an eminent marsupial authority.[16]

Pursuing further this tale of tails brings us to the famous tailless Manx cats on the Isle of Man. Islanders call them "rumpies" and, as usual, capitalizing on the obvious, folklore has it that the Manx is a distinct species. The first "rumpy," it is claimed, came from a cross between a rabbit and a cat, taking its high-hind-leggedness and taillessness from the rabbit and its other somatic characters from the cat. But the Manx cat doesn't breed true. Often it has low hindquarters and a tail. With justified contempt, folk call these throwbacks "stumpies." Since the Manx is an article of commerce exported at a profit to the far ends of the earth, breeders summoned scientists to devise methods of getting a pure tailless high-hind-legged strain that would bring forth after its kind. The disappointing genetical investigations developed that the Manx breeds with ordinary cats to produce fertile offspring, and is hence miscalled a species distinct from ordinary cats. Professor Frederick Zeuner, a London zoologist, explodes the cat-rabbit folklore by defining Manx cats as "simple mutations with a tailless characteristic apparently linked with high leggedness."[17] He even detracts from the glory of the Isle of Man by ruthlessly pointing out that they "are quite common throughout the Far East." So pure science has its say, but the Isle of Man Manx Cat Association produces still another version and one calculated to maintain the price of stud fees, which is sagging. According to this revised genetical information the first Manx cat was a "sport" and a tom "who managed to impress his dominant male characters on a large number of impressionable queens." This version gives taillessness a more secure footing, if the metaphor is not mixed, and may be called a kind of "Chamber of Commerce" folklore.

The ancients believed in mashing up a quantity of ticks to secure a curative salve useful in the treatment of certain skin affections. Pliny the Elder recommends tick blood as a depilatory and as a curative ointment. It was also used as an aphrodisiac. I suppose very few sophisticated people consider this other than worn-out folklore coming down to us from unscientific ages. But Dr. Cornelius B. Philip, of the U. S. Public Health Service, doesn't think so.[18] Having spent his whole life studying ticks he now assures us that tick blood contains an antibiotic that inhibits growth of many species of bacteria. So it is quite possible that, with a little more experimentation with the gore of the humble tick, folklore may be able to stick another feather in its cap and say, "I told you so."

Actual experimentation has proved that a vulture can take off from a tower or other eminence and fly for miles with a weight in his talons which he could not possibly lift up from a level surface. Tales of baby-snatching by eagles met their quietus in these experiments. Weight-lifting experiments and observations seemed also to discredit folk tales of how any decadent descendant of Reinecke Fuchs could make off with a ten-pound goose. But science, apparently, doesn't know its fox as well as folklore knows him, as will later appear.

The big owl, whose bulk is mostly hollow bones and feathers, has been accused of making away with much more than his weight of hen. Confronted by the skeptic who has actually seen a good-sized owl unable to lift a medium-sized fryer off the ground, much less a full grown hen, a very pretty little story is invented which seems to obviate the difficulty.

True enough, you are told, no one of the big owls can get off the ground with the weight of a hen in his talons; but, being a very wise bird, the owl takes advantage of certain well-known laws of flight by snatching his hen on the wing.

You immediately object to this on the ground that hens fly very little during daylight hours, not at all at night when the owls are feeding.

"But you don't know your owl," comes the ready response. "The owl catches his hen as she flies down from the roost, and soars happily off without violating any law of flight."

Now you think that you have your taletelling nature-faker backed up in a corner. "So," you say, with the triumphant air of a lawyer who has just trapped a troublesome witness, "you call the owl a wise bird, and still you would have her wait around the barnyard until daylight for a hen to fly down from her roost. A likely story! when the farmer is already up and feeding his horses. Wouldn't he make short work of an owl perched up in a tree waiting for one of his fat hens to fly down!"

But your witness slips out of the noose even as you begin to tighten it.

Oh, no, the owl doesn't wait until daylight — by no means. He simply flies quietly in about midnight and perches right beside his sleeping victim. You know owls fly very quietly. Presently he gives the hen a little nudge, which means "move over." The sleeper, accustomed as she is to being pushed around on the roost by members of her own clan, squawks a weak little protest and promptly moves over. The intruder now waits until the hen of his choice goes back to sleep. Then he gives her another nudge towards the end of the roost, and gets the same satisfying reaction, a little squawk and a little move over. Thus patiently and very gently he gets his "intended" right to the end of the roost. The brute now changes his tactics and gives his hen a violent shove off the roost and swoops down after her. At just the point where he has gained the necessary momentum, he fastens his talons securely in her back and away they go on his wide wings to the hungry brood hidden safely in the deep, deep woods, far, far away.

I had never thought of doubting this story until I became folklore-conscious. Then I found that I couldn't remember a single farmer who had ever "seen with his own eyes" this owl-hen drama occur. Owls hooted over in the bottom and next morning a hen was missing: "after this, therefore on account of this" — typical folk reasoning. I began cross-questioning everyone who told the story but failed to get even one eyewitness. There were those who had heard squawking and flapping in the old dead hackberry tree where the chickens roosted and had rushed out there *just after* that damned old owl had made off with the fattest hen on the place. And "surenuff" next morning feathers were scattered all over the place — surely light evidence to sustain so heavy an indictment.

In 1942 I struck a hot trail. Miss Edna McCormick, at that time professor of mathematics in the Southwest Texas State Teachers College at San Marcos, said her father had actually seen an owl do this very thing. My heart fluttered a little as I asked her if her father were still living, for I needed a firsthand observation from a living witness. Yes, he was alive, living in Denton, Texas.

With reference to the owl and the chicken [his reply to my letter began], your letter received and the facts are as follows:
At my father's home in Denton on a moonlight night, about 67 years ago, I was in the yard near an unfinished crib. The ridgepole was exposed, and chickens were roosting on it. I saw an owl light beside a hen, and begin pushing it. The owl tried several times to push the hen off the roost, and every time the owl pushed the hen would squawk. [These lovely details! what a witness!] The owl seemed to know, the only chance to carry off the hen was to force it off the roost, and catch it on the fly. [Here I drew a deep breath. Now I have it nailed down, I muttered. But alas! there was a final sentence.]
I frightened the owl away to save the hen.

Very truly yours,<br>W. L. McCormick.

James R. Simmons, Contributing Editor of *The Land*,[19] quotes and flatly contradicts the eminent naturalist, Roy Chapman Andrews' debunkation of two folk stories: (1) that of how handily a fox can make off with a fat goose; and (2) the old, old story of the snake's swallowing its young.

Regarding the first, Simmons quotes Andrews as saying that the fox never undertakes to make off with anything larger than he can handle. His jaws and body size are not built for a quarry as big as a goose, turkey or heavy fowl.

Just the other morning [replies Editor Simmons], I saw a red fox emerge from a timothy field, cross the farm road and disappear into a patch of woodland, dragging a fowl that would weigh at least ten pounds, and *I'll swear that it was slung from his shoulder!* I was near enough to observe how this was accomplished....

Two reliable persons have recently told me that they saw a fox carry off a goose, "on his back." One, a Canadian woman, has described the entire procedure from kill to get-away, as she actually saw it in the barnyard of her farm home.

How is it done? Not of course by main strength of body or jaw but by sheer skill in the distribution of weight. The fox first kills the goose. Then he grasps it by the neck, close to the head. With a clever twist he slides his body underneath. Then he rises and goes forward in a comparatively straight line. He never backs up, tugging at his load as a dog or even a man so often does. The quarry hangs across his shoulder somewhat as a man would carry a partially filled sack of grain. The body of the goose drags. But the weight of the pull is actually on the body of the fox.

Again, you see, Reynard the Fox comes up triumphant. Folk don't credit the fox with cleverness without warrant. He may have a fragile body, but what a mind!

As for the snake-swallowing story, Mr. Simmons quotes Roy Chapman Andrews as saying that many years of scientific observations fail "to produce evidence that a snake ever swallowed its young." Then Mr. Simmons gives an eyewitness account with himself on the witness stand.

"Recently," he reports, "I came upon a three-foot snake, stepped on its tail and held it captive for examination. The snake immediately opened its mouth and out wiggled four small specimens of the same species, each about two or three inches in length and in excellent health and vigor.... I can name other observers who have seen the same thing." J. Frank Dobie can, too. Mr. Dobie has flirted with acceptance of this story as true for years, and has speculated entertainingly about it in various articles, the most thoroughly documented of which appeared in the publication of the Texas Folklore Society for 1946, "Do Rattlesnakes Swallow Their Young?"[20] He contents himself here with quoting authorities. "I repeat," he concludes, "that I affirm nothing, that I merely transmit." Like Paul, Dobie appears at times "almost persuaded"; and the last time we discussed the matter, he was still wavering.

Mr. Simmons' account, in my opinion, would have been improved had he identified the species under his observation. He says definitely that the little fellows were the *same* species as the adult, but he does not say *what* species.

With these few samples of the kinds of folklore that pervade natural history and popular reasoning on the subject, I should like to be able to draw certain profound conclusions relative to the mind of man and the nature of belief. But alas! I must content myself with that which is already apparent to any reader, with pointing out that natural-history folklore consists largely of folk fancy playing about irresponsibly with mere appearances; that folklore jumps at conclusions; that it seems incapable of rational analysis; that it must give every organ a function, whether or no; that its humor leans to the broad and the grotesque; that it paints with a wide brush; that it has an overwhelming yen for mysterious happenings in nature (whence we deduce that man is a natural at wonder-mongering); that folk interpretations of natural phenomena are incurably anthropocentric; and finally and marvelously, that folklore in the field of natural history often discovers facts or principles at which science scoffs for some centuries only to be forced at long last to accept them.

So, looking out from my own restricted field over the vast, vast field of folklore, I am no longer amazed at its persistence, its power, its philosophical implications, and its entertaining qualities. Age cannot wither it nor custom stale its infinite variety. I am appalled at the crude amount, at the mass and smothering volume of that which we call folklore, including, as it does, the traditional customs, vernacular ballads, sayings, and beliefs, especially those of a superstitious or legendary character, preserved unreflectively by a people. And, of course, this mass is by no means homogeneous throughout the world. Cross racial boundaries or language barricades, or change social levels inside specific racial or language groups, and the character of much of the folklore is transformed. Indeed, it would hardly be an exaggeration to say that folklore constitutes the basis of 99 per cent of the mental and emotional life of 99 per cent of the people.

On the time scale of evolution, mind itself is a late-comer, while the modern mind's main instrument, reason, came on the scene only day before yesterday. Considered in the large, that is, taking into view mankind as a whole, reason as motivation has established but limited sovereignty and that only in restricted areas of the vast jungle where human motives arise and give impulsion to action. "Thinking," says Professor Toynbee, "is as unnatural and arduous an activity for human beings as walking on two legs is for monkeys."

Speculating on the universal appeal of folklore, I return again to my trail theory as a helpful analogy. All normal human beings like to wander through the woods following footpaths beaten out by the tread of savage feet, which, in turn, took them over from the hoofed or padded feet of animals. And so does the machine-age mind, tired of rational dictation, like to be turned loose to take its own way in wilderness areas along brain-tracks scored in the primitive or even in the subhuman brain, and now appearing as inherited vestiges of a very ancient traffic.

Dim trails, they are, with twists and turns and many branchings-off, offering free choice at frequent intervals, including that always present one of back-tracking when the prospect no longer pleases. Here the vacationing mind may idle, entertain not-so beliefs, think as wishfully as it pleases without rebuke, indulge prejudices and prepossessions and, when the mood strikes, may even burlesque that great tyrant Reason with clownish abandon. Here its hankering after "hunches" and other mental atavisms finds a congenial climate. This, I take it, makes for the wide appeal of folklore, and this may be its main contribution to sanity.

1. General J. C. Smuts, *Holism and Evolution* (New York, 1926), p. 336.
2. A. C. Bent, *Life Histories of North American Cuckoos, Goatsuckers, Hummingbirds, and Their Allies* (Washington, 1940; U.S. National Museum *Bulletin* 176), p. 349.
3. According to Gordon C. Aymar, *Bird Flight* (New York, 1938), p. 133, the hummer makes "up to 200 strokes per second," apparently counting both down-beats and up-beats as strokes. A. C. Bent, on p. 345 of the work cited above, explains how the flight of the hummingbird has been studied by means of a high-speed camera. He states the results: "Dr. Charles H. Blake examined with great care the films taken of hummingbirds in flight and found that the birds beat their wings 55 times (completed strokes) a second when hovering, 61 a second when backing, and as rapidly as 75 a second when progressing straightaway. Probably this last figure would be found to increase as the bird

gained speed, if the camera could keep the bird in focus." Since Blake is speaking of completed strokes, his figures would have to be doubled to make them comparable to Aymar's.

4. Breland, *Animal Facts and Fancies* (New York, 1948), p. 182.

5. Edward W. Meyer, Jr., editor, *Natural History Magazine*, tells me that the label on an exhibit formerly existing in the Fish Hall of the American Museum of Natural History read as follows: *"The Black Pirates*. These deep-sea pirates are not snakes but 'degraded eels,' that have lost almost everything but their voracious appetites. One of them has just swallowed a fish that is bigger than himself, which stretches him nearly to his elastic limit. His less fortunate mate, yawning fearfully, opens the dark gateway to a cavernous interior."

6. *Op. cit.*, p. 111. Dr. Breland writes "learned published articles" with tongue in cheek.

7. From Eckstein's "Lives" (1932), in *The Book of Naturalists*, ed. William Beebe (New York, 1944), p. 358.

8. For an extreme example of facial hideousness in bats, see photographs of a large carnivorous member of the leaf-nosed family, the "javelin bat" (*Phyllostomus hastatus panamensis*), close relative of the vampire bats, p. 48 and p. 90 in G. M. Allen's *Bats* (Cambridge, Mass., 1940), or Hegner, *infra*, p. 537.

9. Robert Hegner assisted by Jane Z. Hegner, *Parade of the Animal Kingdom* (New York, 1944), p. 538.

10. See Paul Russell Cutright, *The Great Naturalists Explore South America* (New York, 1940), chapter on the vampire bat, pp. 47-57, from which much of the information in the summary is derived.

11. *Ibid.*, p. 47.

12. Charles Darwin, *Journal of Researches ... During the Voyage of H.M.S. Beagle* (New York, 1896), p. 22.

13. See Cutright, *op. cit.*, p. 55.

14. Carl C. Hartman, *Possums* (Austin: University of Texas Press, 1952).

15. *Ibid.*, p. 83.

16. See Harold C. Reynolds, "The Opossum," *Scientific American*, CLXXXVIII (1953), 90.

17. See *New York Times*, 5 May 1953, p. 15, cols. 2-4.

18. "Tick Talk," *Scientific Monthly*, LXXVI (1953), 77-78. See also Ludwick Anigstein, Dorothy M. Whitney, and Don W. Micks, "Antibacterial Factor in Tick Extracts," *Texas Reports on Biology and Medicine*, VIII (1950), 86-100.

19. James R. Simmons, "From a Cabin in the Woods," *The Land*, Vol. VI (1947), No. 1, pp. 42-43. Simmons paradoxically heads his discussion of the fox and the snake "Myths That Are True."

20. *Mexican Border Ballads and Other Lore*, ed. Mody C. Boatright (Austin, 1946; Texas Folklore Society Publication XXI), pp. 43-64.

GEORGE D. HENDRICKS

# The Names of Western Wild Animals

As THE PIONEER westward emigrant first observed a strange animal of the New World, he usually misnamed it. His sole guides were his own past experience, which was deceiving, and the animal's physical appearance — an invalid criterion.

For example, three out of twelve names applied to mountain sheep signify goats; two, deer. Five out of twenty names applied to the opossum belong rightfully to other unrelated species. The stranger the animal, the more names it accumuulated from wider sources. This confusion in misnaming animals was a token of pioneers' tremendous adjustment to a strange, new environment.

## The Bighorn

The explorer found in the bighorn something quite unlike anything he had been accustomed to. Though Colonel Dodge knew the animal well, its mixture of animal traits was to him a puzzle: "The mountain sheep is a curious combination. His body is that of a very large deer; his head that of a domestic sheep, except that no domestic sheep could possibly carry the enormous horns with which his mountain cousin is provided."[1]

Peregrine Herne observed, "This animal partakes of the nature of both deer and goat."[2] Inevitably, naming such a creature must have presented a problem.

In the history of the West at least twelve different popular names have been applied to the bighorn, three of which signify goats and two, deer. In 1697 Jesuit missionaries of California used an Indian name for bighorn, *taje,* later Anglicized to *taye.* A century later, the scientist Thomas Pennant called it *argalia* in his *Arctic Zoology,*

THE NAMES OF WESTERN WILD ANIMALS  41

thus equating the bighorn with the largest Asiatic sheep. In 1800 Duncan McGillivray cited three different names: the Cree Indian *My-attic* (ugly reindeer); another Indian name *Emi-Ki-Ca-Now* (also applied to deer); and the Canadian French *le bélier des montagnes* (mountain ram). The journals of Lewis and Clark include *argalia, Rocky Mountain sheep,* the Mandan word *ahsahta* (which was Irving's favorite), and *bighorn;* and Sergeant Patrick Gass quoted Captain Clark's misnomer *ibex,* the name of a European goat.[3] In 1879 Baillie-Grohman recorded the Spanish *cimarrón,* and about the same time Peregrine Herne cited it as *carnero cimeron.* O'Connor writes that, at present, it is called *borregos salvajes* (wild sheep) in the cities of Mexico and *chivos* (goats) by natives of Sonoyta, Sonora. In the Philippines, oddly enough, the *cimarrón* is a wild water buffalo.

The pioneer had no real precedent for naming such an exotic looking animal as the bighorn. He experimented, therefore, with Spanish, French, and Indian names, and for once came to the happiest and simplest solution of calling it by its own most distinguishing feature. At the same time he circumvented the usual feeling for the need to classify the animal. At any rate, here was a native animal that deserved a native christening — the *bighorn.*

## The Cougar

One of Richard Hakluyt's early English voyagers wrote that the natives of Virginia "sometimes kill the lion, and eat him."[4] Another traveler listed among the "beastes best known in this country [the West Indies] . . . the leopard . . . and a certaine kinde of beaste that differeth little from the Lyon of Africa."[5] Not knowing what to call these new *Felidae,* the newcomer applied names of similar Old World animals.

The cougar, therefore, had several aliases. Mountain man and hunter Ben Lilly gave his testimony:

I grew up in Mississippi and Louisiana hearing the American puma called pantha; in Mexico I heard it called *león,* also *panthera;* in Idaho I heard it called cougar; in New Mexico and Arizona it is generally lion or mountain lion. Under these names I have killed the same animal, measurements varying little, from the Mississippi River to the Continental Divide.[6]

Even Ben Lilly's list is not complete. There were also *painter* (a variant of *panther*), *catamount* (a brief form of *cat-of-the-mountain*), and *red tiger*. John Mortimer Murphy, an educated British hunter, applied the name *pard* to the cougar, taking it from the scientific designation of the Old World panther, *Felis pardus*.

Despite the frontier currency of these Old World names, pioneers encountered and used two New World names, *puma* and *cougar*. The history of these names is of itself a matter of interest. *Puma* came directly from Spanish but primarily was a Peruvian word. In his book on Mexico, C. F. Lummis, in 1898, commented: "The proper name of the American lion today is puma, and that is an Inca word that Pizarro found in the Fifteen-thirties among the Andes ... its Peruvian name ... by now is accepted, not only in all Spanish countries, but wherever English is spoken."[7]

The word *cougar* came to English by a devious path. There is a Tupi-Guarani tribe native to Brazil, which had two words *guacu ara* (OED), which were applied to the animal. European scientists and explorers adapted the name from the natives and from one another in the following sequence: Marcgraf, Pison (1648), Ray (1693), Buffon (1749). It would seem that the name proceeded from Tupi to Dutch to Spanish to English to French and back to English.

All of these names, with the important exceptions of *cougar* and *puma*, were originally applied to Old World animals, none of which were native to Europe during recorded history. Only *cougar* and *puma* have been specifically applied to this distinctively New World animal — the *Felis concolor*. This Latin name itself seems most appropriate, because the cougar is one of the most colorful of the larger cats.

## The Opossum

The lowly opossum is the prime example of human befuddlement in naming strange American animals. It was called by at least five names belonging rightfully to other unrelated animals. It was not until about the middle of the eighteenth century that Captain James Cook introduced the Australian marsupials to Europe, so for two and a half centuries before that the homely opossum had been the only known pouched animal. It was naturally regarded as one of the strangest and most exotic animals in the world. Europeans had no accurate basis to compare or name it accordingly.

Because of its resemblance to a rat, the opossum was called *beutelratte* and *boschrat* in Dutch New Guinea and *rat-de-bois* or *rat sauvage* or *rat-de-forêt* by French Creoles. Since it had a like propensity to abscond with poultry, the opossum was often called *el zorro* in Central America. The Guaranis called it the *micure* (smelly), and the French of Guiana named it *puant* (fetid) — associating it perhaps with the polecat. These names and associations are, I think, unjust. When I was twelve years old, I captured and brought home half a dozen young opossums and kept them in my bedroom as companions, until my mother decided they should be given their freedom. While it is conceivable that pioneers would associate the opossum with the fox, rat, polecat, or even monkey, it is puzzling why anyone might confuse it with a weasel. In South America the native Indian designation for weasel, *comedreya*, was applied also to the opossum. The weasel is a mustelid, has a fine fur, is most agile on the ground and in trees, and is a vicious fighter; the opossum is a marsupial, has a poor fur, is sluggish in movement, and is almost defenseless.

Buffon adapted a native designation from South America, *careguiya*, rendering it in French as *sarigue*. Actually, there were at least ten different spellings of this word in the European languages, but Buffon's *sarigue* in one form or another found more currency in early frontier annals than did *opossum*.

The more unusual the animal, the more legendary it became, the more its misconceptions, and the more names it accumulated. The opossum had at least twenty New World designations. The name *woapink* of the Lenapes was said to mean "white face." True, the animal has a white face; and probably these other Indian names had some veiled descriptive significance: Aztec *tlacuatzin*, Tupi *maritacaca*, Choctaw *shukata*, Brazilian *gamba*, Cuban *zurcan*, Cherokee *seegua*, Ecuador *faras*. The source of English *opossum* was Ojibwa *wabassim*.

Sometimes, as in the case of the pronghorn and bighorn, the newcomer simply named a strange animal by its most unusual physical feature. If he had followed this procedure, he would have named the opossum the *pouch*. The scientist, in assigning the name *Marsupialia* to the order of mammals having pouches, followed this principle, the word coming from Latin *marsupium,* and ultimately from Greek *marsypos,* meaning "a little pouch or purse."

## The Prairie Dog

The prairie dog is not as insignificant as its size might cause one to believe. Though small, as a symbol of the pioneer's difficulty with his new environment, it looms large. The prairie dog is not really a dog, but a rodent. Its misnomer, therefore, seems indicative of the pioneer's misunderstanding of the new and different plains country.

To most people the word rodent means only mice or rats; they do not realize that the *Rodentia* family of mammals consists of at least 7,000 species of gnawing animals, or roughly one-third of all mammals. Captain William Clark, Edwin Bryant, and James O. Pattie called the prairie dog a sort of rat. Francis Parkman and Lieutenant James W. Abert called it a marmot (which is also a rodent). Colonel Dodge wrote that the animal had "no more of the dog about him than an ordinary gray squirrel."[8] And an old stage-driver, telling about prairie dogs, once said to Vernon Bailey: "If them things was called by their right names, there would not be one left in the country. They are just as good as squirrel, and I don't believe they are any relation to dogs."[9]

Captain Meriwether Lewis first called this exotic little beast a barking squirrel and later a burrowing squirrel. And Captain Randolph B. Marcy took great pains to explain how, because of its appearance and physical characteristics, it should be a called a squirrel.

The prairie dog's voice, probably more than anything else, gave him his name. It was like the barking of a miniature dog. Because of this diminutive sound and the co-ordinate jerking of the tail, the prairie dog was frequently likened to a toy dog. Lewis, for example, wrote:

> When at rest above ground their position is generally erect on their hinder feet and rump; thus they will generally set and bark at you as you approach them, their note being much that of the little toy dog, their yelps are in quick succession and at each they give a motion to their tails upwards.[10]

And Josiah Gregg recorded in his *Commerce of the Prairie,* "Its yelp, which resembles that of the little toy-dog, seems its only canine attribute."[11]

The various onomatopoetic versions of the prairie dog's bark are themselves evidence of confusion and puzzlement. Gregg used the words "yelp" and "bark"; Abert, "cheh, cheh"; and Lewis, "whistle." But Zebulon Pike's version, borrowed from Indians, was most singular:

> The wishtonwish of the Indians, prairie-dogs of some travelers, or squirrels, as I should be inclined to denominate them, reside on the prairies. . . . As you approach their towns, you are saluted on all sides by the cry of "wishtonwish," from which they derive their name with the Indians, uttered in a shrill and piercing manner.[12]

Thus we have the words of a merchant, army officers, a scientist, and an Indian. All of the symbols are different. Certainly, the newcomer must have been confused and puzzled by the animal and by its sound.

Pioneer adaptation of native names of animals or coinage of new English words to designate New World animals, though often erroneous, was a small but definite example of the germ theory (as applied to the study of history) in reverse: the influence of the frontier upon civilized Europe. The mere increase in European vocabulary, to say nothing of the increase in the numbers of known varieties of animals, was appreciable. The example could be multiplied many times by such words as skunk, ocelot, jaguarundi, cacomixtle, kinkajou, eyra, coyote, peccary, puma, coatimundi, raccoon, tuco-tuco, jaguar, and cougar. All of these were New World names of New World animals, which were soon to find their ways into European natural histories and glossaries.

Western wild animals, therefore, had a significant part in acquainting the people of Europe and other continents with the new frontiers being opened in the Western hemisphere — a part not yet fully realized or analyzed.

---

1. Richard I. Dodge, *The Hunting Grounds of the Great West* (2nd ed.; London, 1879), p. 205.

2. Peregrine Herne, *Perils and Pleasures of a Hunter's Life* (New York, n.d.), p. 20.
3. George R. Stewart, "Popular Names of the Mountain Sheep," *American Speech*, X (1935), 283-88.
4. Richard Hakluyt, *The Principal Navigations, Voyages, Traffiques, and Discoveries of the English Nation* (New York, 1907), VI, 181-82.
5. *Ibid.*, VI, 235.
6. J. Frank Dobie, *The Ben Lilly Legend* (Boston, 1950), p. 186.
7. C. F. Lummis, *The Awakening of a Nation; Mexico of Today* (New York, 1898), p. 164.
8. Richard I. Dodge, *The Hunting Grounds of the Great West*, p. 211.
9. Walter P. Webb, *The Great Plains* (Boston and New York, 1936), p. 39.
10. *The Original Journal of the Lewis and Clark Expedition, 1804-06*, ed. R. G. Thwaites (New York, 1904-5), V, 177.
11. T. H. Scheffer, "Historical Encounter and Accounts of the Plains Prairie Dog," *Kansas Historical Quarterly*, XIII (1945), 534.
12. *The Expeditions of Zebulon Montgomery Pike*, ed. E. Coues (New York, 1895), II, 430.

JOSEPH W. HENDREN

# Bonny Barbara Allen

I

On an international scale "Barbara Allen" is not the most widely circulated ballad, nor does it outrank other ballads in every respect in its own homeland. Yet there is undeniably something supreme about the old song of cruel Barbara and her jilted lover, a genuine greatness that depends not simply upon immense circulation but upon intrinsic quality too.[1]

To this many people have borne witness. Alan Lomax expresses an opinion common among ballad hunters when he writes, "For two hundred years 'Barbara Allen' has been the best loved of all English ballads," and he quotes a Georgian mountain farmer who recently told him, "Every time I hear 'Barbara Allen' it makes the hair raise on my head." Oliver Goldsmith carries us back two centuries when he declares with Irish exuberance, "The music of the finest singer is dissonance to what I felt when our old dairy maid sung me to tears with 'Johnny Armstrong's Last Good-Night' or 'The Cruelty of Barbara Allen.'" Earlier still, Pepys wrote in his diary under January 2, 1666, "In perfect pleasure I was to hear her [Mrs. Knipp, the actress] sing, and especially her little Scotch song of Barbara Allen."[2] And from William Owens comes a modern East Texas vignette, quoted from a letter addressed by L. D. Bertillion to "Friend Dobie": "In the fall of 1938 a friend took me to see Bob Brown, an old-timer who lived on the road between Kountze and Sour Lake at the edge of the Big Thicket. In answer to our request for songs, he replied that he knew 'Sweet William.' Needing little urging, he leaned against a picket fence and sang this version of 'Barbara Allen.' When he came to the line 'Young man, I think you're dying,' tears filled his eyes and he brushed at his wrinkled cheek with the back of his hand. He showed no embarrassment nor offered any apology for his sentiment." The striking thing about these various attestations is their similarity. When people respond to the song, poet or peasant, scholar or share-cropper, they seem to do it in the same way and for the same reasons. Urbane listeners of our own day, I have noticed, often find in a really good singing presentation something more than the quaintness they are expecting.

It is not surprising that a ballad able to affect people in this way should steadily widen its geographical range. "Barbara Allen" has of course done so, though our knowledge of distribution is still very general and, concerning the earlier American period, very scarce. Sporadic references show the song well known in Colonial times, sung by Abe Lincoln, used in old New England as a lullaby and children's game song, and the like. And the evidence of variants collected during the past forty years makes clear that the ballad must have been carried across the ocean during the seventeenth and eighteenth centuries in the memories of many hundreds, or more likely thousands, of English and Scotch settlers. But beyond that the record is mostly blank, for scholars of earlier times seem to have paid little attention to such matters. Early in the present century, in fact, so few learned people were aware of folk balladry that when W. E. Gilbert in the fall of 1912 took down a variant of "Barbara Allen" from the lips of an authentic country singer, the editors of the *University of Virginia Magazine* hailed the event with surprise and excitement.

Academic interest picked up rapidly. In 1915, when field collecting was first beginning to look like the embryo of a scholarly movement, Reed Smith noted the discovery of versions in Georgia, Virginia, South Carolina, Tennessee, and New England, and reported "Barbara Allen" as leading all American ballads both in geographical distribution and in the number of variants. Thirteen years later he was able to repeat this estimate, adding this time that the song could be found in all parts of the country. In 1929, with the harvest of folk song growing sizable, A. K. Davis reported the early favorite still in the lead, with ninety-two versions recovered in Virginia alone, thirty-six of which appear in his own volume. Using a slightly different basis of comparison, H. M. Belden in 1940 confirmed the opinions already cited. He refers to "Barbara Allen" as the "most widely known and sung of all the ballads admitted by Child." John Lomax reported in 1947 that eighty-three versions had been recorded from folk singers by the Division of Music of the Library of Congress. When A. P. Hudson speaks of the ballad as the best known in Mississippi, he is representing the usual, though not the invariable, experience of collectors as they have worked in their own local states or regions.

Today the panorama, despite wide gaps, is rather impressive. Variants have been recorded from Nova Scotia, Newfoundland, Cape Breton Island, and half the states of the Union: Maine, Vermont, New York, Pennsylvania, Ohio, Indiana, Illinois, Maryland, West Virginia, North and South Carolina, Florida, Tennessee, Georgia, Kentucky, Arkansas, Alabama, Mississippi, Louisiana, Texas, Nebraska, and Oregon. Though published collections can give us but fragmentary information about the general areas they represent, some rough observations are certainly warranted by the collectors' work. For one thing, the returns seem to show "Barbara Allen" comparatively rare nowadays in New England. Barry says it is hard to recover in Maine but adds that it was once known everywhere in that region, an observation well supported by aged Mrs. Carrie Grover, of Gorham, who would not bother to sing the ballad for Evelyn Wells on the ground that everyone knew it. At all events, *British Ballads from Maine* (1929) prints but four variants; *The New Green Mountain Songster* (1939) shows none. This is in sharp contrast to the wealth of versions turned up by collectors, Cecil Sharp and A. K. Davis for example, in the South. Perhaps the disparity can best be accounted for by the greater isolation of the mountain regions where so many of the Southern variants have been recovered.

Although modernization has gone far toward eradicating folk arts in the Middle Atlantic and some Midwestern states, field workers have found a moderate traditional circulation over this area. West of the Mississippi direct information is scarce, but the few soundings taken there, added to the many taken elsewhere, give us a pretty clear idea of conditions on a continental scale. That few of the Western states are represented in ballad compilations means only, of course, that organized collecting has not yet started in those areas. The fact that the ballad turns up wherever an effort is made to find it really tells the story. Texas, in this connection, is an eye-opener of particular value. Here, as William Owens tells us, the ballad was known to the cowboys of the old days, and it is certainly familiar in tradition at the present time. What is true of folk song in Texas, moreover, we might well expect to be true to northward and westward, since those vast reaches of country were settled mainly by people of similar racial stocks and cultural antecedents. It seems reasonable to suppose that circulation of the song in former times was roughly coextensive, right along, with the settlement of the country and has remained so.

If we cross the ocean to the British Isles the general scene is much the same and need not be described in detail. The *Journal of the Folksong Society* (1899-1926) shows a generous distribution. Cecil Sharp wrote in 1916: "There is no ballad that country singers are more fond of than that of 'Barbara Allen,' or 'Barbarous Ellen,' or 'Edelin,' as it is usually called." Writing in 1891 Frank Kidson noted that the ballad was common in both England and Scotland, that "few ballads have had more lasting popularity." And he adds, "It is quite needless to say that by the very reason of its being such a favorite there are endless versions of both the song and the tune." The variants in Gavin Greig's *Last Leaves* show the song flourishing in modern Scotland. Evidence of traditional vitality in 19th century Ireland comes from P. W. Joyce, who writes in *Ancient Irish Music* (1873) of a young girl, Ellen Ray, of Limerick, who sang an ancient modal version "with power and feeling." In this variant the direct quotation of the bell tones ("And every toll that the death-bell gave/Was, 'I died for you, Barbara Ellen'") is a highly unusual and vivid rendering of the lost lover's accusing spirit.

Considering what we have reviewed and taking account of the dispersion brought about in recent years by published collections, by college courses in folk song, balladry, and literature, by hillbilly performers, radio, television, stage shows (e.g. *Dark of the Moon)*, and phonographic recordings, it seems inferable that "Barbara Allen" must nowadays be familiar to a greater number of people than ever before in its history — to some extent, one might suppose, in all parts of the world where English is the common speech. Curious irony, that mechanical entertainment, while assisting in the demolition of folk song as a traditional art, should be awarding to it a publicity beyond anything previously dreamed of.

## II

The most historically distinguished model of "Barbara Allen" in existence is the old Scotch version, and it carries more than one mark of distinction. It has appeared in the largest number of famous ballad books, was the first version ever to be published in an anthology, and probably represents, traditionally speaking, the oldest form of words and music in which the ballad has come down to us. There is, indeed, the possibility that this venerable specimen may be a close approximation to the unknown original composition. We have no factual knowledge about the old Scotch version, however, until 1740, the year in which it was published by James Oswald in *A Curious Collection of Scots Tunes* and also by Allan Ramsay in *The Tea Table Miscellany*.[3] The ancient text has been abundantly preserved in tradition, as well as in many reprintings, down to our own time. The antiquated Aeolian tune has proved less durable. It appears in English songbooks of the 19th century, and Gavin Greig's scores show it still common in Scotland (where it was formerly used also for "Binorie" and "The Rantin Laddie"), but I have not encountered a survival of it in America, and its replacement by many other tunes furnishes a striking example of the greater fluidity in tradition of melody as contrasted with poem. From the following score we can gain a fair idea of what "Barbara Allen" sounded like in 17th century Scotland.[4]

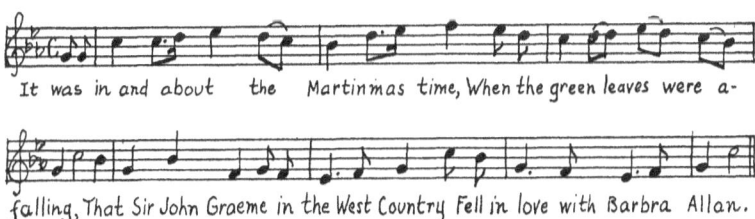

It was in and about the Martinmas time, When the green leaves were a-falling, That Sir John Graeme in the West Country Fell in love with Barbra Allan.

    He sent his man down through the town
        To the place where she was dwelling;
    O haste and come to my master dear,
        Gin ye be Barbara Allan.

    O hooly, hooly rose she up
        To the place where he was lying,
    And when she drew the curtain by,
        Young man, I think you're dying.

> O it's I'm sick and very, very sick
>   And 'tis a' for Barbara Allan.
> O the better for me ye's never be,
>   Though your heart's blood were a-spilling.
>
> O dinna ye mind, young man, said she,
>   When ye was in the tavern a-drinking,
> That ye made the healths gae round and round
>   And slighted Barbara Allan?
>
> He turned his face unto the wall
>   And death was with him dealing.
> Adieu, adieu, my dear friends all,
>   And be kind to Barbara Allan.
>
> And slowly, slowly raise she up
>   And slowly, slowly left him,
> And sighing, said she could not stay,
>   Since death of life had reft him.
>
> She had not gane a mile but twa
>   When she heard the dead-bell ringing,
> And every jow that the dead-bell geid,
>   It cried woe to Barbara Allan.
>
> O Mother, Mother, make my bed,
>   O make it soft and narrow;
> Since my love died for me today,
>   I'll die for him tomorrow.

Runner-up in antiquity and prestige is the old English or Roxburgh text. This version appeared in the later 17th century as a blackletter broadside, of which two copies are extant in the Roxburgh collection. The Ballad Society's reprint shows a facsimile title page, embellished with a truly quaint woodcut and worded "Barbara Allen's Cruelty or The Young Man's Tragedy; with Barbara Allen's lament for her unkindness to her lover and herself." Place and date are not mentioned, but London can be assumed and editor William Chappell dates the copy as contemporary with Pepys. "To the tune of Barbara Allen" suffices for music. It also shows the song well known at the time of printing. This old version contains fifteen or sixteen stanzas, the sixteenth, when present, expressing Barbara's familiar warning to "shun the fault I fell in." A few stanzas have evidently been retouched, if not added altogether, by hack writers for commercial reasons. The text, which lacks the tavern scene, is less firmly woven than the Scotch poem, and the tincture of rhetoric and didacticism also tends a little to dilute its effect; but for all that it rounds out into a good ballad and, probably because it was originally imported in larger numbers, has been more influential in America than its Scottish counterpart. For this reason the entire song will be given here.

In Scarlet Town, where I was bound, There was a fair maid dwelling, Whom I had chosen to be my own, And her name it was Barbara Allen.

All in the merry month of May
    When the green leaves they was springing,
This young man on his death-bed lay,
    For the love of Barbara Allen.

He sent his man unto her then,
    To the town where she was dwelling:
You must come to my master dear,
    If your name be Barbara Allen.

For death is printed in his face,
    And sorrow's in him dwelling,
And you must come to my master dear,
    If your name be Barbara Allen.

If death be printed in his face,
    And sorrow's in him dwelling,
Then little better shall he be
    For bonny Barbara Allen.

So slowly, slowly she got up,
    And so slowly she came to him,
And all she said when she came there,
    Young man, I think you are a dying.

He turned his face unto her then:
    If you be Barbara Allen,
My dear, said he, come pitty me,
    As on my death-bed I am lying.

If on your death-bed you be lying,
    What is that to Barbara Allen?
I cannot keep you from [your] death;
    So farewell, said Barbara Allen.

He turned his face unto the wall,
    And death came creeping to him:
Then adieu, adieu, and adieu to all,
    And adieu to Barbara Allen.

And as she was walking on a day,
    She heard the bell a ringing,
And it did seem to ring to her
    Unworthy Barbara Allen.

She turnd herself round about,
    And she spy'd the corps a coming:
Lay down, lay down the corps of clay,
    That I may look upon him.

And all the while she looked on,
    So loudly she lay laughing,
While all her friends cry'd [out] amain,
    Unworthy Barbara Allen!

When he was dead, and laid in grave,
    Then death came creeping to she:
O mother, mother, make my bed,
    For his death hath quite undone me.

A hard-hearted creature that I was,
    To slight one that loved me so dearly;
I wish I had been more kinder to him,
    The time of his life when he was near me.

So this maid she then did dye,
    And desired to be buried by him,
And repented her self before she dy'd,
    That ever she did deny him.

    I cannot ascertain what tune is so cryptically referred to in the broadside, but probability lies with the one shown in this paper. Among other indications, E. F. Rimbault speaks of it as "a common traditional tune well known in the northern counties of England" and prints it, as an example of the English ballad, in his *Musical Illustrations of Percy's Reliques* (1850), from which the score above is taken. The melody is well known nowadays. It seems, however, to have gained its American popularity mostly among the educated through publication in songbooks, including the influential *Charlie Fox's Minstrel's Companion* (1861) and *Heart Songs* (1909). The two traditional specimens I have seen (from Maine and Nova Scotia) look as if they got their start with Fox's book.

The earliest publication of the old Roxburgh text in book form was Bishop Percy's in the *Reliques* (1765), and it was a great event in the career of the ballad. He was first to publish Scotch and English versions together and call attention to their separate existence. From then on, they were recognized as typical forms, and so great was the prestige of this anthology that songbook editors since have usually represented both texts exactly as Percy showed them, including verses which he doctored up according to the polite taste of his age. Jemmy Grove as hero first appears in print with Percy. No doubt he had been traditional for a good while previously, and his vogue since has been very great.

Two other favorite melodies deserve a passing glance. The first, clearly a very old one, is well distributed in American tradition and has not, to my knowledge, been found admissible to the popular songbooks, probably because of the archaic Dorian and Mixolydian modes in one of which it is usually cast. In various times and places it has been set to "The Baffled Knight," "The Cruel Mother," "Sir Neil and Glengyle," and "The Braes of Yarrow," from the latter of which it may have been derived. Attachment to so many ballads illustrates what an interwoven pattern of texts and tunes has sometimes been developed among singers when an attractive melody has got into circulation. The following Maine variant is Barry's. It is found in *British Ballads from Maine,* page 195, and is reprinted here through the courtesy of Yale University Press.

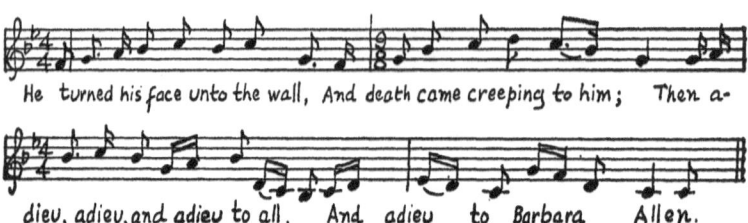

He turned his face unto the wall, And death came creeping to him; Then adieu, adieu, and adieu to all, And adieu to Barbara Allen.

The following air seems to have dropped out of living tradition in America but is familiar to many through its preservation in such well known publications as Kidson's *Traditional Tunes* and Sandburg's *The American Songbag*.

As she was walking on a day, She heard the bell a-ringing, And it did seem to ring to her "Unworthy Barbara Allen."

One more important melodic family remains to be illustrated, by far the most significant one in this country, but it will be introduced later in the paper in connection with a typical American textual variant.

Great tune families have been dominant in tradition, but many airs do not belong to them, and even within the families variety is great. Some have few traits left by which they can be recognized. Others are phrasal composites of two melodies. There are circular tunes, bimodal curiosities, and anomalies of many other sorts. An Iowa text is set to the familiar tune (slightly modified) of "The Bear Went Over the Mountain." The vitality of this tune, incidentally, is amazing; Ben Nilajagi, a native of India, tells me it is alive in the folk music of his own land, learned no doubt from resident Englishmen or Americans.

Modern English collections show wider diversity than anything to be found in those of our own country. There is a surprising assortment of unrelated strands and the sharpest variety in scales and rhythms, which is a little hard to account for unless it results simply from the greater age of the ballad in the Old World. Perhaps in earlier days, when people moved about less and communications were meager, the song in a given locality was comparatively freer, as the English language itself evidently was, to develop local idiosyncracies. The following beautiful melody in 5-time will illustrate the unusual rhythmic and tonal effects to be encountered in present-day English tradition. It was first recorded by Cecil Sharp in the *Journal of the Folksong Society* and has been reprinted several times in America, notably in Sharp's *One Hundred English Folksongs,* from which the following is taken. It is used here by permission of the Oliver Ditson Company, Bryn Mawr, Pennsylvania.

In Scotland I was born and bred, In Scotland I was dwelling, When a

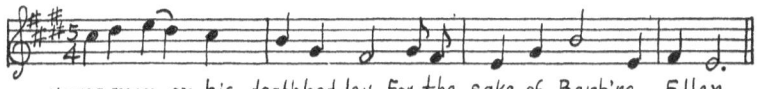

young man on his deathbed lay, For the sake of Barb'ra Ellen.

As ballad melodies go, Barbara Allen's assortment can hardly be rated as surpassingly fine. A few have the inimitable beauty of folk song at its highest level, but most of them are good in precisely the way that average ballad melodies are good, i.e. in being natural vehicles for their stories. Nowhere in balladry, or elsewhere, can we find better illustrated the fusion of musical and language meanings into a perfect unity of narrative rendering.

## III

Being a folk song, "Barbara Allen" has, in the usual literary sense, almost no history. Its great tradition has moved invisibly through the generations, and out of it scholars and collectors have occasionally taken samplings for publication. These samplings, plus a handful of chance comments scattered across centuries, constitute our only documents and hence our only evidence of the ballad's earlier existence. From them a few facts may be ascertained, some conjectures made, and some guesses hazarded if one chooses to do so out of pure curiosity. It is a fact that "Barbara Allen" originated somewhere in the British Isles and, except for a few French and German translations mentioned by Child, has since remained domestic, also highly popular, among the English-speaking people of the

Old and New World. It is also true that the song was known in Restoration England, for it was remarked by Pepys and published in a broadside at that time.

It is but conjecture that the ballad was composed in Scotland, though the grounds are good. They consist of the Scotch claim to national origination, the scarcity of challenge from the only source whence it could come, i.e. England, the strong traditional belief that "Barbara Allen" began as a romantic Border ballad, the occurrence of the Border name *Graham,* and — what appears to be the only direct comment in existence — an unexplained remark by W. Christie: "The scene of the story is supposed to have been at Annan, in Dumfriesshire." To which may be added that the plentiful survival of the old Scotch text in England and America, in contrast to the dearth of English and American models in Scotland, while not exactly proving anything, certainly gives an impression of Scotland as a center of radiation. True, there is the alternative chance that the ballad might have been composed, as a broadside or otherwise, in England early enough to have migrated slowly into Scotland, absorbed Caledonian markings, then recrossed the border, adorned with linguistic kilts and bagpipes, in time to be recognized in London in 1666 as a Scotch song. This might have happened, but it is more far-fetched and in the scales of probability rises on the lighter side.

And it is outright guesswork, guided only by general principles, that the ballad was made in the 16th or early 17th century by some humble Scot with a local reputation as an out-of-the-way songster, and that the story represents a romanticized and otherwise artistically distorted version of an actual incident. As Phillips Barry once said in support of this view, if Barbara Allen was not a real person, it took genius to invent her. "No other woman in balladry stands out so in the round, with incident, motive, and action all so consistently sequent."

If the ballad originated in some fashion in Scotland, as there is good reason to suppose, what subsequently happened to it in the Old World is not difficult to reconstruct in rough outline. Within several generations it spread, no one could guess through what devious channels, over considerable areas of Scotland and England and across the Irish Sea to Dublin. Inventive singers in some regions pleased their fancy by adding narrative ideas, often borrowed from other ballads, such as the dying man's legacies to Barbara and the rose-and-briar ending. Though most of these increments were short-lived, others hardened into permanent parts of the story. Across central and southern England the text soon lost its Scottish coloring. John Grame was supplanted by Jemmy Grove and the locale shifted to Reading or London or Carlisle. In fact Carlisle Town, gradually corrupted into Scarlet Town, became one of posterity's favorite settings. Thus arose an amplified and multiform English version, set to many new tunes, eagerly exploited by broadside printers in the larger cities, who sometimes, to help sales along, expanded their texts with original quatrains. Sometimes these innovations were tastefully executed; in other cases they must be called execrable deformities; and there were all degrees between. The forty-stanza monstrosities preserved in the Motherwell manuscript illustrate excrescences rejected as grotesque in folk tradition as shown by their failure to survive.

Meanwhile in Scotland the old song went on its way, without radical modification, until picked up somehow in 1740 by Oswald and Ramsay for its initial publication in book form.

## IV

As we have seen, the reputation of "Barbara Allen" points to a traditional song of unique interest and significance. What is there about the swift tragedy of a cruel girl and her hapless lover that could arouse such response among such a diversity of people over so long a period of time?

No doubt fortuitous factors of publication, theater performances, and the like have somewhat influenced the career of this ballad, but there can be nothing basically adventitious about the fame of a song which endures through centuries. The explanation of its hold upon the public lies in the ballad itself, in the simple beauty of its language and melody and the emotional impact of its dramatic situation. The story combines in a remarkably effective way the two imaginative sources of emotion dearest to the heart of the human race, namely romance and tragedy: the bewitching sweetness of love betwixt man and maid, and the impressive shock of death, with its attendant pathos. The two responses are authentically passionate;

they have their roots deep in the physical and spiritual nature of man; there is a kind of biological and cosmic compulsion about both of them. And they are given maximum freedom of action by the strange catalytic magic of the music in which their existence is poised.

To a reader versed only in the fictional methods of books and periodicals it might seem that a story so stripped of the embellishments ordinarily connected in a reader's mind with interest and vividness would lack power to survive, for there is little physical action in the tale, no scene, no approach, no introspection or psychological analysis, almost no color or elaboration of any kind. Yet it is paradoxically this very nakedness, this universality of nuclear human situation separated from all special occasion or place or known personality that has given the story in tradition its perdurable vitality. In contrast, the ballads with local association have been the ones to lose interest among succeeding generations, as we see illustrated in the Robin Hood and historical pieces, which show few survivals in America. The Barbara Allen story, if bare to the bones, is made of permanent ingredients independent of location, time, or passing fashion, and scarcity of incident is compensated for by the force of moral decision and passion involved in what action we do have. Carl Sandburg, in *The American Songbag,* notes the "paradox of tender and cruel forces operating together in life" and surmises that "perhaps something of that paradox working in the hearts of people has kept the Barbara Allen story alive and singing three centuries and more."

To those who know and love folk songs it is needless to point out that the true effect of a tragic ballad can only be experienced in hearing it sung with feeling and also with dignity and a fair share of tonal beauty. This fact is not to be deplored, but it renders aesthetic criticism, on the sole basis of a printed text, rather unsatisfactory. The objection does not hold, however, in the case of the text itself, which is our next object of attention. The following example is presented to illustrate what I think is a typical modern American variant and to give us a vantage point for closer observation of the story in connection with what has been happening to it in our own land.

## BONNY BARBARA ALLEN

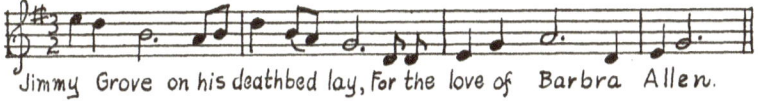

He sent his servant to the town,
    To the place where she was dwelling,
Saying, Come, my master bids you come
    If it's your name be Barbara Allen.

Slowly, slowly she got up
    And slowly she came nigh him,
Though all she said when she got there
    Was, Young man, I think you're dying.

Oh yes, I'm sick and very sick
    And death is with me dwelling.
Though death is printed on my brow,
    What need the tale you're telling?
Just one sweet kiss from your sweet lips
    Would keep me from my dying.

Don't you remember the other day
    When you were at the tavern?
You drinked your health to the ladies all round
    And slighted Barbara Allen.

Yes, I remember the other day
    When I was at the tavern;
I gave my hand to the ladies all round
    And my heart to Barbara Allen.

If on your death-bed you do lie,
    And oh, your heart is stilling,
I cannot keep you from your death;
    Farewell, said Barbara Allen.

He turned his face unto the wall,
    His back unto them, saying:
Adieu, adieu to my dear friends
    And farewell to Barbara Allen.

> As she was walking in the fields
>   And heard the death-bell tolling,
> And every stroke that did seem to say
>   One word to Barbara Allen.
>
> She turned her body all 'round and 'bout
>   And spied the corpse a-coming.
> Lay down, lay down the corpse, she said,
>   So I may look upon him.
>
> Oh Mamma, go make my bed,
>   Go make it long and narrow,
> For Jimmy has died for me today,
>   I'll die for him tomorrow.
>
> Young Jimmy was buried in the white churchyard
>   And Barbara was buried beside him,
> Out of Jimmy's grave sprang a deep red rose
>   And out of Barbara's a briar.
>
> They grew to the church's steeple-top
>   And couldn't get no higher,
> And there they tied in a true-lovers' knot,
>   Rose wrapped around a briar.

The tune, or more accurately the melodic pattern of which it is a variant, evidently did not originate in the United States, since Kidson has an English and Greig a Scottish example of it.[5] It seems to be rare in the Old World nowadays but has earned the best right to be called the favorite American folk tune for this ballad, especially in the South. It occurs in collections from eleven states, ranging from Massachusetts to Texas and, to judge by that, must be known practically everywhere else.[6]

As we have seen, the dichotomy of Scotch and English archetypes, first recognized by Percy, has become a critical commonplace. The line of cleavage is traceable to our own day, some modern texts following one, some the other, with widely varying degrees of accuracy or recomposition. Usually only the pull of tendency is visible; in a few cases the resemblance to an ancient version is remarkably close or exact, for in the tenuous convolutions of transmission, versions have sometimes entered oral circulation from printed sources,[7] just as printed versions have been derived from oral tradition at various points in the life of the ballad.

Most characteristic of all in modern America is the text in which tradition has blended both of the old types together, utilizing the most dramatically valuable elements of each. The resultant amalgam, without losing integrity, gains a hybrid variety and vitality. This has happened in the text shown above. From the ancient English archetype come Jimmy Grove, the month of May, the request for the kiss, and the glance at the corpse. The young man's statement of his plight and the crucial tavern scene derive from the old Scotch model. The tolling bell and Barbara's request of her mother belong to both types, but the wording shows they have descended from the English. There is, in fact, such an overbalance of English ingredients, especially in phrasing, that the text appears clearly to have been a British original onto which the Scotch features have been superadded. The most important American accretions or changes consist of the young man's defense of himself[8] and the altered diction and idiom, to which should be added the rose-and-briar motive, for although the latter did not originate in America, it is fairly regular in American texts and merely sporadic elsewhere.

We turn now to catch a glimpse of our text in the company of its fellow variants, looking first at the narrator's point of view toward his story. One of three slightly different methods is commonly employed. (1) The Scotch like to begin simply with the hero and hang tightly on to the grammatical third person throughout. (2) Typically in English models the tale is related in the third person except for a passing intrusion by the narrator in stanza 1, e.g., "In Scarlet Town where I was born." This touch may lend additional verisimilitude by its suggestion that the teller lived where the action happened, or might have been a witness. It is the favorite scheme in America. (3) Like (2) except that the teller begins by speaking in character, e.g. "I fell in love with a fair pretty maid." And other texts exist, as one would expect, in which the angle of narration shifts in almost a random manner.[9] A rare feature, which I have not noticed outside of America, is the mention in an early stanza of "three maids," among whom "the only one I called my own" was Barbara Allen.

"Barbara Allen" does not belong to the class of ballads represented by "Edward" and "Lord Randal" which unfold their story wholly in dialogue. The teller assumes the task of introducing the essentials of the situation, though this is done, balladwise, in the barest possible manner. We are usually told at the outset the names of the protagonists and of their relationship. We learn where the action happens[10] or at what season of the year,[11] or in some generous texts, both. Singers have shown a liking for considerable variety in background detail of this sort and they often show it in interesting ways. It is a curious thing that, whereas the hero masquerades under a bewildering variety of names,[12] or perhaps no name at all ("a young man"), Barbara never changes except for slightly variant pronunciations (Barbery, Barbry, etc.) and one not unnatural confusion with "Barbarous" noted by Cecil Sharp among the English peasantry, who also in some localities use Ellen or Edelin in place of Allen.[13] The contrast is explainable, I think, by one of the simplest axiomatic laws of ballad transmission: that the elements most important to the indispensable core of the narrative are always slowest to change or be lost, whether they be names, objects, or incidents. Here the figure of Barbara dominates the drama; she is of the two the dynamic soul, clearly defined throughout in the central focus of interest, and she therefore has exerted, in contrast to her lover, a far more tenacious hold on the memories of traditional narrators.

The personal slight to Barbara, originating in the old Scotch version, has proved so widely acceptable that it is integral today in a majority of American texts. As in the oldest examples, it is still usually a tavern event, "the toast," or "a treat," or "the cups" going round to all the ladies except prideful Barbara, who takes great offense at the omission. The drink, if specifically mentioned, is nearly always wine, though sometimes cider or another homely beverage. In rare instances a dance or wedding accounts for the gathering.

The tavern scene, in motivating Barbara's anger, helps to produce a stronger situation than exists in versions where such justification is lacking. And yet, in typical ballad fashion, more is left to curiosity and imagination than is anywhere explicit. The relationship here is the most provocative in the ballad. By most readers the slight is somehow felt to be unintentional. In the Scotch ballad it is nowhere explained as such and evidently it must be so felt because an ungallant gesture of open insult is out of character for the generous, devoted worshipper visited by the girl in his final moments. What may be presumed to happen between the time of the social error and its repercussion in the doom of John Grame? Barbara's reminder to the stricken man is spoken as if she were acquainting him for the first time with the true cause of her indignation. Had the lover been miserably existing in a state of honest bewilderment over Barbara's seemingly unwarranted behavior — perhaps begging for an explanation which the girl, in the full perversity of feminine wrath, is withholding as an instrument of emotional punishment? At any rate, sympathy for the young man's plight has been active enough through the centuries to have generated the verses that in some American versions allow the wretched man to express his sense of wronged fidelity.

The heroine's grief and remorse is a standard story ingredient, expressed or implied in all but fragmentary texts. Its most remarkable variation consists of the exhortation stanza which first appeared in one of the Roxburgh broadsides, was popularized by Percy, and has survived in tradition to the present time:

> Farewell, she said, ye virgins all
> And shun the fault I fell in;
> Henceforth take warning by the fall
> Of cruel Barbara Allen.

Though few modern folk versions show this feature, it has appeared in variants from eight Eastern and Southern states. The sort of diction and didacticism exhibited in the stanza is not characteristic of folk composition. Visible here is the hand of the poetaster who fashioned or refashioned the old Roxburgh text, and the persistence of the variously modified stanza in oral circulation furnishes an example of the influence on tradition of a famous printed text and also of its narrow limitations.

Barbara's remorse, after her general conduct, her unpitying words, and her sometimes scornful glance at the corpse, comes as a reversal of expectation late and sudden enough to produce surprise. Reversal is, of course, a commonplace of ballad narrative. Its particular interest here lies in its neatly interwoven involvements, for it not only introduces the pleasure of surprise but also establishes in a flash the unknown fundamental character of the heroine, raises her from merely a vindictive belle to a second tragic protagonist, and terminates the ballad climactically in a complete lustration of error and guilt which leaves behind it a sense of purification similar, in its microcosmic way, to the catharsis of authentic tragedy. In the end neither soul triumphs over the other; they share destruction as they had shared intimacy and disruption before. In this is a curious and abysmal tragic beauty whose springs are somewhere in the contradictory heart of human creatures and especially in that of cruel, unwise, and noble Barbara.

Legacies or gifts from the young man to his sweetheart mark a rather curious feature in the tradition of the song. This motif, occurring sporadically in only a few variants[14] and in none of the older ones, appears to be an accretion of the later 18th century. Handled with taste and restraint, it can be an effective device. As Davis observes: "The victim's generosity stands out in contrast to Barbara's cruelty and adds to the poignancy of the tragedy." An instance of clumsy mishandling is the version in the Buchan and Motherwell manuscripts, where the lover offers as a tocher his watch, ring, Bible, penknife, mill and thirty ploughs, nine meal mills, and the freight of nine ships. Child would not admit these texts to his collection and replied to C. K. Sharpe's observation that such stanzas were sung by the peasantry of Annandale by saying that they doubtless learned them from "some stall print." Favorite items in the legacy are the ring, watch, rolls of money, and dish of heart's blood or napkin soaked in heart's blood, among which the latter is the most frequent. It is also the most interesting in view of its symbolic character and its evident connection with ancient folk belief. As Gordon Gerould has pointed out, blood in earlier ages was felt to be vitally connected with the principle of life and therefore to have occult virtue to the extent that it "might be preserved with advantage by the enemy who had killed a person."[15] As regards Barbara's lover, however, the old principle has lost its pristine literalness and applies with a somewhat different significance:

> Look down, look down at my bedside,
>   You'll see a bowl o'erflowing;
> And in that bowl there's my heart's blood,
>   That's shed for Barbara Allen.

Clearly here is no question of evil intent. As Gerould says, "It is bequeathed by the man simply as a symbol of his personality." Perhaps to the taste of some readers a sanguinary image of this sort may hold more historical interest than artistic satisfaction. To others the symbol may appear appropriate, as it probably did to its originator, because it represents so well the uncompromising absoluteness of everything in the situation.

The familiar rose and briar motif occurs in none of the early texts and furnishes a good example of an intrusive device that suited the ballad admirably and came in to stay. Though rare in modern British texts and scarce in Maine (as noted by Barry), the ending is generally abundant in America, especially in the South, where in some regions it is well-nigh universal. Some collections indicate a tendency among singers to end the ballad either with this feature or with the warning by Barbara, but not to include both. Rose and briar are found in a number of other romantic ballads also.[16] Needless to say, no original can be fixed, but Davis is well justified in wondering whether the stanzas might not originally have been supplied by "Fair Margaret and Sweet William," as suggested by the hero's name and the striking similarity of theme. Imagery shows occasional variation, sometimes slight, as in the substitution of a white lily for the rose, or more radical, as in this charming little tableau from one of Cecil Sharp's North Carolina texts:

> On William's grave a turtle dove,
> On Barbara's grave a sparrow.
> The turtle dove is a sign of love,
> The sparrow was for sorrow.

## V

In its career "Barbara Allen" has not degenerated. Texts have been forgotten, some half forgotten, others ignorantly corrupted, but in the main the song has held its form well. Historical comparison on a pure folk basis is difficult, since versions of the earlier period, represented necessarily in print or manuscript, have in some instances been editorially altered. Still, with reasonable discounts, it is safe to say that the best variants of today are as good, both in poetry and in music, as those of earlier centuries, if not sometimes better. Sound taste and artistry have gone along with ceaseless variation in the evolutionary process. Comparison of modern texts with those found in old books really leaves little to choose in the matter of quality. They are simply different — it is like comparing *Ivanhoe* with *Huckleberry Finn*. The ancient poems are usually better in the mechanical sense, with more accurate rimes, smoother diction, closer conformity (barring Scotch dialect) to standard usage; but such merits tend toward colorlessness. American variants are richer in the cherishable qualities of variety and folk idiom, but offer also a more generous seasoning of loose rimes, grammatical solecisms, irregular meter, and outright corruptions. Preference comes down to a matter of taste. It is merely a question of whether you prefer "So slowly, slowly she got up / And so slowly she came to him" or "She got right up and walked out the door, / Hardhearteder than ever"; whether you like "He turned his face unto her straight / With deadly sorrow sighing" better than "He turned his face to the cold, cold wall / And busted out a-cryin'." Individual verses, however, do not provide as fair a comparison as do the whole poems quoted earlier in this study.

Variation in America has produced no important rhythmic or structural differentiations. The common meter stanza, favorite of balladry, is virtually universal. In length of story there is, of course, every degree of gradation. The word *average* can hardly be used here in any useful sense, but one might point to a text of about a dozen stanzas as something to be found more often than not. In some regions collectors recognize shorter and longer models as definite types. The shorter texts (5 to 9 stanzas) are condensed to a skeleton beyond which abbreviation cannot, or can hardly, go without serious damage to the story. The dwarf variety is probably a product at first of faulty memory, but once evolved it tends to become more or less fixed.[17] The longer texts, apparently developed by singers of invention and gusto, range from twelve to sixteen stanzas, the longest sometimes reaching eighteen and containing a great melange of Scotch, English, American and regional ingredients.

In choice or exclusion of incident and motive one encounters every conceivable combination, though not many aberrations reach outside the usual repertory. Very rarely there comes along some startling minor metamorphosis like the turning of "Barbry" into a man, in a Mississippi version, so that the roles are reversed, a singular freak resulting no doubt from someone's misunderstanding. But usually the differences amount to whether, say, the tavern scene is involved or ignored, or whether Barbara's parents are mentioned, and, if they are, whether they prepare her bed and grave or offer counsel or die of grief after her. Small differences in the shading of emotion or in its manner of articulation are not uncommon. For example, in a South Carolina text Barbara tells her lover, who has asked for the saving kiss, "If one kiss would kill you dead, / I'd freely give a hundred" — an abnormally extravagant expression of wrath, to say the least. In a Florida story Barbara, on catching sight of the approaching funeral procession, departs from her usual hauteur to express herself with remarkable colloquial naturalness and psychological realism: "She cried, Oh Lord, what shall I do? / Shall I go and meet his coffin?"

Except for melody, it is in the realm of dialect and local color that variation operates most freely, and the effects produced, though merely incidental in terms of the story, are often among the most interesting features a particular text can show. Many pages would be required to illustrate such markings in any adequate way, but we can at least glance at a characteristic few. There is nothing startling about such Carolina verses as "Sweet William went down to his well today, / He's down to his well a-drinking," but they are different from the familiar Old World imagery in a fresh and spontaneous way, carrying with them a feeling of back-country quietness and dreamy summer warmth, a far cry from Scotland or Scarlet Town. Sometimes we catch, too, a glimpse of occupational background, as in this seagoing figure from the maritime province of Nova Scotia: "Oh I am sick and very sick, / And my mast is at the breaking." From the South come the most picturesque dialectal renderings. A Florida variant, for example, tells us of Barbara that "She went a-traipsin' through the fields," and a Virginia Negro version remarks sympathetically: "He co'ted her for seven long years; / She said she would not marry. / Poor Willie went home and war taken sick/ And ve'y likely died." Juxtaposition of old stock epithets and vernacular often appear in such combinations as "He handed her out his lily-white hand / All for to tell her howdy" (Virginia); and in verses like "Come bridle to me a milk-white colt, / To see if he is dying" (Newfoundland) we see curious interweavings of familiar text with intrusive elements from other ballads.

By and large, American influences have not radically modified the Old World song. Our singers have tremendously expanded its currency, have made famous some great tunes, have added or popularized valuable narrative elements, and have contributed an interesting range of fresh local color and language. In other words they have taken good care of the ballad and made it feel at home. From the outset "Barbara Allen" has been treated with hospitality, respect, and often affection. As it deserves, the fine old song has fared nobly in its career among us and bids fair to do so for a long time in the future.

1. Systematic footnote documentation has been omitted because the space it would require seems out of proportion to its value. Usually references are to the song or its attendant discussion, and these can be located simply by looking for "Barbara Allen" in table of contents or index. I have found variants of the ballad in nearly fifty scholarly collections, in a score of articles, and in sundry manuscripts, popular songbooks, broadsides, and phonographic recordings. I have also collected a few variants from folk singers. The present study is indebted in one way or another to all this material but most directly to the sources mentioned in the text, plus the following authors and publications not mentioned, or incompletely identified, therein: Alan Lomax in Library of Congress, Division of Music, Recording Laboratory, Album I, Leaflet. Oliver Goldsmith, *Essays*, No. III, 1765. W. A. Owens, *Texas Folk Songs* (Dallas, 1950). A. C. Morris, *Folksongs of Florida* (Gainesville, 1950). E. H. Linscott, *Folksongs of Old New England* (New York, 1939). Reed Smith in *Journal of American Folklore*, XXVIII (1915), 203, and in *South Carolina Ballads* (Cambridge, Mass., 1928). A. K. Davis, *Traditional Ballads of Virginia* (Cambridge, Mass, 1929) — a particularly valuable criticism. H. M. Belden, *University of Missouri Studies*, XV (1940), 60. W. E. Gilbert, *University of Virginia Magazine*, V (1913), 329. John Lomax, *Adventures of a Ballad Hunter* (New York, 1947), 423. A P. Hudson, *Folksongs of Mississippi* (Chapel Hill, 1936). Barry, Eckstorm, and Smyth, *British Ballads from Maine* (New Haven, 1929). Evelyn Wells, *The Ballad Tree* (New York, 1950), 307. Campbell and Sharp, *Folk Songs from the Southern Appalachians* (New York, 1917). Cecil Sharp, *One Hundred English Folksongs* (Boston, 1916). Frank Kidson, *Traditional Tunes* (Oxford, 1891). Gavin Greig, *Last Leaves of Traditional Ballads* (Aberdeen, 1925). W. Christie, *Traditional Ballad Airs* (Edinburgh, 1876). Carl Sandburg, *The American Songbag* (New York, 1927). Thomas Percy, *Reliques of Ancient English Poetry* (London, 1765). C. F. Rimbault, *Musical Illustrations to Percy's Reliques* (London, 1850). F. J. Child, *English and Scottish Popular Ballads* (Boston, 1883 ff.). J. H. Cox, *Folk-Songs of the South* (Cambridge, Mass., 1928). Greenleaf and Mansfield, *Ballads and Sea*

*Songs of Newfoundland* (Cambridge, Mass., 1933). Dorothy Scarborough, *On the Trail of Negro Folk Songs* (New York, 1925). Anyone interested in phonographic recordings should consult Ben Gray Lumpkin's catalogue, *Folksongs on Records,* Issue 3, published by Alan Swallow, Denver, Colorado. Rebecca Tarwater sings the ballad beautifully in a recording contained in the Library of Congress album mentioned above.

2. There has been some speculation, with Mrs. Knipp in mind, as to whether the ballad could have begun as a stage song. It seems highly unlikely. Pepys's entries give us no right to suppose that the piece was even in Mrs. Knipp's theater repertory, and he recognized it, we must remember, as a Scotch song. Pepys's remark is significant, however, in showing the existence of a Scottish version at a time when only English texts, as far as our records go, had gotten into print. It disposes of any notion that the first known Scottish printings, dated 1740, must have been derived from English models of the preceding century and strengthens the Scotch claim to "Barbara Allen" as an indigenous product.

3. This version is also known as the "Ramsay text" as a result of Ramsay's fame in the antiquarian revival of his day. He seems to be generally regarded as the earliest publisher of "Barbara Allen" in any form, but this prevalent opinion is inaccurate on two counts: (1) as noted above, the Scotch version was also published in 1740 by Oswald, who is therefore entitled to share the honors; and (2) a broadside text known as the "English" or "Roxburgh" version (presently to be shown and discussed in this article) was printed nearly a century earlier and thus really represents the earliest printing of the ballad which has survived, though the Scotch version, in my opinion, was already old in tradition before this broadside was composed. The Scotch song was republished by Oswald in *A Caledonian Pocket Companion* (1743), by Percy (slightly edited) in the *Reliques* (1765), by David Herd in *The Ancient and Modern Scots Songs* (1769), by Joseph Ritson in *Scottish Songs* (1794), and by James Johnson in *The Scots Musical Museum* (1787-1803), a publication which Robert Burns contributed to and helped to edit. Walter Scott knew "Barbara Allen"; he has not said why he omitted it from the *Minstrelsy,* but it was evidently because he was seeking new pieces not already in print. G. Thompson continued the series in 1822 with *Select Melodies of Scotland,* followed (1876-81) by W. Christie's *Traditional Ballad Airs* and G. Eyre-Todd's *Ancient Scots Ballads* (*ca.* 1890). Child (1882-98) made the first attempt at critical colltaion of texts. Gavin Greig's variants in *Last Leaves* (1925) are well preserved but show slight intrusions of textual features developed in England. The foregoing list mentions famous or typical books; it is not exhaustive. Oswald's books seem not to be available in this country, and my knowledge of his work has been pieced together from the comments of other editors.

4. The text shown here is Ramsay's. The tune, from Eyre-Todd's *Ancient Scots Ballads,* is chosen because it is a good common denominator of the type. In some versions the first long phrase (half melody) is repeated and followed by the second half melody, also repeated. This

produces a double-length melody which is set to a corresponding eight-line (or double) stanza.

5. The words of the ballad shown above were given me by Thomas H. Tyler, of Partlow, Virginia. The tune is from my own memory. Like the text, it is out of Virginia tradition but was learned so long ago that I cannot recall an exact source. Abundant examples could, of course, be found in collections. I use Tyler's because it has not been published before.

6. Other states are Virginia, North and South Carolina, Georgia, Kentucky, Florida, Alabama, Tennessee, and Missouri. The tune differs from some of the older ones in being cast in the major scale. It is often pentatonic, sometimes in common time, but characteristically in triplicate time, as above. What I take to be a radical mutation of it has developed in parts of the South. In this variety the most marked departures occur in measures 3 through 6. For an example see Campbell and Sharp (D).

7. Undoubtedly many people have learned the ballad from print. Reed Smith, Phillips Barry, H. M. Belden, and others have commented on the matter. Belden puts the case well by saying that printed versions have been both the cause and the effect of the ballad's popularity. In the United States during the nineteenth century the song appeared in at least fourteen popular songbooks, beginning with *The American Songster* (Baltimore, 1836). In the British Isles publication has been active for two centuries. But the extent to which such texts have crossed over into pure folk tradition is another matter and has, I think, been overestimated in some quarters. In reading through Davis' thirty-odd Virginia variants, for example, or Sharp's Southern specimens, one finds but few verses certainly traceable to published sources, and the case is the same with other collections. By and large, these texts show, as their music does, the marks of long traditional handling. If they have passed through print, it must have happened a long time ago. On the other hand, versions exist, even in the South where the tradition is strongest, which preserve the phrasing of a Percy text almost exactly. (Davis' M-version furnishes a good illustration.) These must have come into oral circulation in relatively recent times from some book using one of the old Percy texts, as many of the old songbooks have done, running in a straight line of literary rehandling from 1765 to modern times. *Heart Songs* (1909) is a fair example. It reproduces flawlessly six stanzas of Percy's English text. Mackenzie's A-version (Nova Scotia), barring a few stanzas perhaps derived from some other ballad, is almost word for word the same as the version in *The Forget-Me-Not Songster,* once so popular in Maine. "Barbara Allen" has always shown a strong affinity for print. With so much publication and traditional knowledge running along side by side, interchange would be inescapable.

8. C. A. Smith's response to this more lately developed feature is interesting. At the time (1916) Dr. Smith was apparently habituated to Old World versions. Having quoted Child's A (Scotch) text, he remarks: "... the story has always seemed to me flawed by the silence of Sir John under the accusation brought against him. The reader infers, of course, that Barbara's charge in stanza five is unjust, but in view of the

tragic denouement, artistic balance demands some sort of exculpatory answer . . . at any rate, I felt a sense of profound relief when a version came in from Buchanan County Virginia, with four additional stanzas." (*Musical Quarterly*, II, 109-29). In some texts, as Davis points out, two stanzas of accusation are replied to by the man. It is, of course, possible that the defense motif is of Old World origin. I can only say that I have not found an instance of it outside of America.

9. Davis (D-version) describes the following example: "The young man begins the story in the first person (stanzas 1-3); the 4th stanza begins in the third person, but slips back to the first person in the 3rd line; dialogue follows to the end of stanza 7; here the first person is resumed, but with Barbara as narrator (stanzas 8-10); then back to the 3rd person again (stanzas 11-14)."

10. Nothing in the ballad shows greater variation. The list of settings includes Scotland, London, Scarland Town, Scarlet Town (a great favorite), Reading Town, Yonders Town (common in the South), Honor Town, Lonely Town, Gordon Town, Garland Town, Charlotte Town, Limerick City, Dublin, Story Town, Way Down South, Western Country, Quelick Town, Foreign Country, Strawberry Town, High High Hill, Our Town, West Country Town, and Yorkshire. Occasionally two places are connected, e.g., "In Scotland I was born and bred,/ In London was my dwelling." Or sometimes after the town is named, comes the line, "That's where I got my learning."

11. The favorite season in America is "the merry month of May, when the green bunds were a-swelling," but June is sometimes mentioned, and in a few instances the events happen "early, early in the spring," a line doubtless borrowed from the opening stanza of the old English ballad of that name. Martinmas, "when the green (or yellow) leaves were falling," is the usual time in texts of Scotch descent with "Lammas" and "fall" as occasional variations. In rare cases we are also told something about the duration of the courtship, e.g., "months and years" or "seven long years."

12. The Scotch call him John, Sir John, or Sir James Graham, Graeme, etc. From these come such derivations as Johnny Green or Grey, or Sir James the Grave, or Young Johnny. These in combination with favorite English names produce such hybrids as Jimmy Green or Sweet William Gray. Straight English or American are Sweet William or Willie; Sweet Jimmie, Jemmy, or Jamie; Jemmy, Jamie, or Young Jamie Grove or Groves; Jimmy Grooves or Grew; Poor William or Willie; Pretty William; Young Jimmy or Willie; William Riley; a youth or young man.

13. *Ellen* may result from exigencies of rime in the natural course of folk recomposition or it may be simply dialectal. It is commonest in Yorkshire, rare in the U.S. From Sharp's account *Edelin* seems to be a peasant singing mannerism. The title "Bonny Barbara Allen" was popularized by Child but was evidently first used by Ramsay.

14. Collections show it to be traditional in Scotland and England, in Nova Scotia, Newfoundland, Maine, Virginia, West Virginia, and South Carolina. It occurs in *Charlie Fox's Minstrel's Companion*.

15. For a discussion of this notion in balladry see *The Ballad of Tradition* (Oxford, 1932), 154-55. "Sir Hugh," "Lamkin," and "Little Musgrave" are cited as examples of stories in which blood is preserved for sinister purposes.

16. Among Child's A-texts it occurs in "Earl Brand," "Fair Janet," "Prince Robert," "Lady Alice," "Lass of Roch Royal," "Lord Lovel," "Fair Margaret and Sweet William."

17. Fragments show that forgetting is not a haphazard process in tradition. There is a definite order of relinquishment. To speak in averages, singers forget first the stanzas not essential to the core of action. Of those remaining, the opening stanza is remembered longest. If the whole text vanishes, the tune is often retained. These are my own observations. They are, however, about what one might expect, for (1) the folk singer is primarily interested in his story and therefore most attentive to its indispensable units; (2) both in learning and singing, the first stanza gets the fresh, initial effort of memory; and (3) in a single performance the singer repeats the tune many times but goes over the words of each stanza only once.

MODY C. BOATRIGHT

# Aunt Cordie's Ax and Other Motifs in Oil

IN ALL THE OIL REGIONS of the United States there circulate certain archetypical stories which are told as truth and often printed in good faith, but which in many instances prove to have little or no basis in fact. Such stories are not without interest in themselves; and if they are folklore (as I believe they are) a study of their content and distribution should throw some light upon the development of folklore in a literate and increasingly industrial society. Pending a more thorough study, which must await further collecting, this paper is offered as a preliminary report on some of these tales. In it I shall deal with only three typical and widely distributed motifs.

One of these is the story of the new ax. It is meant to be comic, the humor depending upon the discrepancy between the wants and the means of the formerly poor but now rich landowner. I first heard the story in the McClesky version from Ranger, Texas.

In 1917 Uncle John and Aunt Cordie McClesky, as their neighbors called them, were living on a farm a mile south of Ranger. They had an unpretentious but substantial farm house with a garden and orchard, for, like most of their neighbors, they produced much of their food at home. For cash income John McClesky grew cotton and peanuts, and worked as a bricklayer on the rare occasions when there were any brick to be laid in the little village. He was not used to handling large sums of money, but his condition was hardly one of poverty. The owner of property valued at some $20,000, he ranked among the more prosperous farmers of his community.

It was upon his farm that the Ranger discovery well came in on October 22, 1917, with a flush production which gave him an income of about $250 a day. Some weeks after his good fortune he built a cottage in Ranger, where the McClesky Hotel, representing the first sizable investment of his oil money, was under construction.

It was at this time that a newspaper woman from Fort Worth called upon Mrs. McClesky for an interview. The reporter quoted her as saying that when the well came in, her husband asked what he might buy for her. Mrs. McClesky replied, "Well, the blade of the old ax has a nick in it and I would like to have a new one to chop kindling with."[1]

I have heard this story in several variants (in one the handle of the ax is so old and rough that it leaves splinters in her hands) from at least a dozen informants who believe it to be true. I accepted it as truth myself until a few years ago when on the trail of Gib Morgan I found the same story in Pennsylvania. I have since heard it from Desdemona, where a farmer is reputed to have said that he was going to get not only the best ax that money could buy, but also a grindstone and a gasoline engine to turn it. Then he was going into a thicket and see how it felt to attack a post oak with a really sharp ax.[2] Bob Duncan has a version of the ax story from Beaumont.[3] Haldeen Braddy heard it in Vann. George Sessions Perry must have heard it, for in one of his short stories, he has a character say to another who had oil land in East Texas, "He's got so much money he can't hardly spend it. He bought three new axes an' a barrel of lamp oil an' a barrel of flour, that didn't even make a dent in his money."[4]

Doubts therefore arise as to whether or not Mrs. McClesky did in fact ask her husband for a new ax. She and her husband are dead and their children have left the state. Among their neighbors the story is widely believed, but I have found no informant who will vouch for its authenticity. Mrs. Hagerman, the widow of the first mayor of Ranger, for example, said that since Mrs. McClesky did not consider herself too good to go to the woodpile and cut up an armful of wood, the story was not impossible. She said, however, that many stories were told about the McCleskys which she knew to be false. She said that at one time in the Ranger-Breckenridge area "a McClesky" was used as a common noun to designate any comic story of the newly rich.

John Rust, who lived on the farm adjoining the McCleskys and was twelve years old when the well came in, said in a tape-recorded interview:

> Yes, I heard the story and I've always doubted that it's true. It could be true certainly, and I'm not sitting here to say that it's not a true story. . . . I will tell you that I didn't hear her make the remark, but then of course she could have made it . . . without my presence. But knowing her . . . and her husband as I have known them for years, all my life, and the kind of people they are . . . I just don't believe that she made the remark at all. She might have made it, however, in a joking sort of way, just for fun. But to seriously make the remark, I doubt if she would make it.
>
> I know that they didn't do silly things with their money; they were good, thrifty people. They always had plenty to eat and they looked presentable in their clothes. Old John McClesky was the kind of man that didn't have his ax blade gapped up anyhow. He had an old-fashioned grindstone — I remember where it used to sit — and I've been over there before the oil boom at their home, and maybe old John would be gone somewhere or out in the field working or something, and Aunt Cordie would need some wood to cook the evening meal. I've gone out there and picked up that ax, and I remember that it always had a sharp blade.
>
> And I just have every reason to kind of doubt that she made the remark.

Joe Weaver, retired oil operator who came to Texas from West Virginia by way of Oklahoma, and who was beginning operations in the Ranger area before the McClesky well came in, said that he did not believe the story. Then he said he would tell me what he called "an old West Virginia story." Oil was discovered on a widow's farm, "and her boys went to Harpersburg to celebrate. They had had a tough time and the widow had been a very hard worker. And the boys were enjoying themselves when one turned to the other saying, 'We must take mother a gift,' and the other one said, 'Well, what in the world will we take her?' And the first suggested, 'I know, we will take her a new ax.' "

Tradition does not indicate that the first purchase of every suddenly enriched landowner was an ax. It might be a stalk of bananas, a cookstove, linoleum for the kitchen floor, a XXXX beaver Stetson. But the ax seems to be the most constant symbol of the new status. Its appeal may rest partly on irony. Oil brings a new fuel and makes the family chopping ax obsolete.

Another motif is that of the lucky breakdown. As drilling equipment is being moved to a wildcat location made by a geologist, transportation fails and the well is drilled at the scene of the breakdown. It is a producer, but when the original location is later drilled, the well is a duster.

This story, observes Samuel W. Tait, Jr., "has been related about every oil field I know, whether it be sandy desert, boggy swamp, muddy prairie, or rocky mountain, and it has probably happened in every one of them."[5] The one instance that Tait vouches for happened in the sandy desert of California in 1895.

There are several occurrences of the story in Texas. Of these I have been able to verify only one, and it is little known. J. R. Webb of Albany, Texas, entered into a partnership with a relative to drill a well in Shackelford County, where oil, when found at all, was encountered at shallow depths. The partner, a geologist, now a man of high position in an oil company, made the location on the top of a hill. When machinery arrived it was found that the trucks could not be driven up the grade, and in those pre-bulldozer days the construction of a road involved more money than they cared to risk. They set up the rig at the base of the hill and got oil. Part of the returns from this well were used to build a road to the original location, where drilling brought a dry hole.

Few people have heard of the Webb-Crutchfield experience, but nearly everybody in Texas and Oklahoma knows the legend of the Fowler Farm Oil Company.

S. L. Fowler, owner of a large and rich cotton farm in the Red River valley just north of the little town of Burkburnett, Texas, in 1918 decided to give up farming and become a ranchman. He figured that the proceeds from the sale of his farm would buy sufficient grassland to sustain a herd large enough to make him a good living. The only difficulty was that Texas has a community property law, and Mrs. Fowler would not consent to the sale. She was quoted by one journalist as saying: "I believe there's oil under our land, and I won't agree to dispose of the farm until a test is drilled. If oil isn't found, I'll sign the papers; but the people of this section have undergone so many hardships with such patience that I just know there is something good in store for them."[6]

Finding his spouse adamant, Fowler decided that the only way to sell the farm was to meet her condition, so he called on his neighbors for help. He figured that it would take $12,000 to put down a well deep enough to satisfy his wife. He put up a thousand dollars and his friends subscribed varying amounts until the sum was raised. One of the subscribers was Walter Cline, a drilling contractor who happened to have an idle rig in North Texas at the moment. In exchange for a thousand-dollar interest in the venture, he agreed to furnish the rig and the services of his drilling superintendent.

A geologist was employed, according to legend, who staked out a location in the cotton field. The wagon hauling the first load of equipment bogged down in the sand. "Oh well, unload her here," Fowler said, for for his purpose one place was as good as another.

The well came in and opened the Burkburnett Field. After a few months the Fowler Farm Oil Company sold out for $1,800,000, paying the shareholders $15,000 for each one hundred invested.

The figures are history and a part of the legend is true. Neighborliness did enter into the formation of the company. Sand had something to do with the location of the well, and a well drilled later north of the discovery produced only salt water. The rest is imagination.

As Walter Cline remembers, the project began to take shape one day in front of Luke Daley's drug store, "where we usually congregated and did our whittling and settling really heavy problems."

S. L. [Fowler] broke the news to the bunch [Mr. Cline continues] that he wanted to dispose of his cotton land and get him a piece of ranch land but that his wife thought they ought to drill a well on the land and that he didn't have money enough and he was going to have to get some help, and he wanted to know if any of us would be interested. Well, there was nothing particularly favorable to encourage anyone to want to spend any money or time or effort on the Fowler land. On the other hand, there was nothing that definitely condemned it. So we sat around and decided that just as friends and neighbors, we'd just do our boy scout good turn by putting in a little, not enough to hurt any of us, but maybe enough to poorboy a well down. . . .

And we got enough money committed to look like we could afford to drill a well. The question of location then came up and we decided there wasn't any use in pulling a whole lot of sand, going way out in this cotton patch, and we'd drill it reasonably close to town. So we went right north of the hog pen that was east of S. L.'s house with a lane through there and a gate, drove out in the field where we had driven a stake and drilled there.

I'd like to interject here the statement that there's been very few discovery wells brought in that the myth hasn't started that they decided to drill a well on a given ranch or a given farm or on a given part of ground and they started out and it rained like the devil or they broke the wagon wheel or the truck broke down, and they were already on the property where they wanted to drill and they were a half-mile or a mile from the location, and they said, "Oh well, hell, let's just unload it. One place is as good as another. We're on the right land. We'll drill it here."

Well, now I heard that. I've heard it about the Fowler well and I've heard it about practically every discovery well that's been drilled in Texas in my time, and I have yet to find a single instance of where that's true. I just don't think there's a bit of truth in it. I know it's not true so far as the Fowler well is concerned. We drilled the Fowler well right where we intended to drill it, and right where we drove our stake. And that definitely settles the Fowler well.[7]

Another and more elaborate version of the lucky breakdown story is the one concerning Santa Rita, the discovery well in the Big Lake Field, the first of the oil fields to be opened on the endowment lands of the University of Texas.

The earliest published version of this story that I have found is that of Owen P. White in the New York *Times* for May 3, 1925.

> When the lease was signed Krupp [Hyman Krupp, organizer and president of the company] went to work. He hired expensive oil experts . . . to go out and locate the proper anticlines for him and then after this had been done, busied himself in getting together enough money to drill the well. . . . The months flew by until the date on which the lease would automatically expire was dangerously near. Krupp redoubled his efforts and finally, with only a few days to go, he took the road with three trucks loaded with drilling equipment.
>
> When Krupp was still several miles away from the precious stake, which had cost him several thousand dollars to have driven in the ground, one of his trucks broke down completely, and — there he was! At that time, as the story goes, he had only two days left. What should he do? There was no possibility of being able to reach the desired destination with his outfit. The breakdown had occurred on land covered by his lease and so, with no high-salaried geologist at hand to advise him,

but merely because the ox was in the ditch and he had to act at once to prevent forfeiture, Krupp set up his rig at the scene of the disaster and went to work.

Another version of the tale was included in the general report of the Sun Oil Company covering operations in West Texas and New Mexico up to November 1, 1929. A paragraph reads:

> An unusual incident occurred when the Big Lake Field in Reagan County was discovered in 1923. Location for their first test was made some two miles westward, but owing to a breakdown while transporting the materials to the location, they unloaded just where the incident happened, and this well, while it led to a small producer, led to the discovery of the Big Lake Field. Had the first test been drilled where the location was originally made, possibly new chapters would have been written regarding the field. Subsequent tests have proven their first location would have been a failure.[8]

A writer in the *Daily Texan,* student newspaper of the University of Texas, for February 9, 1940, told the story as follows:

> The site, in the southwestern part of Reagan County, at which the first oil well was completed in May, 1923, was chosen purely by accident. The drilling party, headed by Frank Pickrell, was bogged down. Since the lease was to expire in a few hours, members decided to drill where they were stranded.
> They drilled not on their own lease, but on a part of the 2,000,000 acres provided by the Constitution for the University endowment fund and now known as the Big Lake Field.

But for a real professional handling of the story, we turn to the Austin *Statesman* for January 23, 1940.

> The ragged country with its old worn jutting hills, crouched beneath the terrible drenching from the rains. Little rivers ran where dry gulches with their platted grasses formerly cut through the terrain.
> In slicker and chewing the end of an old cigar, a man named Frank Pickrell peered from the switch house into a torrent of rain, walked impatiently back and forth.
> "All right, boys," he said, "I've got a lot of money tied up in this. We've got to take a chance. We've got to get this machinery going."
> And the boys got up and in the heavy rain began loading the rig and drilling machinery on the cumbersome wagons. In a little while they got started.

Mud clawed at the wheels and sucked at the mules' feet. The animals grunted and strained at the traces and the wagons creaked through the slime over the treacherous roads.

"Just seven miles to go," encouraged Mr. Pickrell. The rain poured. The men cursed and cracked whips, and wiped the mud from their eyes.

The geologist had said that oil would be found on a certain spot. Mr. Pickrell was determined to reach that spot. Then the rain came down in torrents. It almost hid one team from another. West Texas had never seen it rain like that before.

Up front there was much cursing. Hazy figures floundered here and there. Mr. Pickrell stalked up front. The lead wagon was mired. There wasn't any use, the straining mules could not budge it.

"We'll have to wait," said Mr. Pickrell. The boys huddled together to wait. The skies were puffed and swollen with clouds, and the rain chattered along the gullies and around the wagons.

They waited all day. Mr. Pickrell knew his West Texas. "Boys," he said, "this thing'll keep up. Another day and we'll be here two weeks getting to that place. Unload her here. We'll dig our well right here."

Now the testimony gathered by Schwettman from Pickrell and other participants in the event is to the effect that (1) it was not raining when the equipment was being moved; on the contrary, the ranchers were complaining about a long dry spell, (2) horses rather than mules or trucks were used to draw the equipment, (3) there was no breakdown, (4) the well was located where the geologist had driven the stake.

Pickrell had previously certified that the well had been located at the stake driven by the geologist and that it was upon the recommendation of the geologist that the well had been drilled. Moreover, the breakdown story became an issue in a lawsuit in 1926. The court found the story false and so stated in its judgment.[9] This, however, did not dispose of the legend. Three of the four written versions I have quoted came after the decision, and folks in Texas still talk about the lucky breakdown that first brought oil to their university.

The third motif is that of the million-dollar drink. This is no Coal Oil Johnny episode in which a million dollars is spent; instead, a million dollars is gained, though not for the celebrant.

In one form of the story that celebrant is a geologist. He is called upon to make a hurried decision, when, unfortunately, he is too drunk to study his data. He makes a random mark on the map, and when he sobers up he realizes that it is not on the structure as he had plotted it. He remains silent, however, and hopes for the best. The best happens, and subsequent drilling on the location he would have made had he been sober results in a dry hole.[10]

In the more common form of the story, the big brass in a distant city decide to abandon a well. But the driller or someone in the chain of authority between him and the president of the company fails because of drunkenness to see the order carried out. Drilling continues a few hours longer and a million-dollar sand is tapped.

This tale is told of the McClesky well, but it has met with no wide credence in the Ranger area.

The classical Texas example, like that of the lucky breakdown, comes from the Big Lake Field and involves Frank Pickrell. In 1928 a deep test known as University 1-B was being put down with cable tools. At a depth of 8,245 feet the bailer hung, the sand line parted, a long and expensive fishing job ensued, and the company decided to abandon the well. The order was not carried out, and the discovery of a new producing horizon resulted.

The reason the order was not carried out, according to a widely circulated report that reached print in the *San Angelo Standard-Times* for May 28, 1933, was the million-dollar drink.

Late in Nov., 1928 Frank Pickrell, Texon vice president, ordered a halt at 8,343 feet. The deep wildcat had cost over $100,000. Cromwell reported that the formation looked promising and argued successfully that drilling continue. On Saturday, Dec. 1, the bit reached 8,518 in black lime. Pickrell again telephoned and this time insisted that work stop. Cromwell stopped to revive his spirits with what someone later aptly termed "a million dollar drink," and decided he could notify the crew the next morning. Meanwhile the drill kept pounding.

Early the next morning the driller phoned Cromwell that the well was spraying oil. "Hit 'er another foot," Cromwell instructed and No. 1-B began to flow for a new world's record depth of 8,525 feet.[11]

Schwettman also investigated this legend. What basis it has in fact is indicated by a letter he received from Waldo Williams, chief driller.[12] Williams said that the "big boys had a meeting in New York and decided that $140,000 was enough to spend on a non-paying well." They ordered Pickrell to stop drilling at 8,500 feet. Pickrell then called Cromwell by telephone and gave the order. Cromwell then talked over the prospects of the well with Williams, and was so confident of success that he said instead of giving the order he would disappear for a few days. On the second day of December the well flowed forty barrels of oil.

Williams began trying to locate Cromwell. After two days he was found at an editors' convention in Sweetwater. In a few hours after he received the message, he was on the location directing the completion of the well.

These are some of the local exemplifications of some of the motifs that seem to be coextensive with the oil industry in the United States. The tales have been only meagerly collected, and little can be said with assurance concerning the localities of their origin. Although I have not been able to verify any instances of the ax or the million-dollar drink stories, it is not improbable that they, like the legend of the lucky breakdown, have happened somewhere, perhaps more than once.

The stories I have dealt with and many others have been disseminated through both the spoken and the written word. The mobility of the personnel of the oil industry and the high rate of circulation of newspapers and magazines among the American people account for their wide diffusion. In no case have I been able to determine with certainty whether a local version was circulated first in oral or in written form. The newspaper account of Mrs. McClesky's ax followed so close upon the discovery of oil that my informants cannot say whether or not the tale had been previously in oral circulation. My belief is that the reporter had heard the story before and was the first to apply it to Mrs. McClesky.

The story of the lucky breakdown in connection with the Big Lake discovery was in oral circulation by midsummer following the completion of the well in May, 1923. The earliest version I have found in print is that of May 3, 1925. The earliest printed version of the million-dollar drink story that I know of was published May 28, 1933, nearly four and a half years after the event. The reporter intimated that the tale was then in oral circulation.

Whichever preceded, the history of these tales illustrates the manner in which the spoken and the printed word complement each other in the development of one type of folklore in a literate society.

AUNT CORDIE'S AX AND OTHER MOTIFS IN OIL

Like most folk motifs, they involve the unusual, the unexpected. Yet why some stories are interesting and are widely repeated and others are not cannot be fully explained. But in any group there will be those who know a good story when they hear one and are not too strictly bound by facts to alter them if it makes the story better. And there will always be feature writers who are not averse to changing and embellishing facts to make salable copy.

1. Boyce House, *Were You at Ranger?* (Dallas, 1935), p. 15.
2. *Ibid.*, p. 78.
3. Bob Duncan, *The Dicky Bird Was Singing* (New York, 1952), p. 268.
4. George Sessions Perry, *Hackberry Cavalier* (New York, 1944), p. 42.
5. Samuel W. Tait, *The Wildcatters* (Princeton, 1946), p. 113.
6. Boyce House, *Oil Boom* (Caldwell, 1941), p. 39.
7. Tape-recorded interview, Wichita Falls, August 13, 1952.
8. This and the two newspaper stories following are quoted by Martin Schwettman, "The Discovery and Early Development of the Big Lake Oil Field," M. A. Thesis, University of Texas, 1941.
9. Schwettman, *op. cit.*, p. 20.
10. Duncan, *op. cit.*, pp. 37 ff.
11. Quoted by Schwettman, *op. cit.*, pp. 101-3.
12. *Ibid.*

ROBERT C. STEPHENSON

# The Western Ballad and the Russian *Ballada*

HISTORICALLY, the Russian *ballada* is an interloper. When the energetic survivors of the Grand Duchy of Kiev, harried by continual invasion from the East, retreated to the woods and lakes of the North, they left an epic vacuum behind. In the course of time, this was filled by Western ballad materials, which flowed in from Poland and Galicia. Even in the North, where the transplanted native *bylina* survived as a creative force down into the seventeenth century, it was steadily being pushed out to the fringes of European Russia, until, in the eighteenth century, it was a curiosity, apparently savored, or even known, in central Great Russia, by very few. The upper classes no longer needed it: they were busy acquiring a taste for French neoclassicism; and the lower classes, who had supplied singer and song, now had a fragmentary new subject matter: their domestic woes. These the limits and mood of the Western ballad were designed to express as the *bylina* could never have done, and so, once more, this time from the Ukraine, where it had already shaped itself to East Slav needs, the ballad flowed in.

How much earlier than the eighteenth century the supplanting had actually begun, it would be impossible to say. Certainly there was never a time, from the moment when the *bylina* began to disappear from general knowledge, that apprentices, house servants and peasants were without their songs. Perhaps some of these were of an unbroken epic tradition, and, in fact, the survival of formal devices and some themes from the *bylina* supports this notion. But, in any case, and this is the point, the *ballada* of Great Russia is a *parvenu* in the ballad world. The Russians themselves call it their "low" epic genre, and Entwistle dismisses it as inconsequential.[1]

An unintended effect of this disparagement, which would apply

THE WESTERN BALLAD AND THE RUSSIAN *BALLADA* 87

equally well to the cowboy ballad or the Mexican *corrido,* is that the very features of borrowing have been neglected. Yet the give and take of ballad substance among Western ballad families, the extent and the nature of such interchanges, has always been a subject of interest to the student of folkways. Interest flags, it seems, only when the process continues down to the present in a ballad culture that is still alive.

In general, what the *ballada* borrowed came in by oral diffusion at the folk level, at first along the roundabout way from Poland and Galicia to the Ukraine and thence up into central Great Russia, and later, when the pattern was widespread, directly across from Western Europe. But since the genre flourished throughout the nineteenth century, it was reinforced by a new invasion: the Western folk ballad as Russian romanticism appropriated it. In one instance, at least, literary translations may have shaped a *ballada;* in others folk poet and writer made independent borrowings of the same material; and, finally, there are recognizable bits of Western ballads that the folk poets alone took over. I shall consider some cases, beginning with the one of possible literary influence.

In the revolutionary year of 1789, a young Russian gentleman, Nikolai Mikhailovich Karamzin, who was making the Grand Tour of Western Europe, set down his impressions, with an eye to publication, in a series of elegant letters. After the most advanced fashion of the moment he was a man of sentiment, but his sentiments were of a delicate and elegiac temper rather than a stormy one. Consequently he found what was going on in Paris very little to his taste, but in Weimar he thoroughly enjoyed himself. There, every aspect of Romanticism seemed equally *gemütlich* and tender and he embraced them all without distinction. One manifestation in particular charmed him. This was the German discovery of sixteenth- and seventeenth-century Spanish poetry, and the felicitous translations that were appearing. One of these, a German version of the old Spanish ballad "Guarinos," he turned into faithful and melodious Russian and sent along home with his other exquisite impressions.

For Russian readers this was the first literary translation of a *romance,* and if it was done by a man most probably unaware of the simple strength of the Spanish form, it was in other respects a happy find. For the principle upon which the German translation was made facilitated the further translation into Russian with the least loss of form and sense. This principle was, briefly, to keep to a trochaic octosyllabic line, alternately acatalectic and catalectic, and, since the long *laisse* of Spanish mono-assonance could find no natural counterpart in German, to dispense with rime. An understandable German prejudice in favor of the quatrain disfigured the original only visually, inasmuch as, in respecting the half-pauses of the odd-numbered lines and stressing the full-pauses of the even-numbered ones but leaving these unrimed, it avoided dismemberment into the discontinuous auditory units of less purely narrative patterns. The features of the German translation Karamzin scrupulously carried over into Russia. If he had known or divined the nature of Spanish assonance — as, outside of Spain, only a few specialists then did — he might have made an almost technically perfect borrowing.[2] The Russian folk songs, of which he was a connoisseur, make rich, though undisciplined, use of this device, and would have furnished him with a more than ample store of it. But this is asking too much; it is enough that after the German he came very close to the Spanish rhythms — something that English translators, like Lockhart and Southey, could never twist the predominantly monosyllabic English tongue into doing.

It has seemed desirable to labor this point at pedantic length, for the reason that it was a genuine, if modest, historical event: in the year 1789, which thereby becomes memorable, Russian prosody formally appropriated a fair copy of *romance* meter. The practical importance of the happening lies in the fact that the new form was easily incorporable into the *ballada*. Strictly speaking the latter was ametrical, like the *bylina*. It had no fixed line length, no meter, not even a recurrent rhythm (except for a tendency toward dactyllic line-endings), no patterned use, though a profuse incidence, of rime and assonance, and usually no strophic divisions. But it was song, and the influence of music held it within manageable limits. Herein, with the unpredictable facility of protean matter, it would frequently assume the most regular of forms. Upon its capacities *romance* made minimal demands, and in its resources found all that was needed.

More than merely assimilable, it was congenial: in a poem about an incomprehensible occurrence in the far-off and equally incomprehensible land of Spain, the Russian folk must have responded

THE WESTERN BALLAD AND THE RUSSIAN *BALLADA* 89

to a kindred accent. Well along in the second quarter of the nineteenth century, a traveler in Siberia heard peasants, who had learned them from gentlemen in exile, *singing,* quite as mournfully as if they understood them, the lines

> Khudo, khudo, akh, frantsuzy!
> V Rontsevale bylo vam!

which are Karamzin's Russian for the Spanish

> Mala la hubisteis, franceses,
> en el val de Roncesvalles.[3]

Here the significant word is *singing:* the peasants had accepted the poem as one of their own songs. Now this does not mean that "Guarinos" had become a Russian *ballada,* but it is a step toward a folk acceptance of *romance* meter.

There was arguably another such step. In 1831, the much more influential and widely known poet Zhukovsky, who had been translating artistic ballads ever since 1808,[4] turned fourteen of the traditional *romances* about the Cid into vigorous Russian. Like Karamzin he drew upon German sources, and his metrical solution was even better, since he abandoned the strict alternation of acatalectic and catalectic endings for a predominantly acatalectic series, that is, for the complete octosyllabic line of feminine endings. Zhukovsky, it happens, was an inspired translator, the greatest, perhaps, as the most industrious, that ever lived, and his versions of the *romances* catch, even at second hand, the headlong sweep and the homely vigor of the originals. With them we have *romance* meter not only taken over, but tawed to the state of Russian leather. But did the folk adopt it?

It is natural to look for their use of it in a *ballada* with a Spanish theme, and that, to take the unquestionable example, would be the "Dyevushka-Voin" (C 6), that is, "The Warrior Maid," a version of "La doncella guerrera." "La doncella guerrera" is a sixteenth-century *romance* that moved all the way across Southern Europe, leaving, like a gypsy, the patrin of a new version at each linguistic and geographical halt. Russia it reached, as was to be expected, by way of the Ukraine, and into Great Russia it must have come tardily, for Chulkov's collection of folk-songs, printed in 1770, does not register it.[5] But as late as 1895 there were a few variants in the oral tradition of the environs of Moscow.[6] What do they show? Is there any sign of the *romance* pattern in them?

It is pleasant to be able to answer both yes and no: pleasant to find two or three *romance* lines in the *ballada* since this means that, very likely, the ballad reached Russia Spanish in form as well as in content; pleasant, on the other hand, that the lines are a mere vestige, which indicates nearly complete assimilation[7] and suggests that wherever a parallel to *romance* occurs in folk Russian it may do so as an independent prosodic movement, not a secondary characteristic of some particular subject matter.

A little search in Chernyshev's *Russkaya Ballada* turns up the example we are looking for. It is an item entitled "A Husband Finds a Visitor with His Wife" (C 33-35). The visitor is, naturally, a young gentleman, whose presence even the quick-witted wife is hard put to it to explain. In other words, we have here the old English ballad "Our Goodman" (Child No. 274). Chernyshev gives three variants, one in the native ametrical form, another in what we may call Karamzin's *romance*, and a third in Zhukovsky's (but with the extraneous detail of frequent internal rime). Each of these last two is somewhat disguised by refrain-like repetitions, a feature not characteristic of *romances* as printed in the *romanceros,* but, in oral tradition, frequently having the same source with the Spanish as with the Russian, namely, the musical pattern to which the verse is sung.

Here, then, we have a curiously mixed borrowing: our *ballada* takes its pattern from one Western European ballad family and its subject matter from another. The confusion is even greater than this, since it extends to the form itself. For one of the two variants that concern us, the Zhukovskian, has frequent interval rime, and the other, the Karamzinian, contains a couplet of brisk half lines. The first of these oddities looks like a feature common in English outlaw ballads, the second is a humorous device from "Our Goodman" itself.[8]

We might conclude that in taking an old English ballad and reworking it by grafting English riming practices onto *romance,* the folk poets had been influenced in each case by the translation of Karamzin or Zhukovsky or both; and it actually does seem more than merely possible that in one instance, that of what I have called the Zhukovskian pattern, which appears in a ballad discovered as late as 1925, the literary model was influential. But what of the other variant? Does this really owe its form to Karamzin's metrically parallel translation? Actually, it cannot do so, since it appeared in Chulkov's collection, nineteen years before Karamzin's "Guarinos" was written.[9] In other words, a folk poet had discovered the rhythm before Karamzin did, and presumably without a written model, inasmuch as his version precedes any German translation of a *romance*. Still, the undatable folk pattern, while anticipating Karamzin's discovery, does not deprive it of luster or preclude the possibility that it may yet be shown to have influenced folk song. The coincidence chiefly suggests a sort of inevitability in a form that the fastidious versifier Karamzin and some probably illiterate journeyman independently hit upon.

"Our Goodman" was the material for another parallel between folk verse and literature when, in 1835, Pushkin made a translation of its climactic stanzas, working, it seems probable, from Friedrich Wilhelm Meyer's German translation of 1789 — though he could have known the original.[10] No evidence has appeared that this translation found any echo in popular verse. Equally without such effect was Pushkin's translation of "The Twa Corbies" (1828), which has its parallel in folk verse. The folk had been singing it, greatly modified, but still recognizable, since before 1770, under the title "A Mother, a Sister and a Wife Bewail the Slain One."

With this I conclude my scanty findings in the influence of Russian literary translations upon the *ballada* and in literary parallels to the folk work. I now turn to a brief listing of themes, details and devices of the Western ballad that the Russian folk singers have taken over without the intervention of sophisticated poets.

One borrowing is partly anticipated in what I have said of "A Husband Finds a Visitor with His Wife," a variant of which has internal rime. I noted that this is a frequent device in English outlaw ballads, or, as I should have put it more precisely, in some of the late Robin Hood ballads, where it is regularly accompanied by an anapaestic movement of the line. But precisely this combination, of internal rime with anapaestic movement in a ballad about outlaws, is what we find a recent *ballada* to be. The Russian collector, who discovered the *ballada* in 1901, judges it to be of recent and bookish origin (C 337). The possibility that it is an imitation of a Robin Hood meter is supported by this appraisal and by the further fact that the Robin Hood ballads have been known in Russia since the 1830's.[11]

Final lines of ballads have a specially stubborn way of carrying over into foreign versions, almost as if they were the passionately cherished point of the song. Striking instances of this are to be found in the two *ballady* "Sister and Brother" (C 259) and "Sophia and Vasily" (C 250). "Sister and Brother," on the well-known theme of the brother that finds he has ravished his sister, ends with the lines

> Farewell, maid, farewell, fair one,
> Farewell my own blood-sister.
> The hunter slew himself,

and the well-known Scottish version of this theme, "Babylon; or, the Bonnie Banks o Fordie" ends

> 'O sister, sister what have I done!
> O have I done this ill to thee!
> O since I've done this evil deed,
> Good sall never be seen o me.'
> He's taken out his wee pen-knife,
> And he's twyned himsel o his ain sweet life.

The parallel between the endings of "Sophia and Vasily" (C 249) and "Fair Margaret and Sweet William" is even closer. The *ballada* ends

> There grew over Vasily a golden willow,
> Over Sophia a cypress bush,
> And leaves with leaves wrapped round
> And twigs with twigs were bound,

and the ballad

> On Margaret's grave there grew a rose,
> On Sweet William's grew a briar,
> They grew till they joined in a true lover's knot....

These are, of course, immemorially old devices of sentiment, in Oriental as well as in Occidental literature, but here we find them growing out of ballad and *ballada* and binding the two together.

To that large family of Western ballads that includes the English "Sweet William's Ghost" and the Danish "Aage and Else" we must relate the Russian "The Ghostly Visitant" (C 329). This time it is not the final words themselves so much as their tender and homely tone that recalls familiar Danish ballads. When the cock crows and the specter lover vanishes, the exasperated Russian maiden cries

> If I'd known 'twas crowing time
> I'd have wrung the rooster's neck.

Still another *ballada* as close in tone as in subject matter to a ballad is "The Dismembered Darling" (C 212). Like a comic English version of "The Twa Sisters," this is the gruesome tale of a murdered girl whose remains —her bones, her tendons, her hair and so on— are made into a tell-tale harp. The extraordinary feature of the resemblance is that each of the two is a jester's song, with a common grisly sportiveness.

*Ballady* in which recognizable Western themes or moments occur without any notable echo of language are the following: "Prince Michael's Mother Slaps His Wife" (C 244), a fusion of bits from the two Danish ballads "Valdemar and Tove" and "The Elfin Shaft"; "The Unwed Mother" (C 171) in which mother and newborn child converse, as they do in the English "The Cruel Mother," but in a gentle and lyric, not a melodramatic style; "The Beloved Ransoms Her Lover from Prison" (C 121), a Russian "The Hangman's Tree," but without the effective device of incremental refrain; "The Two Sisters" (C 334), a sober variant of "The Dismembered Darling" possibly influenced by a translation from the Swedish (N. Berg, Moscow, 1854); "The Maiden Drowned on Her Wedding Day" (C 262), a version of the Danish "The Mighty Harp" that is all the more dramatic for stopping short of the rescue; "The Deceived Maiden Drowns Herself" (C 324), a recent work that may owe one situation to "The Fair Flower of Northumberland"; "The Maid Who Would Not with a Lackey Be Wed" (C 325), related to both "The Gay Goshawk" and similar Danish and German ballads; "Malvina" (C 328), a new find (1915) where the very title suggests a bookish source, perhaps a version of the Spanish *romance* "Los amantes de Teruel"; and "The Lad Outplayed by a Maid" (C 4), remotely descended from the ancient Western group of the riddle ballad.

One *ballada*, finally, stands apart from the others for the mysterious relations it suggests. This is "They Killed Brother Roman" (C 213), a strange old piece, from Chulkov's collection, another jester's ballad. In more than the jingling resemblance of titles it reminds us of the nursery rime "Who Killed Cock Robin?" Like the latter, again, it seems to hide a historical reference in the discreet guise of nonsense. I quote it in full:

>     The shaggy duck,
>     Where did it spend last night,
>     Where has it been the night?
>     Yonder on the marsh,
>     By Kuzma-Demyan,
>     By St. Barbara.
>
>     They fired the stove red,
>     They boiled the porridge thick,
>     The pies are hid on the shelf,
>     The beer's at work in the barrel.
>
>     They went, went, went, the jesters,
>     Got tangled in the bushes.
>     Whistles, don't you blow,
>     Don't wake up mama.
>     Mama's little and old,
>     Papa's a young one,
>     Three brothers are in service,
>     Three sisters are married.
>
>     They killed brother Roman,
>     Buried him under a bell,
>     Censed him with a censer,
>     Remembered him with a wafer.

Who will weep for brother Roman?
Two hairy wolves,
Two hump-backed swine,
Two tailless hens,
Two headless cocks.

1. *European Balladry* (The Clarendon Press, 1939), pp. 379-80.
2. Russian verse being accentual by his time instead of syllabic, he could not have managed the rhythmic variety of *romance*; but this, for all its freedom, is so predominantly trochaic in movement as to be reasonably represented by trochaic meter.
3. Cf. Menendez Pidal, *Flor Nueva de Romances Viejos* (Buenos Aires, 1938), p. 116.
4. The ballads distinguishable as either translations or imitations, but omitting the quasi-ballads he calls songs, are as follows:
Bürger: one in 1808, one in 1811, one in 1831.
Goethe: two in 1818.
Goldsmith: one in 1813.
Mallet: one in 1814.
Moncrieff: one in 1814.
Schiller: one in 1809, one in 1810, two in 1818, one in 1828, three in 1831, one in 1833.
Scott: one in 1822.
Southey: one in 1813, two in 1814, one in 1821.
Uhland: three in 1816, one in 1831, four in 1832.
5. M. D. Chulkov, *Sobranie raznykh pesen* (St. Petersburg, 1770).
6. A. I. Sobolevsky, *Velikorusskie Narodnye Pesni* (Moscow, 1895-1902; 7 vols.). Quoted by V. I. Chernyshev, *Russkaya Ballada* (Leningrad, 1936), to which my parenthetical numberings of *ballada* titles refer.
7. What I call assimilation looks like disfigurement to such scholars as Professor Entwistle. They are distressed to find the story stripped of its neat little Western folktale triads and of some undeniably interesting details of folklore, and reduced to a cryptic rendering of one moment from the original. But the odd fact is that the "deformed" Russian retelling is closer to the style of traditional *romance* than is the neatly finished short story in verse of the sixteenth-century Spanish.
8. This second structural detail is fair evidence that the *ballada* stems pretty directly (perhaps by way of the eighteenth-century German translation) from "Our Goodman" and not from the metrically different "Ein Bauer und sein Weib."
9. To put it the other way round, Karamzin must have known this song, but probably did not relate it to "Guarinos," of which he had the prosodic model in the German directly before his eyes.
10. The only collection of English and Scottish popular ballads in Pushkin's library was Sir Walter Scott's *The Minstrelsy of the Border*,

in the French translation of M. Artaud (Paris, 1826), which does not contain "Our Goodman," but does contain "The Twa Corbies."

11. Professor M. P. Alekseev, *Istoriya angliskoi literatury* (Moscow, 1943), Vol. I, Part 1, p. 229. Professor Alekseev quotes Gorky's account of how a fragment of a Robin Hood ballad fell into his hands in his youth. Unfortunately the rudely translated fragment that Gorky remembered is from the wrong pattern of ballad to support my assumption.

ROBERT C. STEPHENSON

# Signature in Ballad and Story

*Well here comes Dr. Melton!*
— *"The Midnight Express"*

ANTHROPOLOGISTS INTERPRET TALES of magic in terms of myth or ritual or both; and as far as origins are concerned the explanation is impressive, though sometimes as marvelously constructed as the stories themselves. But how are we to explain a much more functional and an equally important fact about such tales — their survival? Rites and cosmogony long ago dropped out of them, communal participation supports them less than it does the ballad even, they have paled and retreated into the ghostly realm of useless beauty, and still they hold on. Unless we are to posit a buried folk memory of lost meanings, a deep, dim alphabet soup of Freudian mishmashic, we must conclude that, apart from aesthetic values, they answer to an actual need of hearer or teller.

The hearer in general is easily ruled out. Even before the days of the radio he was helpless, a member of the captive audience. As the Russian folklorists have shown, we must give up the sentimental picture of every old gaffer as his own storyteller. Folk tales are preserved by professionals, artists of the spoken and acted word who are esteemed as such by the people. This is a fact that would have been recognized sooner, except that the professional always looked like someone or something else, like a cobbler, a tramp, a nursemaid or any other member of his own audience; in other words, like a mere amateur of his art. What made him a professional, in his own estimation and in the eyes of the audience, was nothing in his economic or social status, but simply his talent and the authority of performance. As a professional he consequently imposed upon his meek and submissive listeners a repertory of his own free choosing. In Russia, where the folk-tale-teller still thrives, only three or four great artists seem to have known as many as a hundred stories or more; most of them have known between five and ten only; and some have made a reputation on the strength of two or three.[1] This means that the storyteller was known for a *characteristic* repertory, which made a suitable vehicle for *his* talents, was congenial to *his* spirit, and survived because precisely *he* could keep it alive with feeling and special understanding.

So, the relation between storyteller and materials being significant, it is the purpose of the following discussion to dwell upon one type of story in the light of this relation. But relation means intrusion, and it therefore seems helpful to begin, in the roundabout manner of the storyteller himself, with some cognate intrusions into ballad and story.

Surely the most curious of these is the wandering cognomen. All at once a mysterious — and often superfluous — minor personage will pop out of nowhere, without, as far as the listener can tell, a stitch on his back, a trait to his character, or a penny in his jeans, but fairly flaunting that most unlikely of possessions in a ballad, an obtrusive personal name. In a fifteenth-century Spanish *romance* beginning with the magical line *"Alora la bien cercada, tú que estás en par del rio"* (Alora the nobly walled, thou that standest by the river), an account of a siege proceeds in the gaunt impersonal style of the historical epic until the *adelantado*, who is leading the attack, is struck by an arrow, and then, with an instantaneous shift to the method of the war correspondent, it identifies two chance bystanders who had not thitherto appeared and will never again be mentioned in either history or song: *"Tomole Pablo de rienda, de la mano Jacobico"* (Pablo seized the rein for him, Jacobico held his hand.) But who was Pablo, who was Jacobico? Why, attendants of his, you answer, children he had raised in his own household, as the ballad goes out of its way to tell us. Yes, of course, but who were they *really*, to come bursting through the tissue of style and self-containment like this, trespassing from another dimension, swimming to the surface of the poetry like insoluble lumps of prose? Who were they?

No one can say who they were, and so they afford us something of the same shuddering pleasure as the three unexplained knocks on the castle gate. Nor can anyone, footnoters to the contrary, tell singers and listeners who a host of carefully named ballad creatures are. Do you happen to know Alice Fry by any chance? All I myself know about her I heard in "Frankie and Albert," where the barkeep says:

> I will not tell you no story,
> I will not tell you no lie, —
> Albert left here about an hour ago
> With a gal named Alice Fry.

I have devoted a good deal of speculation to Alice Fry, as I have to another tantalizing citizen of the American ballad world, a certain Mr. Crego. Ever since the gullible buffalo skinner wryly informed me of how "a man by the name of Crego came stepping up to" him, Crego has been one of my favorite villains. Sometimes these autonymities are explainable in purely traditional terms. There is the Mr. Howard,[2] for example, who was shot by a dirty little coward. Him I find less eerie than some of the others: like Friar Tuck and Little John he coexists to tie the fabulous hero to local habitation and a name. But *his* monicker too, *his* sudden label too, partakes of the wonder. The list of his fellows is endless, we can all add to it, in fact it is only a pleasant parlor game to do so. What is significant is the effect the names have. They come like clods of unprocessed imagination, as the old Greek poet already knew when he invented the epic inventory. They come as more than names, being discourse on the very nature of name.

Characters thus prosily introduced, stripped to the symbol of bare reference, like an entry in an address book, are a symptom of the ballad in the rough, not yet quite detached from impertinent reality, like a partly finished statue with one foot still buried in unworked marble. But there is another kind of involvement, with another cause. This is the first awkward intrusion of the ballad maker, or of the ballad singer, or, in the simple impression we receive, of the ballad singer as ballad maker. Sometimes the old English and Scottish ballads, while holding to an over-all effect of detachment, would begin in the first person singular — as if absent-mindedly, almost as if in unconscious rebellion against anonymity. To say nothing of mere burdens, like "I heard a cow low, a bonnie cow low" in "The Queen of Elfan's Nourice," there is "The Twa Corbies," with the opening lines:

> As I was walking all alane,
> I heard twa corbies making a mane....

But it is hardly worth while to quote instances of this turn. They sound a constant murmur of discontent throughout the whole impersonal canon of the ballad. The example just quoted is to be explained as a device of calculated irony; but in the Robin Hood cycle and the like, which were notoriously the property of strolling singers,[3] vanity and business sense dictate the pronoun. When the entertainer announces

> Of an ancient story I'll tell you anon,
> Of a notable prince that was called King John,

among other things he is making an assertion of proprietary rights in the materials. Whether he himself composed the little notice of copyright, or it was furnished by a self-effacing poet, is sometimes a question. Certainly the introductions and the conclusions have, many of them, the look of standardized, interchangeable parts. In any case they demonstrate that professional recitation and lyric feeling alike were always at work, washing against the monolith of the ballad and wearing it away. Once they have eaten through it, they pour into the Americas — into the lament of the cowboy and the *corrido* of the vaquero — with a great rush of released sentiment.

Sometimes it is clearly the poet, the composer himself, that intrudes, and when he unmistakably does, the intrusion is signature. At the very beginning of the thirteenth century, the first Spanish poet to be remembered by name, pious and pleasant-spoken Berceo, who had much in common with anonymous poets of his own and other lands, set a pattern that is curiously repeated today. With a sly look of appraisal at his reader, Berceo explains in the introduction to one of his poems:

> Quiero fer una prosa en roman paladino
> en qual suele el pueblo fablar con su vezino,
> car non so tan letrado por fer otro latino:
> bien valdra, como creo, un vaso de bon vino.
>
> (I want to tell a story in the speech of every day,
> The Spanish that the people use with those across the way;
> I can't put things in Latin, but for what I have to say
> I think a glass of good red wine would not be too much pay.)

In Spain itself, when the heroic age of the ballad was followed by a period of decline and, specifically, by the derivative form called the vulgar ballad, the anonymous and near-anonymous authors of this form, being vain out of all ratio to their talent, turned signature into a pretentious feature of style. The pattern of such signature is an imitation of Golden Age epilogues. So it is that the obscure poetaster Alonso de Morales brings one of his crude ballads to a stop with the lines

> Y Alonso de Morales,
> que este suceso halló escrito,
> quiso reducirlo a versos
> al mandato de un amigo. . . .
>
> (And Alonso de Morales,
> Who found this happening printed,
> Has tried to do it in verses
> As one of his friends has bidden. . . .)

Flat this envoi may be, but for us it has a value, since we see it as the archetype, related or not, of signature in our own folk songs. Substitute Billy Gashade for Alonso de Morales and you get

> This song was made by Billy Gashade
>   As soon as the news did arrive;
> He said there was no man, with the law in his hand,
>   Who could take Jesse James when alive.

Tom Moore, instead of Billy Gashade, would make no greater difference:

> Of all the comrades that I've had
>   There's none that's left to boast;
> And I'm alone in my misery
>   Like some poor wandering ghost;
> And as I pass from town to town
>   They call me the rambling sign —
> "There goes Tom Moore, a bummer shore,
>   Of the days of '49."

In both the *corrido* and our own indigenous ballads there are great numbers of these pathetic claims to authorship. From ballad to ballad the names, and so the consequent rimes, change, but the pattern is constant.

One considerable deviation does, however, occur. To accommodate his ending to the unknown singer, to furnish the latter with a role as well as a ballad, the poet may turn suppression of his name into a little farce, as he does in "The Ram of Darby":

> The man who owned this ram
>   Was considered very rich,
> Or the man who told this story
>   Was a lying son of a —— yup se doo-la lally.

For doing so, he has high and mighty precedent in "The Twa Sisters," where the inventive miller is identified with the singer in the last couplet:

> Now pay the miller for his payne,
> And let him be gone in the divel's name.

More interesting than precedent in the past of the ballad, he also has parallels in the present of the Russian folk tale, where the intrusion of the performer finally becomes explicit. Here we find the ending to be a time-honored formula, which, while not obligatory, is usually respected in the tale of magic. In as far as merely traditional, it may seem to tell us nothing of the relation between story-maker, or storyteller, and story. But though immemorially old, it is far from being a dead letter. Its purpose is to make a playful association of the reciter with the scene and characters in his recital. Skilful storytellers therefore shape it to their own tone and idiom.

It has two basic patterns. The simpler one of these is a little rime, roughly to be rendered as "Now my story's done, give me a bun," where "bun," more exactly "doughnut," may be replaced by "a crock of butter," "a bit of honeycomb," or some other tidbit. A bolder version, from a clown's tale, runs, "A glass of beer for us fine fellows, a glass of wine all round now the story's done." Berceo would have approved of this reasonable request. The second of the basic patterns, the more adaptable one, goes as follows in the shortest version: "And I was there, and drank beer and mead; it trickled down my beard but none of it fell into my mouth." In other words it was all of it, story and feast, a tissue of fancies, but the narrator lived through it as if it had been real.

Upon this second version of the formula the reciter was free to embroider to his heart's content, just as the pianist in Mozart's time was free to improvise cadenzas. Sometimes a waggish storyteller would turn the ending into raucous nonsense: "I was there myself, I had some beer. It ran down my whiskers. None of it fell into my mouth. They gave me a red coat.[4] A raven flew by and cawed, 'Red's your coat, red's your coat!' I thought it was saying, 'Shed your coat, shed your coat!' and I went and shed it. They gave me red shoes, the raven flew by and cawed, 'Red-soled shoes, red-soled shoes!' I thought it was saying, 'You stole the shoes, you stole the shoes!' and I went and kicked them off." Or again, a literate storyteller may be betrayed into bookish language: "When his relatives had gazed upon the knight, they too recognized him, and such was their joy that your humble narrator can find no words to shape it to telling in a tale or writing in a record. And the whole community partook in the feasting, and there were liquors of all kinds. And your narrator was there, and drank of the mead, and it ran down his beard and not a drop fell into his mouth. With which, gentle listeners, my story of true love has come to an end."[5] In a much simpler vein, finally, the poetic storyteller might turn the little ritual into a touching defense of art. "I was at that feast, too, and they gave me mead and wine. It trickled down my beard, and none of it fell into my mouth. But my soul was as if it had eaten and drunk."

There is one all-important fact to repeat about these versions of the formula and the innumerable others that might be quoted: whether or not an original myth-maker or a ritualistic role partly encompassed the storyteller himself at the outset, catching him half in and half out of make-believe, like the stage-carpenter of a Chinese play, he was at all events free to strike a graceful pose in his predicament. It was a command performance, but he attended willingly, and he put his best foot forward. No matter how he handled the ending, he was almost sure to impress his own style upon it and so make the story his, partly his in language even, and wholly his in feeling. By doing this he becomes the co-author or at the very least the co-signer. There is only one further pattern that signature can take, and this brings us back to where we started.

The storyteller, who, as we remarked at the outset, holds to his congenial repertory, makes it even more intimately his own with the sign manual of personal valediction. In it he pictures himself — and who can say with what degree of self-deception — as hailing from the never-never land of which he talks so enchantingly. One way or another — in fact or in fancy — he has followed in Thomas Rymer's traces:

> And see not ye that bonnie road,
>   Which winds about the fernie brae?
> This is the road to fair Elfland,
>   Where you and I this night maun gae.

It would be strange if the man who has made this perilous journey were content with being only an unbidden guest at the wedding, if he didn't take the natural next step of picturing himself as the hero. As it happens, one of the heroes is actually done in the storyteller's likeness.

This is the character frequently known in Russian folklore as Ivan the Fool.

Sometimes, of course, the storyteller agrees with the Bible, that "honor is not for a fool." It is the teller of anecdotes that does this, the cynical humorist among folk artists. In his stories the fool is punished according to his folly, and sturdy good sense triumphs. But there is another Ivan, with another artist to paint him. This Ivan, too, is mentioned in the Bible, for he is the fool that "is full of words." Only they are words of a child's wisdom, good-natured and friendly ones.

You will recognize Ivan. As in Western stories, he is the backward youngest son. His two brothers are his superiors in every way. They have all the petty merchant's or the peasant's virtues: they are energetic and frugal, sensible and sharp, suspicious but enterprising. They get up bright and early on the morning of adventure, pack their lunch, dutifully give their mother a peck on the cheek, and set out with determination and self-confidence. If there were any justice in the world, that is to say, if God were a merchant, they would certainly succeed. But they fail. Hurrah, they fail! (Parenthetically I remark that they should have been professors instead of adventurers. In the ant heap of erudition they would have afforded the sluggard a very considerable lesson.) But, I take pleasure in repeating, they do fail.

They fail for the very good reason that they suppose a straight line to be the shortest distance to the point of a story. Muscular and brisk, heel and toe, they bounce along, too intent on far-off sun-gilded towers in which the princess awaits them to see or hear the wonders all around them. The dung beetle struggling with an impossible load, the buzz of supplication from a fly enmeshed in a spider's web, the thrashing of carp on a trot-line — no irrelevant little tragedy can delay them from their course. Deaf and blind to everything but the main chance, they husband their strength as they husband their attention. Where they stop beside a brook for a bit of lunch, a hollow-eyed old man is waiting. He asks them to fetch him a drink of water, and his jaws work as he watches every bite they take, but they have no time for him, and they are careful not to drop so much as a crumb. Who knows how things may go?

When the sun is down, and the way narrows and steepens, and gibbering and moaning horrors begin to pluck at them, they are quite lost. This is not their reasonable kind of world, they grow panicky, they forget the warnings the charitable old man has given them, they turn around, and they turn to stone.

You remember how different it was the day Ivan set out. After his indolent habit he slept quite late that morning, and it was midday before he sauntered out onto the hot and dusty road. His mother saw him off with only half a crust of bread and an absent-minded nod, for she had every reason to believe that he would never go very far, if, indeed, he remembered his purpose at all. She was quite right, of course. By every sign he should never have reached his destination. Where his brothers could make only bee-lines, he could make only dog's legs. Where they had an eye to business, he had an eye to pleasure, to the idle pleasure of contemplation. Where they were blind, he was all eyes; where they were deaf, he was all ears. At every step he turned aside, and everywhere he turned, he halted. Not that it was entirely his fault. There were his many friends that it was only polite to stop and pass the time of day with. All those leaves of grass, for instance.

The dung beetle was still struggling with its unwieldy load, and he helped it along a stretch of sand, and they talked about the terrible state of the highways. Things really were in a tangle with the fly, which he wished to release without tearing the web, but he finally succeeded in launching it on its way with a confidential tip about his mother's boiled cabbage. The carp lay quiet in his hand as he gently loosed the hook, and, before sliding back into the water again, paused a moment to say, "I'll be seeing you," as dung beetle and fly had done in their turn. So it went. He spent a specially pleasant time with the old man, who ate Ivan's crust of bread, drank water out of Ivan's cupped hands, and gave him some very useful advice about getting safely past midnight. What with these and others there were really too many encounters to list, but perhaps one more should be set down for oddity: he listened very politely, for at least half an hour, to a moral lecture by a couple of pissants, who sounded for all the world like his brothers.

It would seem, to anyone but Ivan, that he was making no progress at all, and yet such is the nature of time and distance in the land of make-believe that at every stage of his journey he was quite as far along as his punctual brothers. Perhaps his digressions were short-cuts. Be that as it may, he successfully surmounted every obstacle, he threaded his way through the phantoms, with whom, by the by, he would just as soon have spent more time, and, with the help of the dung beetle, the fly, and the carp (the pissants abstaining), he performed a most complicated task in due course. For the trials that followed upon this he needed no outside help. These were well within his province, since one of them was a riddle to solve and the other was merely to coax the sad-faced princess into smiling. Nothing could have been easier for witty and eloquent Ivan. As the Russian folk-saying goes, "He never had to reach into his pocket for a word."

So, when all was said and done, he married the princess, whose name was Beauty, and they invited the whole kingdom to the wedding feast. And I was there and sampled their fare, and so on.[6]

Now what is all this? Obviously it is what the anthropologists say, a fairly fixed ordering of traditional motifs[7] which can be traced to creation and initiation rites. But it holds the naive listener for more intimate reasons. To begin with, Ivan is sometimes a shoemaker, sometimes a merchant's son, sometimes a peasant lad, sometimes a soldier, and so on, as the experience and the sympathies of the narrator go. In this there is already a crude identification for both the latter and his listeners.

But the identification goes farther for the narrator. One might argue that Ivan is rewarded merely for being a good-natured fellow, a Fool of God.[8] Still it is the storyteller, precisely the storyteller, that has the qualities of the Fool of God: a gullible simplicity, a mystical love of little things and creatures, a complete helplessness in what are called practical matters, an un- not to say otherworldly character. It is the storyteller that has these qualities, and it is even he, by the way, as *clerical* storyteller, who celebrated and consecrated such qualities in the Fool of God in the first place. To find the story a moral one does not keep it from being self-portraiture, since the moral qualities in question are modest projections.

The portrait is not destroyed by Ivan's occasional slyness and his dodges, either. For the storyteller has traditionally played the fool in the technical sense of the word, too. In mediaeval Russia he was most often the *skomorokh,* or wandering buffoon; in the court of Ivan the Terrible (who could not go to sleep without his good-night story) and down through the middle of the eighteenth century, he was also the court jester. Hence — possibly — the frequent break in tone between story proper and conclusion.

This, though, is inconsequential. The proof of the portrait is in the living features. To begin with, Ivan is no fool at all, as the storyteller makes clear, but a wise and happy youth who has found himself and fulfilled his nature even before the adventure begins.[9] If he rambles so often on his way to his destiny, it is because he is not greatly concerned to reach his goal. Actually, he has less need of the princess than his brothers had, or, if you like, she was his even before he found her, since she is Beauty, and Beauty is only his way of looking at the world.

Though Ivan is no fool, the storyteller is ironically willing to call him one. Here, he says with a smile, is the fellow you practical folks look down upon. He doesn't, I grant you, make a very good clerk, but I have my own rueful reasons for preferring him. Let's see whether you can guess why. Whereupon he proceeds to paint just such a poet as old La Fontaine was, though without the fabulist's moral purpose. Not for anything in the world would he have allowed the methodical tortoise to beat the frivolous hare.

All of the qualities with which he endows Ivan are those of the naive folk poet. There is his eager curiosity that overcomes all fear; the gift for companionship; the friendly smile and the wheedling tongue, which he and his sister Scheherazade inherited from the same mother; the fellow-feeling for beast as well as man; the knack for riddles; the amiable weakness for digression; and the magical powers.

These magical powers might give us pause. When we consider the shabby, shuffling fellow that the storyteller really is, we wonder. Still, for that matter, what does it amount to, his boasted magic? Only this, that grateful birds and animals are on his side; only that he understands and speaks their language. But this is the simple truth. The humble poets, like Saint Francis, have always spoken the language of the birds and the beasts, and birds and beasts have always been on their side. Everyone, even the merchant or the professor, knows this. It is an established fact that in the hour of his need the poet calls upon supernatural forces, the forces of the imagination, and that these forces come swooping down out of the sky on hawks' wings, or scrambling up out of the well on green little lizards' legs, to do his bidding. They do this for the poet, the storyteller, first, and for Ivan only afterwards.

With the painting of the portrait, the storyteller's portrait, invasion of folk art by subjective reality, which was here and there no more than border raids by occasional proper names, becomes total occupation. Does the invader realize what he has done? Well, back in 1908, the Sokolovs interviewed Sozont Kuzmich Petruschichev, an illiterate storyteller in Byelosersk. One of the tales he told them was of "Ivan the Fool," and this is the way he began. "There was this peasant, you see, and he had three sons. Two of them were smart, but the third was a fool, like me, Sozont."[10]

1. Yu. M. Sokolov, *Russki Fol'klor* (Moscow, 1938), p. 309.
2. Even on the assumption that Mr. Howard is Jesse James himself, I find him a startling intruder as a *name*.
3. This being true, perhaps there is a double sense in the old saying, "Tales of Robin Hood are good for fools."
4. I have changed the color to keep the jingle.
5. Paraphrased from Sokolov, *op. cit.*, p. 576. I give no references

for the shorter formulae, inasmuch as their like can be found in hundreds of places.

6. No folklorist will need to be told that, even apart from readings between the lines, my story is highly synthetic, a composite of Russian and Western features.

7. V. Ya. Propp, *Istoricheskie Korni Volshebnoi Skazki* (Leningrad, 1946), chap. x.

8. Even the realistic story about the fool never quite loses the Fool of God from view. In E. A. Chudinsky, *Russkiya Narodnya Skazki* (Moskva, 1864), p. 62, the humorous story "Durak Nabity" (The Utter Fool) ends, "As all the world knows, God takes care of fools and protects them from all harm."

9. Dostoevski put something of this character into his Alyosha Karamazov.

10. Sokolov, *op. cit.*, p. 313.

AMÉRICO PAREDES

# The Love Tragedy
# In Texas-Mexican Balladry

THE COMMUNITY DANCE is an important feature in the life of most folk groups. The Border folk of the Lower Rio Grande area were no exception, and for many generations the community dance was one of their chief social functions. Aside from the gatherings of family and friends at nightfall to tell stories and to sing ballads, the dance was the only common form of entertainment that was not connected with daily tasks. In earlier days, before the Revolution in Mexico, the community dance was a much more important and a much more widely attended social function than it was later. The very old men used to tell how, in their childhood, settlements would be emptied at the sound of the drum or at the call of a passing horseman. Everyone would go, the men on horseback, the women in whatever vehicles their station in life could afford. Those of most substantial means went in the few four-wheeled conveyances the country contained in that early period; while a great many went in oxcarts. Women of the poorest vaqueros sometimes rode to the dance on stiff, uncured hides which were dragged from the saddle horns of their men like sleds over the fine dust of the chaparral trails. Thinking of the loose customs of a newer age, the very old men would say that only the women who rode on hides had powdered faces at those dances. However they went, it seems that they all attended those Border dances, which were a meeting place for the whole community.

The anonymous officer of Ohio volunteers who wrote *Sketches of the Campaign in Northern Mexico* (New York, 1853) describes (p. 65) one of the open-air dances on the Border during the United States-Mexican War. He calls it a *fandango,* and that seems to have been the popular name for it at that time. In Border Spanish *fan-*

*dango* now usually means "uproar" or "disorder." Its connection with the community dance—especially after the war brought many strangers to the Border—is easy to see. The fandango (now naturalized in English) or *función,* as it was later called, not infrequently ended in tragedy or disorder. This could be the result of rivalries, wounded feelings, a slighted sense of propriety, or just plain cussedness caused by a sudden release from hard work into merrymaking and mescal drinking. The fact that the closely knit Border communities on these occasions welcomed all comers (people from neighboring communities and passing strangers alike) combined with the customs of the dance to create all too many opportunities for friction. The dance was one of the few occasions when Border girls could meet strangers who might be potential husbands, and it was only natural for the local boys to feel jealous.

Taking a girl out for a dance was the most common cause for violence. The girls sat with their mothers or with other older women, and it was not until the music started that the men crossed over and asked the girls of their choice for that particular dance. Being refused a dance was considered as much of an affront as a slap in the face. On the other hand, custom gave a girl's truelove the right to prohibit her from dancing with anyone else, or to keep her from dancing with certain persons only. Her brothers or other close male relatives had the same privilege. So a girl often found herself in a position where she could start an uproar whether she danced or not.

Men were sometimes killed in these arguments over who should dance with whom, and sometimes the victims were the girls themselves. A Borderer who caught his girl dancing with someone else could very well react as might a Castilian of the medieval ages who caught his wife in bed with her lover. And a drink-muddled suitor, publicly affronted by a girl who refused to dance with him, might feel that his own sense of honor required the stain to be washed in the guilty woman's blood. Such incidents made the community dances unpopular with the more sedate families, and they early began to discourage attendance by their daughters at the fandangos or *funciones.*

A strong argument against attendance by nice young girls at the community dances were the *tragedias*, the crime ballads which told the stories of girls who were killed at such affairs. On the Border these *tragedias* were importations for the most part. The Border ballad makers were engrossed in telling stories about cattle driving, Indian raids, and border wars. They seem to have paid even less attention to the "love crime" than they did to the purely criminal outlaw. I know of no dance-and-brawl ballads which are native to the Lower Border. But the ballads from the Greater Mexican stock on the same subject were widely circulated. Stories of disobedient young girls who went to the dance in spite of their parents' wishes and who were killed because they were flirts and danced, or because they were not flirts and would not dance, have been widely sung along the Border.

Whole ballad series have developed on the theme of the girl who is killed at a dance. One of them is built around the famous Jesús Cadena and his girl friend, La Güera Chabela, whom he killed because he found her dancing with other men. Another group of ballads of the same type deals with Juanita Alvarado.

None is more popular, however, than the group telling of Rosita Alvírez, the little flirt who died at the hands of Hipólito, whom she rudely insulted. If one can use the localization of a majority of the versions as evidence, Rosita lived and died in Saltillo, Coahuila, around the year 1900. A few versions, later ones it would seem, place the events in Colima or in Jalisco, on the Pacific coast. These Pacific coast variants usually push the date of the tragedy up to 1935. A few variants say 1800, but most give 1900 as the date of Rosita's death.

In this ballad, Rosita is at a dance, to which (it is important to note) she has gone against the wishes of her mother. Since she is the most beautiful girl present, Hipólito asks her to dance with him. She flatly refuses, telling him with much finality, *"Contigo no he de bailar."*

Hipólito is scandalized; his honor is at stake. "Don't slight me like this, Rosita," he says. "People are watching us."

"Let them say whatever they please," Rosita answers. "I'm not going to dance with you."

So Hipólito lays his hand upon his belt, takes out of it a pistol, and shoots poor Rosita three times. As she is dying, Rosita turns to her girl friend, Irene, and tells her, "Let this be a lesson to you, Irene; when you go to the dances, be sure not to insult the men." Then Rosita's mother comes and weeps over her, but she cannot restrain an "I told you so."

"You see now, dear daughter," the mother says. "Being a flirt has cost you your life."

The ballad ends as Rosita comes before the judgment seat in Heaven to give an account of her actions to the Creator. Meanwhile, Hipólito is in jail, telling his story to the police.

The melody to which *El Corrido de Rosita Alvírez* is sung is a rousing, vigorous tune that shows all signs of origin in Northern Mexico. It forms part of a cycle sung to this same tune. The best known of these, aside from *Rosita Alvírez,* is *El Corrido de Rivera,* which is about Mexico's combination Young Lochinvar and Daniel Webster. Rivera goes Daniel Webster one better and makes the devil back out of a fight. Hearing that his truelove is about to be married to another, Rivera comes dashing out of Tula Pass, Tamaulipas, snatches her away and rides off, leaving the groom making like a crocodile *("abriendo las del caimán")* in his slack-jawed astonishment.

There is no doubt that this same tune, in *Rosita Alvírez,* has had much to do with making the ballad so widespread and so frequently sung. Continuous singing has given the ballad a compactness and a narrative style worthy of a better subject.

At the present time *Rosita Alvírez* is sung throughout Mexico and Southwestern United States. Professional recordings have been made of it, and a moving picture has been produced under the title, "Yo Maté a Rosita Alvírez" ("I Killed Rosita Alvírez").

But not even the movies have succeeded in killing *Rosita Alvírez.* The ballad has indeed an amazing vitality. Like the *Frankie and Albert* and *Frankie and Johnny* ballads (in which it is the woman who kills her man), the ballad about Rosita has become popular among non-folk singers, most of whom have found it funny. As with the *Frankie and Albert* ballads, comic verses have been added by students, partygoers, and comedians. The two best-known comic additions to *El Corrido de Rosita Alvírez* are the following:

> La casa era colorada
> y estaba recién pintada;
> con la sangre de Rosita
> le dieron otra pasada.

"The house in which Rosita was killed had just been painted red; so they gave it a second coat of paint with Rosita's blood." The other verse is even better known.

> La noche que la mataron
> Rosita andaba de suerte;
> de tres tiros que le dieron
> nomás uno era de muerte.

"The night she was killed was Rosita's lucky night. They shot her three times, but only one of the shots was fatal."

One might note the use of the number three, which is a favorite number in balladry of all kinds. Frankie nails Albert with three progressively well-placed shots.

> First time she shot him, he staggered,
> Next time she shot him, he fell,
> Third time she shot him, O Lawdy,
> There was a new man's face in hell.

Crispín (sometimes it is Martín), the hero of another set of ballads, could have taken some shooting lessons from Frankie. When he shoots Juanita Alvarado his aim is far from good. He also shoots three times, but two of his bullets go winging through the air, and only the third one hits Juanita.

> Echó mano a la pistola
> y tres tiros le tiró,
> dos se fueron por el viento,
> uno fué el que le pegó.

But that one shot did the job on Juanita just the same. It is doubtful, however, if the *tragedias* accomplished their job, which was to keep the girls from dancing.

ELIZABETH HURLEY

# Come Buy, Come Buy

A YEAR OR SO AGO a chorus of radio hucksters sought to attract customers for their feed mill sponsor by chanting a western version of a Stephen Foster folk tune. Another peddler of the air-waves appropriated a French folk song to hawk a medicine which its makers promised would give speedy relief to sufferers with headache or indigestion. One of the most popular of the radio singing commercials, hummed and sung by many who heard it, was the chorus caroled on a program advertising a brand of cigarettes.

These radio-crooned jingles are merely mid-twentieth century variants of an age-old salesmanship practice, airwave copies of the songs and chants of yesterday's street hawkers. Through the ages and across the globe the cries of peddlers have enticed buyers to the wares they had to sell. The singing salesmen have been immortalized in literature and music since William Langland recorded the cry of England's medieval pieman in his *Piers Plowman*. Shakespeare's roguish Autolycus sang a merry song to lure customers to his silks, laces, and "perfume for a lady's chamber"; the "Cherry Ripe" cry of a street vendor inspired Robert Herrick's famous poem; Christina Rossetti's goblins mimicked the chants of the fruit peddlers; and the melodious sales appeal of a girl fishmonger in Dublin is preserved in an Irish folk song. Intrigued by the "Who'll buy my sweet lavender?" refrain of the English flower girls, Ralph Vaughn Williams chose it as a theme for his *London Symphony*, and the Parisian street cries were used effectively by Charpentier in his opera of bourgeois life in the French capital, *Louise*.

The vocal appeal of the ragpicker, a familiar figure on the streets of most American towns in the early part of the century, was preserved in verse by W. H. Davies. George Gershwin included the cries of a strawberry vendor, a honey peddler, and a crab man in his opera about Negro life in the South, *Porgy and Bess,* while the song of a lemonade vender is echoed by one of the characters in Tennessee Williams' *The Glass Menagerie.*

Since the tin peddler of colonial days, the huckster has been part of the frontier life in America, following the pioneers to supply their needs as they moved westward. Flourishing most freely in lands and regions untouched by mechanized living, the footsore merchants thrived before electricity and natural gas were harnessed, before health and sanitation laws were exacted and antinoise ordinances, superhighways, and supermarkets eliminated the need for peddlers and drove them off the streets.

Peddlers were prevalent in Texas well into the twentieth century. Although a few still survive, their songs have been rapidly vanishing in the last two decades. Richardson Wright, Carl Sandburg, Rosamond Johnson, and B. A. Botkin have recorded some of the most familiar cries heard in New England and in such picturesque harbor towns as Charleston and New Orleans; but the songs and cries of the peddlers who reflect the products peculiar to the land of the mesquite and the mustang will soon be forgotten. That is why some of them are recorded here.

The earliest peddlers brought dry goods and notions to the settlers who first occupied the comparatively wild country between the Red River and the Rio Grande. Although these traveling merchants, who trudged silently over dusty lanes or jogged along in their wagons over rough unpaved trails, carved a niche in the state's social history, it is the huckster who hawked his goods with a singsong appeal that most clearly mirrors the products typical of Texas.

In his introduction to a collection of frontier songs and ballads, J. Frank Dobie recalled a remark made by an old Scotch woman to Sir Walter Scott as the nineteenth-century folklorist was taking some ballads from her. "They were made for singing and not for reading," she contended. Just as Dobie says this is true of his border ballads, so does it apply to the songs of the ambitious salesmen who traveled by foot, by horse or by wagon, hauling their products to the doorsteps of their customers and attracting buyers by crying out their wares. And they all had one thing in common — strong vocal chords.

Most familiar in Texas, with the greatest number of variations, were the songs of the hot tamale, watermelon, fruit, vegetable, and charcoal peddlers. Those who had food to sell were the most numerous, and many of these were farmers or gardeners who raised their own crops and then peddled them through the streets in residential neighborhoods. Many had regular customers who depended upon the weekly or daily visits of the peddlers to stock their cupboards and pantries.

Each part of the state had its predominant racial huckster. In East Texas, more closely allied with the Deep South, it was the Negro. From Austin and San Antonio south to the border, the Mexican led the parade of peddlers.

Shortly after the turn of the century a Mexican vendor sold his tamales and enchiladas through the streets of San Antonio. He carried them in buckets, one in each hand. His tamales, which he sold at ten cents a dozen, were so moist they would melt in your mouth and so hot they would burn your fingernails. To dispose of his cornhusk-enveloped treat he sang a simple tune:

> Hot tamales and enchilollies,
> Get 'em while they're hot.

On a crisp fall or cold winter day, few could resist the hot tamale man, usually a Mexican, who pushed his little cart of highly seasoned, steaming mixture of minced meat and chili folded in a thick corn meal dough. The name of the product itself was the heart of most of the cries heard in all towns of any size, and more often than not this was preceded by the word that meant both pungency and temperature.

In East Texas there were about as many Negro tamale vendors as there were Mexican. Two still live in the memories of longtime residents of Lufkin — a Mexican everyone called "Hombre" and a Negro named Frank. "Hombre" made his tamales in an old slave-quarter log cabin, where he lived in the earlier part of the century. He would plod through the streets, calling out his "Hot ta-ma-les!" or *"Tamale caliente!"* As late as the 1940's Frank had a regular daily route he walked through the town, with his lard tin of tamales hanging from a strap around his shoulders. In Nacogdoches there was a Mexican vendor called "Old John," while in Texarkana tamales were peddled by a tall Negro known as Mike.

In Galveston many years ago a tamale man rode through the streets in his horse-drawn wagon and blew a horn which attracted attention and customers with its peculiar foghorn sound. He had no cry. "His horn was his signal and everyone knew it," W. A. Nicholson recalled. In recent years the island port still had a Mexican who was somewhat of a landmark in the shadows of the Texas Revolution monument on palm-lined Broadway. There he could be found every day from late afternoon and into the night, as long as his tamales held out. He kept them steaming hot in large tin airtight containers on a small fringe-topped pushcart.

Some of the vendors in Houston had their own peculiar pronunciations for this staple of the Mexican diet inherited from the Aztecs. One Mexican driving a two-wheeled horse-drawn cart would cry, "Hot tamalip!" Another's chant was "Ta-ma! Ta-mal!" For years an old Mexican stood on the same corner near a laundry in Fort Worth, throwing kisses and calling out his "Hot tamales, tortillas, enchiladas, chili con carne! Anybody want some?" Shortly after the turn of the century there was a familiar character who met the trains at the depot in Denton. At a breathless pace, apparently fearing the train would pull out before he could dispose of his food, he would shout, "Hot tamales, chicken and ham sandwiches, nice fresh pies, boiled eggs."

One poetic Mexican in Dallas rang a bell that blended with his tune, which could be heard a block away:

>    Hot tamales, floatin' in gravy,
>    Suit ya taste and don't mean maybe.

Another had two verses to the song he sang. His favorite was:

>    The world goes around
>    And the sun comes down,
>    And I got the best
>    Hot tamales in town.

Indicating he had a bargain when competition grew stiff, a Denton vendor solicited customers with his cry of "Hot tamales, two in a shuck." Another in Lufkin was a little more honest. Although he claimed his tamales had "three in a shuck," he would add facetiously, "Two of 'em slipped and one of 'em stuck." Mody Boatright believes this cry of the hot tamale peddler was being mimicked by boys playing marbles when he was young. As he recalled it, their pleading call for luck when they made a shot was:

> Hot tamales, two in a shuck,
> One fell out, the other stuck.

Although many complained of the unsanitary aspects of the streetpeddled tamales, most people were willing to risk any health hazards to taste the cornhusked treat. George Sessions Perry, who prefers hog's head tamales to those made of beef or chicken, wrote in *Texas: A World In Itself:* "I never saw a tamale peddler in my life who manifested the slightest interest in sanitation, but I also don't remember ever buying any of their wares that weren't, for all their skimping on the meat content, tasty and good."

Once a conspicuous and colorful feature of the San Antonio street scene were the chili stands and the now almost legendary "chili queens," whose voices embellished the atmosphere with their ringing entreaties to prospective customers. Operating first in open-air stands on Alamo Plaza and later moving to other public squares, they enjoyed unfettered popularity in the late nineteenth century, before they were driven indoors by health and sanitation laws. In 1910, chili stands still decorated the plaza in front of the Alamo, Maury Maverick wrote in his autobiography, reminiscing of the Saturday nights when "Papa would give us what he called 'tamale money' — a big nickel each, and with this nickel we would go to the tamale stands where we would all get six tamales and chili-con-carne."

The chili stands on Haymarket Plaza, so called because it was established for the sale of hay before gasoline engines replaced horses on wagons and carriages, are vividly described by Brownie McNeil: "As we approached the plaza, we heard the shrill nasal female voices singing the wares each had to offer: 'Menu-u-u-do-o-o, enchila-a-a-a-das, ta-a-a-a-a-cos, chi-i-i-i-i-i-le!'"[1]

In Laredo, as in the land south of the border, Mexicans would come around in the early morning about sunup selling barbecue.

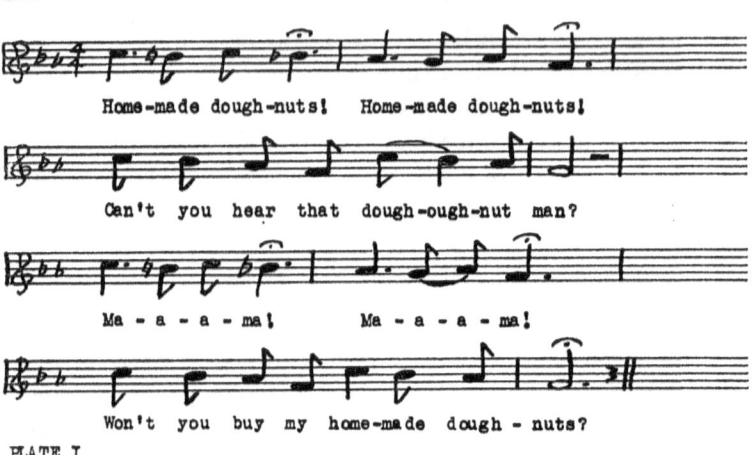

PLATE I

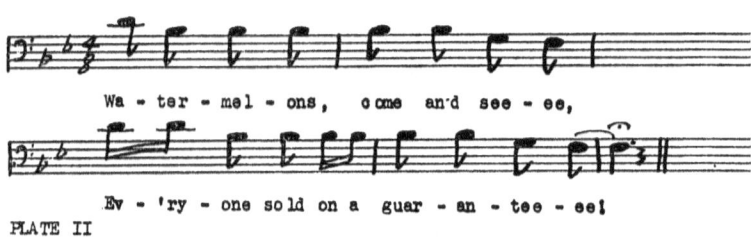

PLATE II

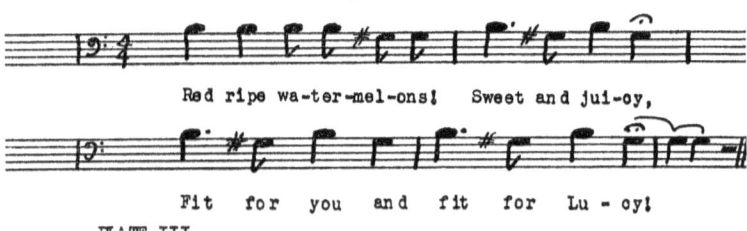

PLATE III

Many people would buy the roasted meat for breakfast. One vendor, driving a horse-drawn wagon, would call out his *barbacoa* as he drove along, but only the "co-a" resounded through the air as his voice rose in a strong crescendo.

The Arabian fashion of selling bread from trays carried through the streets of Jerusalem, which found its way to Europe and then to the New World, apparently was introduced to Texas by the

Mexicans. Many of the *pregons* who specialized in hot and sweet breads were familiar on the streets of San Antonio and smaller towns to the south. In San Antonio the Mexicans carried large baskets of *pan dulce* (sweet bread) or cakes. Some used a ring-shaped attachment fastened to their heads, on which they balanced their large baskets, as they strolled through the streets singing, *"Pan dulce!"* The musical cry of a bakery man in Alice was recalled by J. Frank Dobie. Whoever responded to his *"Pan caliente, pan dulce"* (hot bread, sweet bread) with the purchase of a loaf of lightbread would receive a *pilón,* an extra little round cake.

Anglo-Saxon bread peddlers also hawked their home-baked products. Some rang a bell to announce their approach, while others called out "Hot bread!" or whatever they had to sell. Their wares varied from doughnuts to cakes and pies. In the early 1900's when Galveston still had mule cars as the only means of public transportation, a young Jewish immigrant from Poland started out in business on a literal shoestring. Thirteen-year-old Felix went to the wharf one day to peddle his shoestrings and found that the workers wanted food for their money. At a local bakery he stocked his basket with pies, cakes, and doughnuts, and when he left the docks that day his basket was empty. The next day he carried two baskets, and soon progressed to a pushcart; then to a horse-drawn wagon, with a barrel of water or lemonade added to his shop on wheels. From his original cry of "Get your fresh hot pies!" he soon changed to "Get Felix's fresh hot pies!" Old-timers say that he was a wealthy man when he left Galveston some years later.

Doughnut peddlers were familiar in the island city that had once been Lafitte's favorite hideout. One had a rhythmic chant he used to sell his hot little cakes with the hole in the middle: "Doughnut, doughnut, doughnut man! Get 'em hot while you can!" Another sang a plaintive blues melody. (Plate I.)

Today's highway stands and summer gardens, where people can sit at tables and enjoy the ice-cold pulpy red meat of a sliced watermelon, have driven most of the melon peddlers from the streets, but an occasional wagon still may be seen parked and displaying signs that advertise the huge green-skinned fruit. A few may drawl out, "Wa-ter-mel-ons!" but most of the vendors just sit in silence and wait for customers in passing automobiles to stop and pick out melons to take home. For a long time the vendors would plug their melons to assure their buyers that they were ripe.

Many of the watermelon peddlers rang large dinner bells as they rode along in their wagons, piled high with the large, heavy melons that were as much a part of a Texas summer as a Fourth of July picnic. Most of them emphasized in their cries the color and ripeness of their product, while some added the adjective that spelled refreshment on days when they were baking under a blistering sun.

In Denton and Ennis, and perhaps other Texas towns, certain poetic peddlers caroled a verse that stressed the freshness of their melons and the cost, which now would sound more like the bargains offered at an end-of-the-season clearance sale:

> Watermelons, watermelons,
> Fresh off the vine,
> Get your watermelons,
> A nickel or a dime.

A vendor who plied his trade on the wagon route in Denton in the mid-twenties would solicit buyers with a song which offered a guarantee with every sale. (Plate II.) At the Farmers' Market in Houston there are peddlers who now sell their watermelons, fruits, and vegetables from parked trucks. But several remember the songs they once sang as they drove about in horse-drawn wagons. (Plates III and IV.) One mixed a bit of rhyme with his drawling chant:

> Oh, good old red ripe watermelons!
> Oh, they're red ripe and sweet as honey.
> You can save money.
> You can cut 'em and plug 'em;
> They are red ripe.
> Oh, lady, lady, you can eat the meat
> And pickle the rind
> And save the seed 'til plantin' time.

Many of the Mexican vendors in San Antonio peddled their melons in two languages, depending upon the neighborhood in which they were selling. Two of their most familiar cries were *"Sandías colorados sabrosas"* (Watermelons red and tasteful) and *"Salió colorado y dulce"* (Cut ripe, red and sweet). Some also would add a phrase that carried an appeal to bargain-minded prospects: *"Aquí está él que de barato"* (Here is a man who sells cheap).

PLATE IV

(Plates V and VI.) The depression prices of the thirties make today's housewives sigh as they shop for food at modern supermarkets. When small watermelons sold at a nickel apiece or six for a quarter, and the larger ones at ten cents each or three for a quarter, apples were given away at ten cents a dozen or a bushel basket for six bits; grapes brought five cents a pound or a quarter for six pounds; bananas, ten cents a dozen or a quarter for three dozen. It was about that time when Tony García, San Antonio's market master some years later, was peddling bananas from a Model-T truck for his father. He summoned housewives to his truck with their dishpans by singing a musical couplet. (Plate VII.)

In waterfront towns along the Gulf Coast the banana boats with their brightly striped awnings provided excitement for children who went to the docks to watch them come in. Peddlers, as well as produce men, would meet the boats to load their wagons or pushcarts. Many families bought whole stems of the fruit, which decorated the back porches of their homes as they were hung by ropes to ripen. Nearly everywhere a banana peddler was known as "the banana man." Houston's "Sam, the banana man" was a robust blond German with a magnificent baritone voice who lured customers by singing operatic arias.

In the 1890's when apples were scarce in Texas, the arrival of apple wagons from Arkansas was such an event that teachers in log schools would buy them for their pupils. Perhaps this led to the

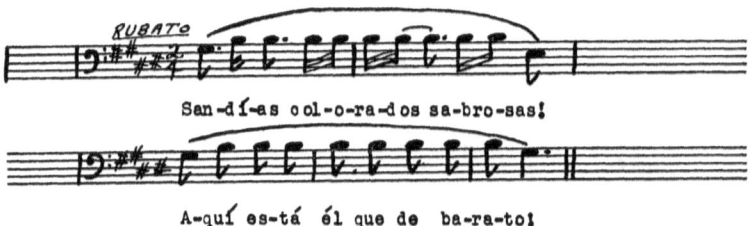

San-dí-as o ol-o-ra-d os sa-bro-sas!

A-quí es-tá él que de ba-ra-to!

PLATE V

later custom of children bringing apples to their teachers, either in repentance for bad behavior or in hope of getting a good report card. The early traveling apple merchants decorated their wagons with the shiny red fruit, and a few cried out a simple "Ap-puls! Ap-puls!" The wide variety of vocal inflections and melodic embellishments distinguished the musical sales talk of the strawberry, dewberry, and blackberry vendors. It was the notes they warbled that made their cries distinctive, for the lyrics usually were restricted to the name of the berries they carried in their baskets, or in pint or gallon cans. Strawberry wagons were most numerous around Houston, as the berries came from a big strawberry patch which today is the thriving young industrial town of Pasadena.

Nearly every woman who was a housewife in the early part of this century remembers the vegetable vendor who supplied her with most of the food that went on her dinner table. When she heard his cry of "Fresh vegetables!" she would wipe the dishwater or brush the flour from her hands with her apron, and go out to the wagon to handpick her vegetables. Many of these vendors rang a large dinner bell to attract attention, and usually spieled out in a monotone the products they had to sell — corn, string beans, cabbage, peas, okra, and tomatoes. Because many of the men who peddled

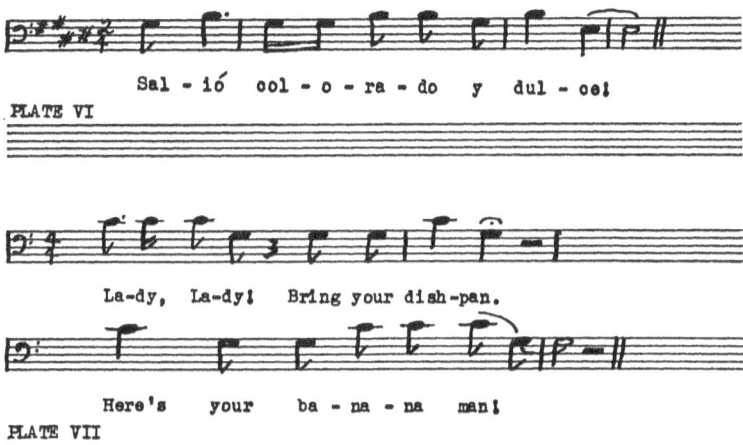

Sal-ió col-o-ra-do y dul-ce!

PLATE VI

La-dy, La-dy! Bring your dish-pan.

Here's your ba-na-na man!

PLATE VII

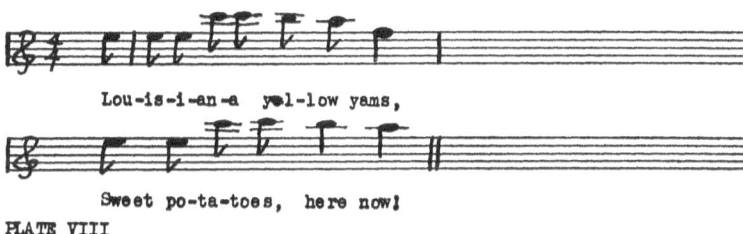

Lou-is-i-an-a yel-low yams,

Sweet po-ta-toes, here now!

PLATE VIII

vegetables in Texas were farmers selling products they raised on their own land, they were exempt from the early ordinances restricting the activity of peddlers. Markets later were established in most towns so the farmers would have a place to sell their garden produce in the city.

In the days before the telephone, the vegetable wagon was the place where women neighbors gathered to exchange the day's gossip. And many of the farmer-peddlers were favorites of the children, who hopped rides on their wagons just as in later years they jumped on the back steps of ice and milk wagons to nibble chips of ice. In Texarkana a woman vegetable vendor left a lasting impression on the people of that city, not only because of her cry, but because of the way she dressed. Mrs. O'Mike was her name, and she wore men's trousers. "In those days she was the only woman in the world — in our world at least — who wore trousers," said F. D. Biddle. As she rode along in her horse-drawn wagon she would cry out in a hoarse shout, "Come on, ladies! Here's your fine collards, sister to cabbage."

In the early 1900's a small Negro woman, whose customers fondly called her "Aunt Mary," would ride through Marshall on her high-seated buggy ringing a bell as she peddled her vegetables and field-corn hominy. But she did not wait for housewives to come to her. She would park her buggy and walk up to the porch, where she would rap with a stick or tin can and call out, "Housekeeper! Housekeeper!" The housewives knew when they heard the tingling of her bell in the distance that Aunt Mary was in the neighborhood, and they would listen for her knock that always followed.

Fifty years ago, before fresh vegetables and fruits were stocked in grocery stores, people either had to raise their own or depend on peddlers to supply them. When only such staples as sugar, flour, and cornmeal could be bought in stores, one peddler in Houston cried from his wagon:

> Okra, cucumbers, squash, and sweet potaters,
> And look at these good old red ripe tomaters.

Another peddled his "yellow yams," or sweet potatoes, with a sing-song appeal. (Plate VIII.)

An Italian peddler who operated in Houston about the same time solved the language problem he faced in his adopted land with an ingenious trick. He would follow an English-speaking vendor, who cried out his beans, potatoes, corn, and other vegetables, and call simply, "Same-a-ting-a! Same-a-ting-a!"

Among the familiar vegetable vendors in Belton were a German woman named Minna Kolls and a farmer who hawked his home-grown sweet potatoes with the cry, "Hart's yellow yams!" Minna knitted as she rode along in her wagon and cried, "Fresh vegetables! Carrots, potatoes, and snaps!" Although the vegetables she had for sale varied, she always ended her cry with an abridged description of the beans she had in her basket. Another vegetable man was easily identified by his cry of "Hoop holes and punkins!" as he peddled his black-eyed peas and large yellow jack-o-lantern fruit.

The mere mention of fresh lye hominy makes the mouths of most old-timers water. Many Texans fifty years ago made hominy in the

# COME BUY, COME BUY

PLATE IX

family washpot behind the house. Those who remember its taste say that the canned hominy found on grocery store shelves today cannot compare with the ash-flavored hominy of the past. William S. Rose of Salado still makes hominy three times a year. He ties live oak ashes in a thin white cloth sack, which is placed in the pot of water with the shelled corn. During two hours of boiling, the lye from the ashes seeps through the sack to give the hominy its tempting flavor, the husks fall off the corn kernels, and the eyes slip out. After this first cooking, the corn is washed thoroughly and put back into the pot in clean water to be boiled five more hours. Frequent stirring is necessary to keep it from burning or getting too dry. When cooked the hominy is put up in glass jars.

Just as Mexicans reigned over the tamale trade, Negroes, including many ex-slaves, led in the peddling of "Fresh lye hominy!" One in Marshall traveled on foot and carried his hominy in a tin bucket, covered with a white cloth. As he made a sale he would dip out the hominy with a tin cup, selling it by the pint. He had a poetic song he crooned as he made his regular rounds. (Plate IX.)

Most people who have lived in San Antonio for any length of time have either seen or heard of Sister Crockett, daughter of Negro slaves, an ordained minister in her own right, and a legend in the city where she peddled lye hominy from her old fringe-topped surrey for many years. Wearing a starched white bonnet and a long black robe-like dress that touched the ground, she carried her hominy in a five-gallon lard can and delivered it twice a week to her regular customers. Sister Crockett, who was born in Columbus the year after the Civil War ended, besides her peddling and preaching, composed many hymns, two of which were recorded for the Library of Congress by John A. Lomax.

With the decline of smokehouses and home-cured meats, many people who lived in cities and towns depended upon their country neighbors to supply them with their fresh meat before butcher shops were opened and meat counters became a part of every grocery store. Most of the time the farmer who brought fresh meat to town also had butter, eggs, and poultry. Many rang a bell to summon housewives to their wagons, but a few called out "Fresh meat!" or the specific name of the kind they might have.

Nearly every town had a favorite meat man that older residents remembered by name. In Marshall it was Mr. Buchanan, who, in the bygone days when steak graced even the breakfast table, came twice a week from the nearby community of Hallsville. When a housewife bought a pan of meat to last for several meals, he would give her free liver. The dietary importance of liver had not yet been widely publicized. Live turkeys also were sold by farmer-peddlers, who carried their birds in wagon beds built into large coops. Women could pick out a large turkey for only $1.25. Recalling a farmer-butcher from whom she bought in Jefferson in the early 1900's, Mrs. Martin Ragley said, "If a housewife took a large roast, he would throw in the liver, brains, and a large tongue. Now we pay ninety cents for a medium-sized tongue and seventy-five to ninety cents a pound for calf liver."

Farmer Brownie, who specialized in pork sausage, was a familiar meat vendor in Texarkana. His mark of distinction was his habit of always asking for "funny papers" to take home to his children. Goat meat, which still is a strong competitor of beef in the barbecue pits on southwest Texas ranches, was peddled in that section of the state, as well as in the hill country northwest of Austin. Anyone who bought a quantity of mutton, beef, or pork would receive free the heart, brains, liver and "lights," as the lungs were called.

About 1910 in Texarkana farmers would come to town with big water buckets of eggs they sold at fifteen cents a dozen, fryers at twenty-five cents a pound, freshly churned buttermilk at ten cents a gallon, and country butter at twenty-five cents a pound. Usually milk and buttermilk were sold from ten-gallon cans, and the housewife would have a pitcher or pail into which would be poured the amount she wanted. Since women made their own buttermilk biscuits, as well as most of the bread their families ate, the cry of "But-ter-milk!" brought them to their doors with pitchers.

From Galveston comes most of the lore on the picturesque fishmongers and their wailful cries. Although their small pushcarts sometimes included oysters, redfish, trout, catfish, and flounder, the most familiar songs were those caroled by the shrimp and crab vendors. The less imaginative fishermen, with strings of their day's catch flung over their shoulders, would cry a simple, "Fish man!" or "Fresh fish!" An Italian woman peddled her fish, which she kept in a small tank of water, from a wagon drawn by an old bony horse. As the wagon rumbled along the streets at a snail's pace, she would repeat over and over, "Feesh! ah, la, la, la!"

But the prolonged "S-h-r-i-m-p!" cry and the refrain of the peddlers who sold stuffed or deviled crabs are the ones that left the deepest impression on the people who heard them. Usually the crab men would come around just after sundown, with baskets on their arms, selling their seafood treats at a nickel or a dime apiece, three large ones for a quarter. Through the air could be heard their "Cra-ibs! Deviled cra-ibs!" as their voices rose an octave to a sharp staccato on the last musical syllable of the fish they were peddling. One would announce his approach with "Crabs! Red hot crabs! Get 'em while they're hot!"

Anyone will admit that suggestion breeds desire, especially when the stomach is empty and the suggestion involves food. That is why Hamburger Bill in Fort Worth sold hamburgers as fast as he could assemble all the ingredients between a sliced bun. He would tease his prospective customers with a reminder that it was time to eat, assisted by the enticing aroma of his product. Then he would shout out the name of the tasty sandwich meal he had to offer: "Are you hungry? Are you hungry? Are you hungry? Hamburgers!" A similar appeal, with a bit of psychology injected, was used by a vendor in San Angelo, who would cry as people passed his small stand, "Are you hungry? Don't you ever get hungry? You look hungry. Hamburgers!"

Those who have tasted both know that a Texas hamburger is as different from one sold in the eastern states as a boardinghouse table is from a depression bread line. With "everything on it," one could expect not only the meat and bun, but lettuce, tomatoes, pickles, onions, mustard, and perhaps chili sauce and no telling what else. As George Sessions Perry described it, "a short-order tantrum, and the sky's the limit." This was the kind of mammoth 'burger sold by a vendor at an Old Settlers' picnic in Sherman in the early twenties. His poetic cry was irresistible as well as descriptive:

> Hamburger lunches and they're all red hot,
> An onion in the middle and a pickle on top.

Although not as streamlined as those pushed through the streets by the Good Humor Man and local independent vendors of today, the first ice cream vehicles used by peddlers in Texas were pushcarts and horse-drawn carts. Before cones were introduced at the St. Louis World's Fair of 1904, ice cream was sold in oblong blocks wrapped in a sort of oil paper. Toward the end of the last century a vendor in Galveston pushed his small cart through the streets and called out, "Ice cream biscuits!" The first ice cream cones were called "saysos."

But it was the "hokey-pokey" man whose ice cream was popular throughout Texas from the 1890's into the early part of this century. In Belton at a Confederate Reunion one vendor cried, "Hokey-pokey ice cream, five cents a stick." The confection was frozen in a small round tin container. When a customer came along, a slice was cut and a small wood stick placed in it so that it could be eaten like a popsicle. Pushing his small cart and ringing a bell, a vendor in Texarkana would pleadingly tempt children, and send them scurrying into their houses to get nickels, with his shout, "Hokey-pokey ice cream! Cry for it, little girl, cry for it." An Italian peddler there would instruct children in a similar manner:

> Go hom-a, baby, cry.
> Cry, baby, cry.
> Tell-a mama to give you nickel:
> For ice-a cream-a.

Years ago *nieve* (ice cream) and *helados* (popsicles, Eskimo pies) were hawked in Mexican sections of San Antonio and in towns along the Rio Grande. But today's ice cream vendors push their slick white carts through the streets in summer months, their voices silent and attracting customers with tinkling bells, chimes, or, as in San Antonio, playing such music box tunes as "Take Me Out to the Ball Game" or "Down by the Old Mill Stream."

Before the town of Alice had water service, in the early part of this century, many citizens were supplied with water by Mexicans who hauled it in barrels attached to small two-wheeled carts drawn by small burros. J. Frank Dobie, who lived near there as a child, described the water boy's drawling monotone cry of "A-g-u-a" as it lingered in his ears:

> As the water hauler went up and down the streets at a snail's pace he called out with a slowness that matched his motion, "A-g-u-a." The housewife who needed water had plenty of time to intercept him. He drove his burro as near as he could get to the upright barrel beside the house and by means of a hose emptied his cart-barrel into it.[2]

When the summer sun in Texas sends the mercury soaring like an air-filled balloon that has slipped from the grasp of a child, nothing is more refreshing than an ice-cold drink. Many hawkers have profited by the heat as they quenched the thirst of patrons with lemonade, soda pop, or other chilled liquids. County and state fairs still retain some of the color of the occupational hucksters of former years, but one chant that has vanished is that of the lemonade vendor. Heard at a Fourth of July picnic in Denton a number of years ago was this one:

> Ice cold lemonade! Made in the shade,
> Stirred with a silver spade.

Many variations of this cry were heard throughout Texas, all similar to the one revived by Tennessee Williams in *The Glass Menagerie*. At a Fourth of July celebration in Belton during the 1920's one vendor poured his tasty potion into tall glasses for his customers as he cried:

> Ice cold lemonade!
> Made in the shade,
> Stirred with a spade,
> Sweetened with the fingers
> Of a pretty little maid.

Other vendors of the same era, who were mimicked by young boys selling soda pop from hastily erected stands along curbs in front of their homes, had a cry that was familiar in many towns over the state. As heard in Huntsville, Belton, Fort Worth, and other communities, it was tempting enough to make anyone want to part with a nickel:

> Ice cold lemonade!
> Freeze your teeth, curl your hair,
> Make you feel like a millionaire.

An orange-juice drink sold at public gatherings in West Texas about the same time was peddled by one vendor at Maryneal who had a romantic sense of humor:

> Orange cider, kiss-me juice,
> Hug me tight and don't turn me loose.

Confederate reunions and county fairs in Belton about fifty years ago had vendors who sold an orange drink they called "moxiemead. "Some say it was flavored water, others that it was made mostly of water, sugar, and soap weed to make it foam. Among the several cries was one bellowed by a hoarse-voiced hawker: "Moxiemead, the honey comb, the honey wine, the ladies' favorite" (with emphasis on the long *i* in the last word). Another was:

Moxie-mead, the honey wine,
The California health drink.
All you can drink for a nickel.

While the songs of the street peddlers have been silenced, most sports fans today would find a football stadium or a baseball park lacking an essential bit of color without the incessant cries of the peanut, popcorn, and soda pop vendors. Recently a wisp of a boy, whose bucket filled with chipped ice and soda pop bottles matched his weight, struggled through the stands at a baseball game in Temple crying: "Ice-cold sody-wa-ter." This is the usual cry. Another boy with a large cardboard box containing small paper sacks of goobers sang a slurred spiel that required close attention to decipher: "Get-your-peanuts-right-here ten-cents-anybody."

As soon as trains began to operate through Texas news butches (or butchers) started hawking fruits, chewing gum, candy, and booklets, as well as newspapers and two-bit novels. Later they added sandwiches to the tray they had slung from a strap around their necks. At first they would board a train when it stopped to discharge or take on passsengers, walk up and down the aisles crying out what they had to sell, and jump off before the train pulled out. But when trains picked up speed and passengers rode them in sufficient numbers to warrant a profitable business, some of the butches stayed aboard between towns to sell their wares as the train rolled along.

On the Fort Worth and Denver line between Amarillo and Fort Worth some thirty-five years ago, one vendor of pork sandwiches amused travelers with the bit of exaggeration he injected into his cry: "Whole hog in a biscuit, one dime, ten cents." Another who operated on a Texas and Pacific route through West Texas puzzled customers with his contradictory sales talk: "Apples, oranges, two for a nickel apiece." Many of the news butches wore stiff-billed caps similar to those worn by conductors annd were considered regular members of the train crews. Children who rode the trains at that time were fascinated by such toys in the butch's basket as climbing monkeys, and candy in glass containers shaped like lanterns and pistols. These child tempters were among the wares of a peddler on the T & P out of Texarkana who hawked his fruit with a rib-tickling appeal: "Boneless bananas!"

Although the majority of the singing peddlers in Texas were those who sold food, others who supplied household necessities were in great demand. The most colorful were those who provided the charcoal used for heating, cooking, and ironing before electricity and natural gas took its place. The principal colony of charcoal burners was in the hill country north of San Antonio and west of Austin, commonly called the cedarbrakes. One version of how the charcoal was made, mostly from mountain cedar, is given by Fritz and Emilie Toepperwein in *Charcoal and Charcoal Burners*. San Antonio was their principal market from 1880 to 1920, where the slow drawling cries of the peddlers could be heard blocks away as they repeated over and over: "Charcoal, charcoal for sale."

The prolonged musical appeal of a Mexican vendor in San Antonio could be heard before his wagon rolled into sight. In the Mexican sections of the city he would sing, *"El car-bón-n-n-n."* As he drove away after making a sale he would sing a sharp, staccato farewell, *"El carbonero! Se va!"* (The charcoal man, he goes.)

Steve Heffington, for many years tax assessor-collector of Travis County, became well acquainted with the people who burned charcoal for a living when he started out as a field deputy in the tax office almost fifty years ago. He recalled the song of one charcoal peddler:

> My hands is black,
> My face is black,
> And I sell my coal
> Two bits a sack.
> Chah-coal!

Some of the people in Austin referred to the charcoal burners who inhabited the nearby hills as "hillbillies." Mrs. Roy Bedichek recalled one peddler who wore galluses and a shirt that was always unbuttoned, and drove a wagon drawn by two horses, one black and one gray. His song was a plaintive melody with a drawling rhythm, and he could be heard far in the distance as his wagon moved slowly through the streets. (Plate X.)

Charcoal peddlers were familiar in other parts of the state, too. In Ennis Negroes riding on horse-drawn two-wheeled carts would drone: "Chaw-coal—, coal—, chaw—coal fo' sale! Fotch out yer pail!" One in Marshall whose face looked like cooked leather hawked his coals from a small dilapidated wagon drawn by two white scrawny mules and sang his wailful cry, "Chah—coal—."

When many Texans used wood stoves for cooking and heating, the wood wagons made their regular rounds. From sawmills around Lufkin, peddlers with small slivers used to start fires in cookstoves and fireplaces sold their "kindling wood" with the cry, "Lightnin' wood." In Houston cries of "Lighterd" (light wood) echoed through the streets. On the campus of the University of Texas during the goldfish-eating, flagpole-sitting twenties, collegiates sang a song that may have been inspired by a wood peddler:

> My name is Kindlin' Willie
> And I come from Tennessee,
> And I'm sellin' kindlin' wood to get along.
> If you haven't any money,
> I will sell it to you free,
> But I'm sellin' kindlin' wood to get along.
> Kindlin' wood, kindlin' wood.
> I'm sellin' kindlin' wood to get along.
> If you haven't any money,
> I will sell it to you free,
> But I'm sellin' kindlin' wood to get along.[8]

Remote duplicates of the medieval mountebanks in England and France charmed susceptible Texas audiences, who were hungry for entertainment and easy targets for the wily salesmanship which accompanied it. The medicine men who brought their camouflaged smoothtalk to this state in the late nineteenth and early twentieth century sold their chill tonics and other drugs almost as fast as they could lift a bottle — after they had hypnotized their prospects with a minstrel performance or other tomfoolery. The "snake oil" men, as they were sometimes called, traveled in platform wagons, on which they gave shows to snare crowds into their selling orbit. If you listened to their claims, you could believe the drugs they sold would cure anything from corns to malaria.

At the old Hyde Park fair grounds in Austin during a summer in the 1880's a medicine man hawked his "Hamlin's Wizard Oil," supposed to be a magic cure-all. After blackface minstrels put on a good show, the "master of ceremonies" would go into his breathless spiel about what his wonder drug would do for the ailing members of the audience. Dave Dillingham described the procedure of one of these medicine shows as he remembered it. "He would look at his watch and shout, 'Go!' After allowing exactly one minute for buyers to grab the dollar bargain, he would halt the sale. Those who had not had a chance to get rid of their dollars would have to wait until next time. Several hawkers mingled through the crowd, each with a dozen bottles. And the bottles were snatched up fast."

When moving pictures presented people with a new form of entertainment, picture-show managers adopted the medicine man's technique to entice patrons into their theaters. Using hand-megaphones to project their voices as far as possible, these criers would walk up and down the street calling out the day's movie fare, "Don't fail to see that ONE attraction! All about the big train robbery!" Or a few years later, "Perils of Pauline, showing tonight. Keystone comedy."

Once part of the street scene in Mexico and South Texas, ballad hawkers have been found occasionally within the past fifteen years in some towns. One was heard not so many years ago around Haymarket Plaza in San Antonio by Brownie McNeil, who writes: "After haranguing the crowd for several minutes with ballads, impromptu speeches on life in general and a tune or two on his fiddle made by himself from a battered two-gallon oil can, he peddles his printed verses. If you care to buy, you had better be quick about it because he will suddenly break off selling, whether all customers are taken care of or not, and will insist on giving another performance."[4]

A more recent replica of the ballad hawkers are the newsboys, one of the few types of vendors who still lure customers in a garbled hodgepodge of slurred words, with emphasis on the most sensational headlines of the hour. The news hucksters almost invariably end their unintelligible gumbo of sounds with an appeal that everyone can understand: "Read ALL a-BOUT it!"

Other types of street singers, who had services rather than products to sell, played vivid roles in the street drama of yesterday, and cannot be altogether ignored here. There was the scissors grinder who rang a bell and rolled his whetstone wheel along the streets, crying, "Scissors grinder! Bring out your knives and scissors!" One in Galveston sang operatic or classical melodies as he walked from house to house, while in Houston a tall Spaniard played tunes on a mouth organ to attract attention.

In nearly every town there were the small Negro or Mexican boys who sat on apple crates with their polish, brush, and rag, appealing to passersby, "Shine, mister?" And the chimney sweeps came around every fall to clean out the flues before winter. Usually they were Negroes. A familiar chant in Houston at that time of the year was "Blow 'em down! Blow 'em down! Blow 'em down!"

Throughout Texas there were the street singers who collected rather than disposed of wares and services. Most prevalent were the ragpickers, remembered for their familiar cry, "Any rags, any bones, any bottles today?" Others, such as the early town criers, sold their services to anyone who wanted to announce auction sales, sports events, or theatrical performances. In San Antonio it was Julius Meyer, who took the place of the church bell that many years before had summoned people to public meetings, warned the populace of Indian attacks, and called them to the plazas for the governor's speeches. Julius had only a weatherbeaten hand-megaphone and his leathery lungs as his tools of trade. He used both to the fullest as he rode through the streets on his sorrel horse during the first quarter of this century.

"Foghorn Kelley" was the unofficial town crier of Houston in the 1920's. As he strolled about the streets he used a small megaphone to announce ball games and other sports events, shows, and auction sales. His booming voice, however, was smothered when public address systems were introduced.

Just as the telephone, radio, and public address systems ended the need for a town crier, so have automobiles, electric appliances, and natural gas abolished the necessity for other types of singing salesmen. The colorful peddlers of the past have been largely replaced and their methods of earning a living curtailed by government restrictions to safeguard the health of citizens and protect them from what was considered unnecessary noise.

Most Texas cities now have ordinances regulating the peddling trade. Only two years ago Temple adopted and other cities were considering an ordinance to keep door-to-door peddlers from bothering busy housewives. It classified peddling as an illegal "nuisance" unless the homeowner had requested an appointment with the salesman.

Although street vendors have been pushed from city thoroughfares, and their songs have been silenced, they have contributed a tradition of successful selling to one of the major forces responsible for their fade-out. Their vocal advertisements to lure customers have been spirited into radio and television channels and transformed into singing commercials, the musical and poetic jingles now poured over the airwaves by hired talent.

But these songs lack the heart-warming appeal of the musical chants that floated through the quiet streets of yesteryear. The peddler who trudged the streets with a pack on his back, a basket in his hand, or a tray on his head — or who rumbled over rough roads in his horse-drawn wagon loaded with watermelons or vegetables — has rightfully earned his place in the folklore annals of Texas.

1. "Haymarket Plaza," *The Sky is My Tipi*, ed. Mody C. Boatright (Austin and Dallas, 1949; Texas Folklore Society Publication XXII), p. 171. He notes that the local pronunciation is *cheé-leh*.

2. *Fort Worth Star-Telegram*, May 13, 1951.

3. Another version sung by Texas students of the same era begins, "My name is Dinah,/ From South Carolina," and ends, "And if you'll try some/ I know you'll buy some/ To help poor Dinah along."—WMH.

4. "Corridos of the Mexican Border," *Mexican Border Ballads*, ed. Mody C. Boatright (Austin, 1946; Texas Folklore Society Publication XXI), p. 5.

E. J. RISSMANN

# Folkways on Bear Creek

DOWN ON BEAR CREEK, south of Cedar Valley in Travis County, was my father's ranch. It was the period 1900-10, a transition era, when horse-and-buggy, team-and-wagon, and horseback times were passing out, and automobile and truck times were coming in. These were memorable years. Our ranch was small, about 1,100 acres, and was not called a ranch in those days — just a "place." Yet the imagination was often overwhelmed with wonder concerning how one family should have ownership and control of so huge a segment of the earth's crust as 1,100 acres that supported such a diversity of life. The owner could truly say with Alexander Selkirk: "I am monarch of all I survey."

What the hacienda was to the early settlers under Spanish and Mexican rule, this ranch was to its owners. Man-made improvements were a limestone ranch house of two stories with attached one-story house, numerous outbuildings including barns, blacksmith shop, buggy and hack stables (buildings housing vehicles were called stables), cattle chutes, cellars, corn cribs, cottonseed lofts, molasses mill and shed, and tenant houses for charcoal burners and woodchoppers.

Rock for the house had been quarried from outcrops along the creek. It was a dense, crystalline limestone, a step further, geologically, than the Austin chalk, which is soft and crumbly. Lime for mortar was "burned" in pits, limestone being piled into the pits and baked by continuous fires on top. Horsehair and tree moss were used as binders in the mortar. Nails were the square-cut kind, and lumber, hauled by oxen and horses, came from Bastrop. Hewn cedar floor and ceiling joists and, in portions of the house, cedar rafters made up the framing.

In the cellars, foodstuffs were kept cool in summer and protected against freezing in winter. Pork was packed in salt or, if smoked, hung from the ceiling; pork spare ribs and beef were preserved in strong solutions of brine. Potatoes were bedded in piles of sand. In crocks were quantities of homemade lard; in barrels and kegs were homemade wine, molasses and vinegar.

In the kitchen, the coffee pot was always on the kitchen range, new coffee being added daily until finally the lot would be emptied into the slop bucket, and the cycle started anew. As this coffee was an "elixir of life," so was it also, because of its potency, a "knock-out fluid." It was called "double-horseshoe" coffee because it was strong enough to float two horseshoes. On the back of the stove was most of the time an iron stewpot of red beans seasoned with chunks of ham or bacon. Occasionally corn bread, made of fresh corn meal ground in the stone grist mill at Dripping Springs, would be baked in the skillet, fireplace coals banked underneath and heaped on the lid, a welcome change from the oven-baked corn bread and biscuits. There were always molasses and jars of jelly and preserves. When the supply of homemade molasses ran out, some was bought in the general store, where the customer's jug was filled from a barrel with a pump worked by a crank. For variety, there was nothing more tasty than corn syrup bought in buckets, and with such intriguing names as Golden Glory and Cascade Drips. Besides grits, corn-meal mush and oatmeal, there was a breakfast food called Egg-O-See, forerunner of later-day cornflakes. Children and grownups loved it with sugar and thick cream. Sometimes, but very rarely, there would be store-bought fruit. The farm wagon, returning from a trip to town, would have under the wagon sheet in the wagon box, along with dried apples, coffee, smoking tobacco and cheroots, flour, and sugar with all the medley of odors, a sack of "mixed candy." This was cheap candy sold from barrels in grocery stores. There would also be gumdrops, jelly beans, and pungently flavored candy hearts with love verses on them. There would be funny papers, too, that Grandma in the city had saved: Fineheimer Kids, Katzenjammer Kids, Slim Jim, Mutt and Jeff, and Juno in Wonderland with spired and domed edifices of Oriental and Arctic lands.

There were many ways to make a living around Cedar Valley those days. Cotton was still a "cash crop." Every man with tillable acres raised cotton. The seed was fed to cows to produce rich milk, though it made the butter oily. Cotton gins were fueled with cordwood, later with gasoline. A heavy belt turned a huge flywheel, the circumference of which gave speed of rotation to the mechanisms that ginned the cotton and worked the press. Corn was raised to feed stock and to be ground into corn meal. Cornstalks were topped for fodder while still green. The fodder was tied into bundles before daylight while the tie-stalks were still pliable from the dew, then "shocked," and finally, having cured out-of-doors, was hauled to the barns to be stacked in the loft or put into tall stacks. Not uncommon was discovery of rattlesnakes, inactive and sluggish because of the chill of the night air, by those whose job it was to "tie fodder" in the pre-dawn moonlight. Sugar cane was grown for hay, and, if of the sorghum variety, for making molasses. A boy's job during molasses making time was to drive the horse round and round to pull the heavy, arched timber beam that turned the mill. His reward, in addition to any self-importance he might feel, was to sample, in conjunction with the light-yellow wild bees that appeared as if from nowhere, the fresh molasses. Usually the neighbors helped make molasses, receiving a share, or, if they furnished the cane, giving a share. The cane juice, crushed from stalks run through the mill, was cooked and evaporated in a segmented copper vat, in which it flowed back and forth around alternate openings of the vat's division ridges over heat generated by the wood-fueled furnace beneath. Raw juice was poured in one end; cooked molasses was drawn out the other.

Charcoal burning and wood chopping were subsidiary to farming and ranching. At times there were as many as eight families on the place burning charcoal. Wood and charcoal were in demand by city people for cooking and heating. Charcoal was also used in blacksmith forges, "stone coal" such as bituminous and anthracite being scarce and expensive. Women heated their irons in charcoal furnaces. There is no more delightful odor than that of charcoal smoke in the country around a coal kiln, nor any sound more melodious than the wood chopper's axe in the brakes. Sometimes the melody of a half dozen or more axes resounding through the hills, on mornings when sound travels easily, was like celestial music.

Stock raising was the main occupation. Cattle, descendants of the

Longhorn breeds, were long, rangy and wild. In the summer they were covered with ticks, which were controlled, there being no dipping vats or sprays, by smears composed of grease, tobacco, sulphur, and other ingredients cooked into a mixture. Some of the cows were milked when "fresh," though the milk was mainly "blue John," milk so devoid of cream that it appears almost blue. Milking was done in the open lots, rain or shine, and the cows were not fed while being milked. The calves were allowed to suck first, to bring down the milk, and then tied, their eyes sometimes bulging if the rope drew too tight to the fence or a snubbing post. Horse raising was the main phase of stock farming, and the most glamorous. Fine saddle horses were in demand and highly prized. Buggy horses had to be of special stock, team horses of another. Ox teams were passing out, and mules were not yet widely used. Herds of horses, varicolored and graceful, grazed in pastures or raced and wheeled on impulse, their manes and tails flying.

There were still many freighters on the highways, which were unpaved but heavily traveled arteries of communication. These men drove long strings of wagons, often with double or triple teams. Conestoga, Milburn, Peter Schuttler, Studebaker, and heavy widetired army wagons moved ponderously in the dust and heat of summer and the cold and rains of winter, drivers hunched like sphinxes on spring seats with hats pulled low over their eyes. The horses plodded with heads down while their drivers stared straight ahead in mute resignation to time and distance.

Country schoolhouses were one-roomed, isolated shacks on a flat or in a grove of trees. The terms were seven months long, three and one-half months at White Hall and three and one-half at Thomas Springs, the terms being split to equalize distances the pupils had to travel. Such schoolhouses were centers of learning, churches, theaters, and forums. They were places for children's education, and for "get-togethers" and sociables for the whole family. During school recess, the children played dare base, Antony-over, marbles, baseball, and sometimes, usually bringing on angry reprimands from the teacher, raced their horses. Boys surreptitiously smoked Durham or Duke's Mixture cigarettes, and played cards, in their privately erected brush arbors. To dissipate the odors of cigarette smoke on the breath and hoodwink the teachers, they put a small amount of

Hoyt's cologne on their tongues, or chewed cedar leaves or peppermint drops. On April Fools' days, most played hookey, and often in turn were threatened with punishment by teacher with tongue in cheek or laughing up the sleeve. Such country schools are now only memories, having been superseded by district schools, with bus transportation for the pupils.

Membership in a church, in addition to satisfying spiritual cravings, provided social life. Churchgoers often engaged in long hours of argument over doctrine and Bible passages at home, or disconcerted the preachers visiting in their homes by entangling them in such matters. Protracted meetings, whole families coming with fried chicken, pies, cakes, and jellies if the weather were favorable, were held in brush arbors; after the services the lunches would be spread in the shade on the grass. On the upper part of Rissmann Ranch was Friendship Church, a two-story rock building erected about 1867, the upper story a Masonic lodge. Other churches were Salem, Oak Hill, and Thomas Springs.

To go anywhere distant as much as fifteen miles took hours, so people provided their own local amusements. There were, of course, neither radio nor television sets, but there were a few graphophones, the cylinder record type with horns that had a tinny sound. About 1904, a traveling motion picture machine showed at some outdoor place one dark night. It was difficult to look at the screen because of the flicker and dazzle.

There were singings, play parties and dances. Singings were held mainly in homes, wherever there was an early-day upright organ or piano. Often a guitar or accordion furnished the accompaniment. The singers, with strong bodies and deep-breathing lungs, had good but not cultivated voices. Occasionally a singing teacher, a peripatetic individual with tuning fork and song books of square-note variety, gave a session of singing lessons at the schoolhouse. Never to have attended such sessions to which folk came in buggies or wagons, on horseback or afoot, along the winding, wooded roads in starlight and moonlight to the lamplit interior of a one-room building in isolation is to have missed some of life's rapturous moments. Romance flowered and hearts were gladdened as songs flowed out through the solitude of night, and then were sung on the longest way home by the happy travelers who would take devious trails or roads to prolong the time and increase the distance, all the while walking or driving slowly, occasionally pausing to steal a kiss, or to snatch a hug. In summer there were the sharply etched but cool shadows along the moonlit trail or road; in winter the stars coldly and incredibly bright and blazing, the moon laying a frozen samite sheen over the landscape, the moonbeams flashing and splintering on frost or snow.

Many of the songs were of a religious nature. But most were sentimental or cowboy songs. They had a depth of sadness in them, a tinge of melancholy fatalism. The following, a passage from one of the love songs, comes to my mind as if from the periphery of an ancient past, its sentiment and tender feeling lingering through the years:

> Thou wilt come no more, gentle Annie;
> Like a flower thy spirit did depart.
> Thou hast gone, alas, like the many
> That have bloomed in the summer of my heart.

Play parties were frequent. Word would get around that some family was giving one, and that was the extent of the invitation. There were singing games at these parties, such as "Shoot the Buffalo," "Sugar Lump-O," "Walking on the Green Grass," "London Bridge is Falling Down," and more vigorous ones like "Snap," and laughable, mystifying games like "Postoffice." One could never forget some of the singers, such as, for example, one Rucker Mayes, a lank, kindly, drawling man of the outdoors, singing for hours from memory, and never repeating a verse. One of his songs was "Sugar Lump-O," a stanza from which goes like this:

> All up and down, my honey,
> All up and down we go,
> That lady's a-rocking her sugar lump-o,
> That lady's a-rocking her sugar lump-o,
> That lady's a-rocking her sugar lump-o,
>     O, turn, Cinnamon, turn.

Dances, too, were given, and sometimes they lasted all night. The space for dancing was usually a large living room, or parlor, augmented in size by an adjoining bedroom, dining room, or a porch in summer. The room itself was lit by kerosene lamps, of both reflector and wall type, and by lanterns or candles. The music was generally supplied by fiddle and guitar, sometimes also by banjo, piano, French-harp, jew's-harp, accordion, and, rarely, a bass or bull fiddle. Once a man selling zithers played at one of the dances, and the music was remembered and talked about for years. The music of these dances was carried forward as a sort of afterglow into the next day by those who went about their work. Its beat and melody kept time with the rhythm and beat of horses' hoofs, the swish and impact of chopping axe, and the squeak of saddle or harness. The mind, constricted by the drudgery of daily work, was for the time released, lifted out of itself, and transported into a magic world of enjoyment. There was always much to remember: the aroma of a faint perfume, the touch of a sweetheart's hand, the charm of a loving look, the bright smile of a beaming face in the glow of lamplight.

Visiting was one of the main diversions, accomplished by driving some miles to the home of a neighbor to spend the evening or a Sunday afternoon, or to stay all night. Sometimes visiting was accomplished by meeting at some designated place for picnic and sports. At this there might be horse racing, roping, and, among the boys especially, though the girls sometimes participated, the riding of yearlings or calves. At an early time there had also been "tournaments," modeled after the jousts of King Arthur's court, survival of early-day chivalry popularized by the reading of Walter Scott's novels. By 1910 there were no more tournaments, but the locations and posts were still there. Women rode horseback in 1900-10, but they rode sidesaddle. A woman riding "straddle" or astride was called by the puritanical a tomboy, or ranked with a "crowing hen." A few, of course, did ride "straddle" without regard to the unmentionable fact of revealing mysterious, enchanting glimpses of lace undergarments or occasionally a bit of bare skin. Most riding "straddle" wore modest divided skirts.

Mumblety-peg and horseshoe pitching were amusements at almost any gathering or sociable. One of these gatherings was the *Verein*, presumably an outgrowth of or affiliated with such organizations as the Grange, Farmers' Alliance, and Farmers' Union. Its members met once a month to discuss crops and stock, and to have a social good time with refreshments.

Among other pastimes of the community, hunting with hounds was almost a nightly occurrence among some of the neighbors. Unforgettable were the deep, bell-toned voices of the hounds ranging through the valleys, over the hills, and along the creek bottoms of the flats and cedar brakes. Some deer hunting, also, was done at night, with the aid of a headlight, a contraption fitting over the head like a hat. In it were two burners using bear oil or kerosene, the reflector adding enough brightness to catch the gleam of a deer's eyes. Hunting varmints with dogs was encouraged, as these roving predators raided hen nests and chicken coops. Often a hunt ranged over numerous ranches, and crossed through many fences. A gun fired at night caused a repeated reverberation through the hills.

In the Cedar Valley community hospitality was the practice. Anyone coming at noon, or at any other mealtime, was invited to come in and have something to eat. If it was after nightfall, the visitor was invited to spend the night. Yet this hospitality had about it a certain code. Unless the visitor was someone very close to the family in kinship or affection, or one who frequented the place often enough to be familiar with the occupants and the dogs, he stopped his horse, buggy, wagon, or himself if he were afoot, outside the front gate, or some fifteen feet from the house if there were no gate. Then he intoned in a loud voice, "Hello-o-." He did not come to the door and knock, or even to the porch. This was especially so after dark. The visitor made sure his presence was known and his identity established.

Chores were endless. They began before daylight for most and ended by lantern light after sundown. Woman's work was never done, and man's work was more than just sun to sun. Fences — wire, rock, rail, and picket — had to be built, extended or repaired; horses shod, and curried and broken; mules' manes roached or tails sheared; buggy and wagon tires, which shrank in summer when the felloes and spokes grew dessicated in the dry air, drenched with water to tighten them, though this would not keep them from rattling. Axle grease had to be smeared on hubs and spindles to grease buggies and wagons; harness had to be mended. Implements and tools had to be sharpened: axes, knives, scythes, sickles, sweeps, double-shovels, middlebusters, and turning plows. In summer, there were cattle and horses to doctor for screw worms and to smear with tick eradicator. New crops of livestock had to be branded at the right time of the year, earmarked, and given all other needed surgery to convert them from young hopefuls to useful adjuncts to man. There was always Johnson grass to kill, Bermuda grass to shear off with double-shovels in the garden during hot months so it would die in the heat. And there was land to clear. Sometimes the trees were cut into firewood, and the brush burned. At other times they were simply girdled and left to die, so that, stripped of foliage, they would let the sunlight reach the planted crops.

Present in the fields were boll weevil, bollworm, and fruit flies. These presented a continuous battle. In the corn cribs were weevils and rats. And, if one could so imagine, these were all protected by savage outriders —the omnipresent and malevolent scorpions or stinging lizards. Ear corn in the cribs was sprinkled with salt water to combat the weevils and to make the shucks more tasty for stock. Corn had to be "shucked" for the horses, which nickered for it and chomped it noisily in the wooden troughs. Corn had to be fed to the hogs, also, to make them fat. Corn for them was supplemented by slop and skim milk from the kitchen. Soapsuds from the dish washing were included, though nobody ever said the hygiene of hogs was improved by the drinking of soapsuds. Chopping of wood for the kitchen, and for the fireplace in winter, was an endless task. Pole wood of live oak, cedar, Spanish oak and elm was hauled out of the brakes and cut and split with the chopping axe. Sometimes it was sawed with a gasoline saw which whined and rasped all day as the saw crosscut the wood. The dust flew, and sometimes the wind blew it into the eyes. On rare occasions a flywheel would hurtle off into space, or a circle saw fly loose from its moorings. This meant danger, sometimes death, to anyone in its path. There were chickens, noisy guineas, and turkeys to feed, protect against the elements, and shield against varmints or hawks and "blue darters." On cold mornings it was no fun to hitch up horses when the bits had to be warmed in the hands before being inserted into the animals' mouths, or harness was stiff and salt-encrusted, sometimes beaded with dew or frost. The horses hunched up their backs, reared and pranced, and shrank from saddles and harness.

In the blacksmith shop there were the clucking bellows to pump with a lever, in the shed by the house a wooden washing machine to operate with a lever, and in the kitchen a churn worked with a dasher. There was cottage cheese to make by hanging up a sack of clabber for draining, cream to dip off the milk crocks in the milk room, milk vessels to sun, eggs to gather, hogs to kill when a cold norther blew up. Killing hogs meant long hours of cutting up meat with numb hands and steaming breath out in the shed, and rendering of lard in an iron kettle. Some of the fat was used for making "ball lye soap" in the wash kettle. In season there were peaches to gather in the orchard and to peel and cut up for drying in pans or trays on the roof.

Always imminent were rattlesnakes on the ranch. They liked to lie on the old roads and trails after nightfall, and, though apparently wishing to be left in peace, would coil, rattle, and then strike the disturber with deadly accuracy. In certain months of the summer, rattlesnakes were purported to go blind and be more dangerous than at other times. Seldom were any rattlesnakes seen in the middle of the day in hot weather; they preferred a cool, shady place to lie. There they would lie stretched out, immobile and expressionless. Often they would be found on summer mornings coiled up asleep outside a house door, or at well or cistern, or even in the house if they could find an entrance. They liked to come around human habitations in search of insects or shelter. Every crib had its chicken snakes which pilfered eggs, ate mice and insects, and surely frightened children. Copperheads, deadly as the rattler but giving no warning, hid around the corrals and fodder stacks. Spreading adders if alarmed hissed and made demoniac faces. Swift coachwhips and prairie runners skittered away into the bushes, or leisurely, as if timeless and ageless, traveled unheeding across dusty spaces. The observant killer of any snake, particularly the rattler, must have noted the snake's bewilderment and reproach, as if to say, "What have I done to hurt you, and why must you attack me? I was only going about my affairs, with no evil intent toward you." And who, with a sense of the aesthetic, can deny that snakes' skins are among nature's artistic handiworks?

To keep up transportation on the ranch, there were always roads to repair, mud holes to fill, ridges to be built along the roads to divert flood water and so prevent erosion. Also the weather had to be watched. Only certain phases of the moon were suitable for the planting of crops or the branding and surgery on livestock. A ring or halo around the moon was a certain indication of rain. The number of stars within the circle equaled the number of days until there should be rainfall. The moon itself was a subject of speculation. Most saw a man in the moon. On the Rissmann Ranch was a cemetery, called graveyard, walled with a rock fence, a huge shade tree in one corner. This graveyard and shade tree were thought to be seen by reflection from the moon, home of the far-off dead. When heavy rains flooded the creek, the spring had to be cleaned of rocks, gravel and soil washed in by violent torrents. Two water snakes once lived in the spring. It was known that they grew from horsehairs dropped into the water. Tadpoles had a permanent home in the spring, for they were said to purify the water and catch the mosquitoes.

At night, when all the family were tired and in bed, lost in heavy sleep, the varmints would get among the chickens. Then the dogs would bark furiously. That meant getting up, taking the lantern or pitchfork and seeing about the intruders. Hardly did one get back to sleep when a hoot owl kicked up a fuss in a tree outside the window, or a screech owl brought his shrilling scream of imminent death. Mosquitoes, there being no screens, and mosquito bars being too hot for comfort and poor in defense anyway, sang their minor melodies or bit fiercely through the sheets. The night crickets and cicadas shrilled antiphonally, sometimes with an almost ear-splitting crescendo of sound. In daytime there were the flies; horseflies, huge, buzzing, swishing creatures that tormented the animals and sometimes gave vicious stings to the exposed backs or posteriors of swimmers in the creek; and houseflies that hummed monotonously and mournfully in the dining room at suppertime. Many were trapped on flypaper placed on the tables and the ceiling. A few, suicidally perhaps, accidentally no doubt, and maliciously it would seem, dropped into the food. They were simply ladled out, without let or hindrance to the eater.

Some years the rabbits would be scarce. It was known that evil spirits had driven them to migrate to other regions; and that after the evil spirits had been exorcised, they would return once again to sit in contemplation and furtive watchfulness, play in the dust at sunset, or meditate on means to outwit Br'er Fox and Br'er Wolf. It was known, too, that when animals put on a thick coat of fur in the fall there would be a severe winter. When the calves and colts raced up and down the flats, or the cattle milled 'round and 'round in the corrals, it was a sure sign that a norther was on the way with all its strange smells of ozone and the atmosphere of faraway places.

Life never grew dull on the ranch. There was always something to do. For boys and girls there were refreshments in the woods: black haws, red haws, wild plums, agarita berries (sometimes called chaparral berries), wild dewberries, pecans and black walnuts along the creeks. There were poke root, said to be poisonous unless cooked, and lamb's quarter that grew as a weed, to gather as greens for the table. There were stretchberries to make chewing gum stretch and pop, and milkweed pods full of silken fibers for making pincushions. In the crib were shucks to make shuck tick mattresses. For smoking there were cornstalks, grapevine, coffee, and tobacco from Kentucky strong enough to knock a mule down. The tobacco was excellent for snitching and smoking behind the barn while watching for Dad. At night there were candles to pour, bullets to mold for the old muzzle-loading rifle, and other guns to clean.

The nights were always the best. They were the times of ease and relaxation around the fireplace while northers howled outdoors or growled sepulchrally down the chimney. Cats and dogs stretched on the floor in front of the gesticulating flames of cedar and live oak gave a feeling of coziness and intimacy. Even better were the nights of summer when we rested on hide-bottomed chairs outdoors. Such nights were times of contemplation and meditation. Overhead were all the wonders of the Milky Way, the Pleiades, and all the other beauties without end that have engaged the philosophers, befuddled the astronomers, and led the astrologers into working out guides to the destinies of man since the beginning of man's residence on earth.

The years of 1900-10 were a time of change, for soon car and truck headlight beams would move eerily through the nights where buggies and wagons had moved slowly in pitch darkness or moonlight and starlight. But they were also years of enchantment on

Bear Creek. In retrospect they are happy times, fading in the memory like a rider vanishing into a limbo of space over the horizon. The folkways of that day have given place to those of a faster-moving culture.

JOHN Q. ANDERSON

# Emerson and the Language of the Folk

THE GENERAL IMPRESSION of Emerson as the philosopher of the Over-Soul and the high priest of nineteenth-century optimism elevates him above ordinary men and makes him a dreamer with no apparent relationship to the folk of America. This unfortunate concept has taken flesh and blood away from a man whose interest in science, politics, agriculture, invention, and trade, as well as in literature and philosophy, makes him one of our most representative American thinkers. Actually, he was very much interested in the common man, and as a writer and speaker he was vitally concerned with the language of the common people. It is the purpose of this paper to show that Emerson's theory of language affected his concept of folk speech and to give examples of his use of the language of the folk.

## I

Emerson's theory of the origin and development of language is first and most explicitly stated in his first publication, *Nature* (1836). Language, he says, is one of the important uses man makes of nature, utilizing nature as a vehicle for his thoughts. Words, he maintains, were originally derived from material appearances, and in the beginning words had only denotations, not connotations. "Children and savages," he says, "use only nouns or names of things, which they convert into verbs, and apply to analogous mental acts."[1] In the natural evolution of language from this primitive state, words became symbolic of states of mind or "spiritual facts," since things themselves are but symbols of spirit. Countless individuals throughout the history of the race have contributed to the word-stock of the language, and others will continue to do so. "Language is a city to the building of which every human being brought a stone," he states.[2] As a consequence, the language is "made up of the spoils of all actions, trades, arts, games, of men. Every word is a metaphor borrowed from some natural or mechanical, agricultural or nautical process."[3]

But the process of building language in this manner brought about great difficulties, for in the course of centuries words got farther and farther away from their origin in nature and thereby lost their pristine qualities of concreteness and vigor. Consequently, words, and especially written words, because of incrustations, ceased to be "one with things"[4] and are no longer identical with "facts."[5] The common speech, however, tended less to lose these pristine qualities than did the speech of educated people. Therefore, the writer, recognizing the necessity for "the right word," always seeks to push words back to their root meanings and to preserve the original freshness of the language.[6]

Since nature was the original source of language and since it continues to be the inspiration for the creation of new words, people who remain close to nature, such as farmers and laborers, have the advantage of city dwellers in maintaining the original force and vigor of language. This bed-rock quality of common speech Emerson attributes to the "Saxon" element, as contrasted with the more highly refined, and thus weaker, French and Latin elements.

Emerson's theory of language has been called "romantic,"[7] and is therefore unacceptable to contemporary linguists. It is a composite of ideas which Emerson characteristically gathered from such disparate sources as Plato, Plotinus, Samson Reed,[8] and G. Oegger.[9] The validity of Emerson's theory is not important to this study, but the influence of his theory on his attitude toward language of the folk is of great importance.

## II

Emerson's attitude toward the language of the folk is intimately associated with his regard for the common people. He had a great deal to say about farmers, laborers, and tradesmen. Nor were his ideas about working people purely theoretical: his lifelong friendship with his farmer neighbor, Edmund Hosmer, his observation of Irish immigrant railroad workers and of the working classes in

Boston, and his thousands of miles of travel in lecturing throughout the nation — all these gave him much more actual knowledge of working people than other members of the Concord group had. His high regard for manual labor made him respect the labor of the hands almost as highly as he did the labor of the mind. Working people he calls the "bone and sinew of society," and he frequently contrasts the "sturdy lad" of the country with the weaker "city dolls."[10]

Emerson's belief in the efficacy of nature causes him to prefer the farmer to any other class of working people. There is a natural nobility about the farmer, he says in the essay "Manners," for he is literally the lord of his house, though it be a cottage.[11] The young farmer, dressed in his Sunday best, exhibits "no arrogance" and is "a perfect gentleman."[12] The farmer's work is "natural and necessary" because he maintains an intimate contact with nature; his company is to be preferred to the superficial society of the town.

Emerson also finds the simplicity of the day laborer refreshing. The many references to the hired laborers on the network of railroads then being built in all directions from Boston usually describe them as "men, manlike employed."[13] He liked the hustle and bustle of the poorer sections of Boston in which he saw the "unrestrained attitudes and manners" of shopkeepers, clerks, peddlers, teamsters, and barkeepers.[14] Such streets, he says, are "full of humiliations to the proud" because the language and manners of these working people, unsoftened by sophistication, "threaten or insult whatever is threatenable and insultable" in more effete society.[15]

These, then, the farmer, teamster, Irish immigrant railroad worker, peddler, and washerwoman, are for Emerson the folk. Since he found their work noble, it is not surprising that he listened avidly to their language and found it pleasing to his ear. In it he found force, vigor, vitality, virility, and simplicity — characteristics which he believed tended to push language back to its origin in nature. The "language of the street," he says again and again, is "invariably strong," because the words are short, simple, readily understood, and spoken unhaltingly.[16] The common people are not fettered by rules of grammar and are not hampered by the proprieties. "I envy the boys the force of the double negative," he says, and "I confess to some titillation of my ears from a rattling oath."[17]

In fact, Emerson himself is capable of *writing* oaths occasionally, if he does not use them in lectures and essays. In the privacy of his *Journals* he confesses:

> What a pity that we cannot curse and swear in good society! Cannot the stinging dialect of the sailors be domesticated? It is the best rhetoric, and for a hundred occasions those forbidden words are the only good ones. My page about 'Consistency' would be better written thus: Damn Consistency![18]

How the proper Bostonians would have been astounded could they have read that entry! Or this one:

> At the Five-Points [in New York] I heard a woman swearing very liberally as she talked with her companions; but when I looked at her face, I saw that she was no worse than other women; that she used the dialect of her class, as all others do, and are neither better nor worse for it; but under this bad costume was the same repose, the same probity as in Broadway. Nor was she misinterpreted by her mates.[19]

Certainly the New England aristocracy, which, as Emerson notes, banished *stink* and *damn* from its vocabulary, could not have been tolerant enough to say as he did: "The oath that is heard in the street, and the jargon profanity of boys, points no less distinctly than a church at the conviction in man of absolute nature, as distinct from apparent and derivative nature."[20] Evidently, then, the pungent speech of the working class appealed to the sedate Mr. Emerson, who says:

> How laconic and brisk it is by the side of a page of the *North American Review*. Cut these words and they would bleed; they are vascular and alive; they walk and run. Moreover they who speak them have this elegancy, that they do not trip in their speech. It is a shower of bullets, whilst Cambridge men and Yale men correct themselves and begin again at every half sentence.[21]

Emerson's *Journals* are sprinkled with examples of folk speech—similes, metaphors, hyperboles, and proverbs. This brief sampling of his numerous remarks about folk speech reveals his lifelong interest in the language of the folk.

## III

Folk expressions recorded in the *Journals* undergo substantial change when transferred to Emerson's lectures and essays. Frequently only the germ of an expression is retained. He felt that the writer should record in his notebook material for future use, as the artist stores up drawings in his sketchbook; the wary writer will, however, adapt this material so that its sources may not be readily obvious.

Always an advocate of the idiomatic, simple style in writing, Emerson admires especially those qualities in Montaigne's work. He also feels that Robert Burns "had that secret of genius to draw from the bottom of society the strength of its speech" and to "clothe it with melody."[22] In addition, Emerson finds in America indigenous material which he thinks might be used. In a lecture in 1843, "he advised American literature to turn westward, and produce writing with the flavor of Davy Crockett's and Daniel Boone's exploits."[23]

Emerson's own style contains much of the same force and vigor which he found in folk speech, especially in its aphoristic quality, but he could not bring himself to use in his lectures and essays the "rattling oaths" whose pungency he admired. Even though in the essay "The Poet" he says, "The vocabulary of an omniscient man would embrace words and images excluded from polite conversation," he left that actual practice to Whitman. On the other hand, Emerson's use of simile, metaphor, and proverb suggestive of folk background is so extensive that only representative samples may be given here. Some examples of his similes and metaphors are:

[The world believes that the scholar is] as unfit for any handiwork or public labor as a penknife for an axe. (*Works*, I, 94)

Total nature is growing like a field of maize in July. (*Works*, I, 203)

The man of talents who brings his poetry and eloquence to market is like the hawk . . . wheeling up to heaven in the face of noon, and all to have a better view of mice and moles and chickens. (*Journals*, IV, 82)

[Theological problems] are the soul's mumps and measles and whooping-coughs. (*Works*, II, 132)

Emerson's use of proverbial speech accounts in part at least for the cryptic nature of his style. The following proverbs are only a few of the many that occur in his *Works* and *Journals*:

The whole value of a dime is in knowing what to do with it. (*Works*, I, 383)
There is always a best way of doing everything, if it be to boil an egg. (*Works*, VI, 169)
If the man at the door have no shoes, you have not to consider whether you could procure him a paint-box. (*Works*, III, 160)
We aim above the mark to hit the mark. (*Works*, III, 185)
Each prophet comes presently to identify himself with his thought, and to esteem his hat and shoes sacred. (*Works*, III, 188)
Better be a nettle in the side of your friend than his echo. (*Works*, II, 208)
Old shoes are easy to the feet. (*Works*, II, 240)
It is for cake that we run in debt. (*Works*, I, 244)
The dice of God are always loaded. (*Works*, II, 102)

Finally, Emerson had a fondness for jokes and anecdotes, some of which have the "numbskull" quality familiar in folklore. One such anecdote concerns a doctor who was lecturing on the ignorance in people of their own complaints. When he had finished, a lady in the audience inquired, "What will be the subject of your next lecture?" The doctor replied, "The circulation of the blood." "Well," she said, "I will certainly attend, for I have been troubled with that complaint for a long time."[24]

This brief account of Emerson's interest in the language of the folk indicates that he was vitally concerned with the manner in which the common people expressed themselves. Certainly, the careful reader of the *Works* and *Journals* will find sufficient proof that Emerson, the chief exponent of the doctrines of self-reliance and optimism, drew much of his imagery and many of his pungent expressions from the language of the folk. And if Emerson himself had the opportunity to answer the charge that his theory of language and his use of folk material are "unscientific," he would doubtless quote his famous statement, "A foolish consistency is the hobgoblin of little minds" and add, "Damn consistency!"

1. *The Complete Works of Ralph Waldo Emerson*, ed. Edward Waldo Emerson (Boston, 1903-4), Centenary Edition, I, 26. The

primitive use of words derived from natural objects is referred to several times in the *Journals* and *Works*. See especially *The Journals of Ralph Waldo Emerson*, ed. Edward Waldo Emerson and Waldo Emerson Forbes (Boston, 1909-14), V, 435, and IX, 114; *Works*, VIII, 140 and 199.

2. *Works*, VIII, 199.

3. *Journals*, V, 213. See also *Works*, VIII, 193; and *Journals*, IV, 23, V, 325-26 and 435; VIII, 506-7; and X, 466.

4. *Works*, VIII, 57. Kenneth W. Cameron, in *Emerson the Essayist: An Outline of His Philosophical Development Through 1836* (Raleigh, N. C., 1945), I, 416, states that Emerson wrote a sermon in 1831 entitled "Words Are Things."

5. *Ibid.*, I, 25. See also *Journals*, V, 102, and *Works*, XII, 5-6.

6. Emerson's doctrine of "the right word" is stated in the essay "Poetry and Imagination": "There is no choice of words for him who clearly sees the truth. That provides him with the best word" (*Works*, VIII, 33).

7. Vivian C. Hopkins, *Spires of Form, A Study of Emerson's Aesthetic Theory* (Cambridge, 1951), p. 114, states: "Emerson's historical conception of language is the romantic view that the savage naturally expressed his ideas in metaphors, which civilization has crusted over until they have lost their touch with life. Although this idea appears in that neoclassic guide to composition and Emerson's college text, Hugh Blair's *Lectures on Rhetoric*, it did not become an operating principle in his thought until he found it more vividly expressed in the mystic writers Samson Reed and Oegger."

8. Reed's *Observations on the Growth of the Mind*, 1826, an exposition of the mystical doctrines of Swedenborg, contains the theory that words were derived from physical objects.

9. This nineteenth-century French mystical writer maintained that the "language of nature" which existed before the fall of man was about to be rediscovered. Emerson refers to Oegger (*Journals*, III, 505) soon after Elizabeth Peabody published part of her translation of *Le Vrai Messie*. Cameron (*Emerson the Essayist*, I, 295-98) believes that Oegger is the "French philosopher" referred to in *Nature*.

10. *Journals*, VII, 66, and *Works*, II, 76.

11. *Works*, III, 134; cf. *Journals*, IV, 444.

12. *Journals*, VIII, 72-73.

13. *Ibid.*, VI, 448.

14. *Ibid.*, V, 538; cf. *Works*, III, 131.

15. *Works*, III, 76.

16. *Journals*, II, 449. Cf. *Journals* V, 419-20, and IX, 306; and *Works*, VIII, 124-26, and XII, 288.

17. *Works*, XII, 288.

18. *Journals*, V, 484.

19. *Ibid.,* VI, 356-57.
20. *Ibid.,* IV, 113.
21. *Ibid.,* V, 419-20; cf. *ibid,* VIII, 532-33.
22. "Robert Burns," *Works,* XI, 442.
23. Hopkins, *op. cit.,* p. 144.
24. *Journals,* X, 17.

JAMES HOWARD

# Tales of Neiman-Marcus

NEIMAN-MARCUS is the name of a specialty store in Dallas, Texas. More accurately, it is a series of specialty shops collected under one management and administered with a single set of policies. The principal store is at Ervay and Main streets in downtown Dallas; a suburban branch, Preston Center, was opened in October, 1951, on Preston Road at Northwest Highway. The company maintains buying offices in New York, London, Paris, and Florence. Neiman's sells clothing for women, children, and men, together with a number of related articles such as jewelry, luggage, and gifts. One of its major characteristics is its emphasis on fashion merchandise.

The Neiman-Marcus Company was founded in 1907 by Mr. Herbert Marcus, his sister Mrs. Carrie Neiman, and her husband Mr. Al Neiman. Mr. Neiman withdrew from the firm in 1928. Mrs. Carrie Neiman, on the other hand, continued her association with, and active participation in, the store until her death in 1953. Since the death of Mr. Herbert Marcus, in 1950, his four sons have taken over the management, the eldest son, Stanley Marcus, having succeeded to the presidency. The other three sons are executive officers in the company. Despite the fact that Neiman-Marcus is a corporation and has issued stock for public sale, it has remained to a marked extent a family enterprise, both in ownership and operation. One noteworthy trait of the Marcuses is their habit of leaving their offices and going out on the floor from time to time to aid a customer with his shopping.

The adjective "fabulous" is applied to this store with considerable frequency. If it is a fabled store, then it seems befitting to ask, what are some of the fables told about Neiman's? With that question in mind, I have collected a group of stories dealing with this Dallas institution. Many of these episodes are drawn from that rich mine of folklore, the Dallas *Morning News,* but more specifically, my chief source has been the column headed "Neiman-Marcus Point of View" which since June, 1950 has twice a week formed part of the firm's advertisement in the Dallas *News.* This column, signed "Wales," is the work of Warren Leslie, assistant to the president of Neiman-Marcus and previously a reporter on the Dallas *News.*

One of the earliest Neiman-Marcus tales concerns a woman from Electra, Texas, an oil town near Wichita Falls. About 1927 this woman appeared in the Neiman-Marcus store barefooted and in a sunbonnet. She announced that she wished to purchase a mink coat, and when she had selected a coat, paid for it on the spot with currency. The sales force at Neiman's, sensing an exceptional opportunity, also sold her a pair of shoes.[1]

At about the same time a young lady who was on the point of beginning a career as a public-school teacher in a small West Texas town decided that a suit from Neiman-Marcus would distinctly improve her chances for marriage. She had never been a customer of the store, and she was without money, but she sat down and wrote this letter:

Dear Neiman-Marcus:

I have just graduated from normal college, and I'd like to have a fall suit. I spent all my money getting a diploma. I can not even make a deposit because my pocketbook is empty and my family hasn't got any cash to spare.

Could you possibly send me a suit in dark blue serge in the latest style? . . .

The store extended her credit and sent her the suit.[2]

The staff of Neiman-Marcus prizes the story of the customer who bought three vicuña coats at one swoop. The vicuña coat, which is made from the extremely soft fleece of a small South American animal, is often priced at from five to six hundred dollars, since in the hierarchy of woolens, vicuña ranks as high above cashmere as cashmere does above top-grade sheep's wool. The incident involving the shopper for these coats started to take shape when a salesman on the first floor of Neiman's telephoned upstairs to the president, Mr. Stanley Marcus, and reported, "A gentleman is down here who speaks with a foreign accent, looks very distinguished, has a swarthy complexion, and wears good clothes. The feeling around the floor is that he either owns the Iranian oil fields or is an actor. We think you ought to come down and meet him."

Stanley Marcus did come down. He was introduced to a tall, slightly balding gentleman, to his wife, and to their nineteen-year-old daughter. They were from French Morocco. The name of the family seemed to ring a bell in Mr. Marcus' memory.

"You have a house in Paris, don't you?" he asked.

"Yes, how did you know?" replied the visitor, his face lighting up.

"I had it pointed out to me when I was in France last year," the Dallas merchant said.

The world having been shrunk to manageable proportions, the conversation proceeded. "If you don't mind my asking," Stanley Marcus inquired, "what has brought you to Dallas?"

"We have come to shop," was the answer. "You see, my wife, my daughter, and I arrived in New York. We desired to have three vicuña coats, one for each of us, all of them alike. Yesterday we started out at New York to obtain the coats.

"At one store on Fifth Avenue," he continued, "they had coats for my wife and daughter, but none for me. At another store near by we found a fine man's coat, none for my wife and daughter. 'Where,' I asked the salesman, 'might we find three identical vicuña coats?'

" 'Oh,' he said, 'at Neiman-Marcus.'

" 'On what street is that,' I asked.

"The salesman laughed. 'It's not on any street. It's in Dallas, Texas.'

" 'Where is Dallas, Texas?' I wanted to know. He told me it was about six hours from New York by plane. 'We will fly down to Dallas,' I said."

The store in Dallas was able to supply the three matching coats, and in two days of shopping the North African visitor purchased seventy-five thousand dollars' worth of clothing, linens, and furnishings.[3]

The figure of the princely shopper appears in other guises. In one story, emanating from the children's department of the store, he is cast as an expectant father. One day, the story goes, a man entered the infants' shop to inform a saleswoman, "I'll take the things in the window out there."

"I beg your pardon?" said the saleswoman, giving herself the opportunity to collect her wits.

"I want to buy everything in that window, if I may," the man repeated.

A hurried conference was held, the conclusion of which was that no good reason existed for not allowing the customer to have the contents of the window. The sale was accordingly completed.

Further talk with the young man revealed that he and his wife were looking forward to the birth of their first child within a couple of months. Since nothing had yet been bought for the child-to-come, the husband was simply trying to acquire a full set of the necessary gear for an infant, all in one package. "Otherwise I might forget something," he explained.[4]

In another episode, the lordly shopper becomes an elderly gentleman who felt a compelling attraction toward one of the store's wax mannequins. This particular mannequin represented a small child. The white-haired gentleman saw a striking resemblance between the mannequin and his little granddaughter, to whom he was devoted. Consequently he came by to see the mannequin every time he was in the store. Invariably he ended these visits by buying all of the clothes on the wax figure, to give to his grandchild, who, it happened, was exactly the same size. This Hawthorne-like situation lasted until the mannequin's dresses were no longer large enough to fit the growing girl.[5]

At Christmas a Texas oilman selected a mink coat from Neiman-Marcus for a present to his wife. He was eager to have his gift placed in a proper setting. Somehow it didn't seem entirely appropriate to confine the mink coat within a mere box. He consulted Stanley Marcus: was there some way of adding the suitable flourish? A day or two before Christmas Mr. Marcus borrowed one of the spare rooms in the oilman's house. There he reproduced faithfully, down to the last detail, a Neiman-Marcus display window centered on a mannequin garbed in the mink coat.[6]

Back in 1939, the story goes, a customer from Houston flew the two hundred fifty-odd miles to Dallas once a week in her own plane, to have her hair done at Neiman's beauty salon. Several years later a woman airplane passenger phoned ahead to the store at Dallas that she would like to buy a fur coat during her brief stopover in Dallas. A detachment of salespeople moved on Love Field, the municipal airport, established a temporary outpost of the store at the terminal. There in a makeshift dressing room they sold the woman a mink coat in the twenty minutes that she had between planes.[7] These stories of princely shoppers form the most numerous group of Neiman-Marcus "fables."

Once a man from Nebraska was in the store to do his Christmas shopping. Mr. Edward Marcus, vice-president of the firm, was helping him, because the customer was unfamiliar with Neiman's. One by one the Nebraskan checked names off his Christmas list. "That's all now," he said at last, with a sigh. "Except for Leonard."

"Your son?" Mr. Marcus ventured.

"No, my lion."

"You said lion, did you?" Mr. Marcus responded, to make sure.

"Yes, lion," the man countered, bristling a little. "Had him since he was a cub."

The fact that Neiman-Marcus has never established a Gift Shop for Lions had Mr. Marcus face to face with a rather perplexing question of what to recommend for a pet lion. His thoughts first turned to Steuben glass. "What would you stay to a Steuben feeding-bowl?" Mr. Marcus suggested.

Examination of the large Steuben collection on the fourth floor was unproductive: the largest glass ash-tray was not wide enough to accommodate Leonard's muzzle. With that avenue blocked, Mr. Marcus tried another.

"Let's visit the Epicure Bar," he proposed. Yet a look at the delicate foods of the Epicure Bar left the customer cold. "Leonard is a red-meat sort of lion," he objected emphatically.

Then a new idea hit Mr. Marcus. "I have the solution," he said. "It's cold in Nebraska, isn't it?"

"Very cold."

"In that case, the gift for Leonard is an electric comforter, much to be preferred to the conventional electric blanket."

The visitor from Nebraska inspected the comforter and pronounced it entirely to his taste. He bought it, noting with satisfaction as he marched off, "Leonard will be pleased with it I know.'

Another tale of Neiman-Marcus revolves around a banker, a New Yorker, and a politician. Early one morning Miss Marihelen McDuff, the store's director of public relations, had a phone call from a prominent Dallas banker.

"I am in a tight spot," he began.

"Why, what is the trouble?" asked Miss McDuff.

"I have recently had a New York banker for a guest," the Dallas man told her. "It is said that he pays no income tax. The government simply rings him up when they run short. Our bank would like to remain on the best of good terms with him. Well, while he was here he developed a mania for Western goods. He has outfitted himself with Western dress, from ten-gallon hat to two-gallon boots. He's adopted the Western theme with a vengeance."

"We'll help as much as we can," put in Miss McDuff.

"Fine. Then I'll depend on you. You see, now he wants a bleached steer head to put above his mantel."

"What is that he wants?" Miss McDuff inquired.

"A bleached steer head. Like you find in the desert. You know, the head part of the skeleton of a steer. Would you locate one for me to send to him?"

He hung up. Miss McDuff pondered for a minute or two. It was the first time, so far as she knew, that the store had been called on to supply this particular article of interior decoration, a real dead steer's head. Where would she go to obtain one? She sifted her mind for ideas.

At this point it occurred to her that Bill Kittrell, politician and man-about-town, might know. She picked up the telephone receiver.

"No trouble about that," Bill Kittrell assured her. "Bob Pool's got one. Talk to him."

Bob Pool runs a restaurant right across the street from Neiman's. Yes, he was the owner of a steer head. Yes, he would be delighted to part with it for a modest fee.

The problem in hand, Miss McDuff called up the banker. She reported that the search had ended in good fortune.

"Well, I'll tell you," the banker replied. "Gift-wrap it, will you?"

Elaborately and daintily gift-wrapped, the bleached skull of a steer was dispatched to New York that afternoon.[9]

Two or three brief incidents will illustrate the ample prestige which Neiman-Marcus enjoys. In 1951 for a few days Neiman's pressed into service a plain black truck to deliver its packages while one of the regular trucks was undergoing repairs. The black delivery truck, which bore no lettering on the outside, drew up in front of a house in Highland Park, a suburb of Dallas, one morning. As the uniformed driver stepped out with a package in his hand, a lady came out of the house.

"Why are you using that old black truck," she demanded, "instead of a real Neiman-Marcus truck?" The deliveryman explained that the other truck had experienced a breakdown that morning and was in a garage being worked on.

"Well," the lady declared, "I'll have you to know I expect my packages to be delivered in a Neiman-Marcus truck. I want to be sure that the neighbors know where I buy my things."[10]

A second incident of this sort grew out of the fire that occurred in the service basement of the store at the end of November, 1946. One of the firemen who helped put out the blaze received a slight burn on his right arm. The next day his wife took him around to all the neighbors, pointing proudly to the arm and bragging, "My husband got this burn in the *Neiman-Marcus* fire."[11]

The prestige of Neiman's is so pervasive, George Sessions Perry asserts, that "chain-store buyers buy one class of goods for other Texas stores, but a simpler line for Dallas, so their customers can look as if they bought their clothes from Neiman-Marcus." Further evidence of the magnitude of the Neiman-Marcus reputation is offered by a want ad that appeared in the columns of the Dallas *News* during 1951:

> Big Shot Public Relations Man from Ohio, currently at leisure but choosy, wants to get in on some of this oil — or what have you? — money in Dallas. Promotion, personnel, house organ and advertising experience that would take all day to tell about. My women folk want to live near Neiman-Marcus. What's your offer?[12]

It is reassuring to the fallible mortal that not all of the anecdotes about Neiman-Marcus necessarily add to the luster of its name. According to one of this less favorable variety, a freshly wed young Dallas man remarked, "When I was a bachelor, I used to be in business for myself. Since I got married, I've been in business for Neiman-Marcus."[13]

The Preston Center branch of the downtown store, which opened in October of 1951, is the locale of another comic story. Above a stairway at Preston Center hangs a piece of mobile sculpture which Neiman's commissioned Alexander Calder to do. In fashioning his "openwork sculpture" or mobiles, Calder works with pieces of metal and wire. The mobile when finished is suspended freely so that it can turn with the air currents in the room. An elderly customer is supposed to have gazed for a time at the Preston Center mobile soon after the store's opening. "If they think," she said, "that they're going to catch flies with that, they're crazy!"[14]

One episode of this sort is a particular favorite of Mr. Stanley Marcus. Some years ago a youthful and well-dressed West Texas cattleman made his way into the store downtown. He walked to the center of the first floor, stopped, then wheeled slowly around as if he were savoring the whole of the contents of the first floor. A blond from the jewelry counter approached. Although Neiman's advises its salesgirls not to say, "May I help you?" — for the reason that it is too easy to answer no — the blond salesgirl fell into that grievous error. She asked whether she could be of any help.

The young rancher surveyed the scene before him again, then replied, "No, I reckon not, lady. I never saw so many things in my life I could do without."[15]

To balance these three stories, there is a series of episodes in which Neiman-Marcus deliberately passes up a sale for the sake of preserving some principle. One has it that Mr. Herbert Marcus, Sr., father of the four Marcus brothers who today share the administration of the store, took one whiff of a new brand of perfume that had recently been introduced by Neiman's and ordered it off the shelves and out of the store. The perfume remained banished, on the grounds that it failed to measure up to the firm's standard of quality. For another example, Mr. Stanley Marcus reports, "We rejected the offer of a manufacturer of costume jewelry who was willing to put a stock in on consignment and guarantee us a profit of $25,000 without risk on our part." But the jewelry was over-ornamented and violated Mr. Marcus' sense of taste.[16]

Stanley Marcus figures in another incident involving restraint or self-discipline on the part of the store. A man and his sixteen-year-old daughter were choosing a coat for the daughter in the store one summer. They were about to settle on a mink coat when Mr. Marcus was called into the fitting room to give his judgment on the choice. As he was checking the fit of the garment, he learned that the girl was soon setting out for her first year at an Eastern preparatory school. Wearing a mink coat at a girls' school seemed decidedly inappropriate to Mr. Marcus. He tried to shift her interest in the direction of a muskrat or a beaver coat, to no avail. The daughter pouted; the father grew angry. Mr. Marcus sought to present the reasons for his advising against a mink. The father in a huff walked out with his tearful daughter.

The next day the man was back to see Mr. Marcus. He was in a chastened mood, and he expressed regret for his behavior of the day before. He had talked the matter over with his sister, who told him, "Mr. Marcus was right. A sixteen-year-old girl has no business going off to school with a mink coat. You go back and buy the one he tells you to." Mr. Marcus sold him a muskrat coat for less than one-sixth as much as the mink would have cost. In doing so, Mr. Marcus adds, "I made a customer for life. Six years later when the daughter married, I sold him a mink coat."

The last word in respect to this willingness to forego a substantial sale belongs to Mr. Stanley Marcus. He writes candidly, "We do not think of ourselves as retail heroes for passing up the profit. We think it good business to lose one dollar to make three."[17] On the basis of this remark, the fur-coat story might be entitled "The Mink and the Slow Buck."

A few of the stories about Neiman's exist in two versions. For instance, a story about a diamond ring has a variant. One form of this incident appears in the pages of Green Peyton's commendable volume, *America's Heartland: The Southwest*. In Green Peyton's account it goes, "Nobody at Neiman-Marcus turned a hair when they received a penny post card from a Texas customer who scrawled: 'Please send ring advertised and charge to my account.' The ring in question — a twenty-four carat diamond — was priced at $127,000."[18]

Miss Marihelen McDuff has an expanded and somewhat more complex narrative of the affair. Along in 1947, she records, Neiman's ran an advertisement of an imposing diamond ring in the Dallas *News*. The advertisement did not make any mention of the ring's price; instead, it described the weight of the stone: 23.08 carats, abbreviating the word carats "cts." A woman from Lubbock, Texas, mailed in a post card ordering the ring. The credit office at Neiman's checked with a bank in Lubbock, to be informed that the woman, though she lived on a modest scale, was sufficiently wealthy to be able to buy the ring. The Lubbock banker, on the other hand, doubted that she had ever put out as much as $35,000, the cost of the diamond, on anything that was not loaded with cotton, saturated in oil, or liberally dotted with cattle. The next move was to call the woman herself long-distance, saying that the store customarily delivered merchandise of such value by personal messenger. Would she indicate a time that would be convenient for the messenger to bring out the package? She was unmistakably surprised at the request. How much was this ring that had to be guarded so carefully, anyway? When the figure of $35,000 reached her ears, she exclaimed, "My God. I thought it was twenty-three dollars and eight cents." She had misread the size of the ring for its price.[19]

One conclusion that can be drawn is that a majority of the stories deal with so-called luxury merchandise — with furs, diamonds, Steuben glass, and the like. Attention is not focused on the persons involved in the incident so much as it is on the goods themselves. The real heroes and heroines of these tales are the rings, the coats, and the other apparel and adornment, not the human beings.

---

1. A letter from Marihelen McDuff to Peter H. Wyden, July 14, 1950, Neiman-Marcus files.

2. *Dallas Morning News*, June 10, 1950.

3. *Ibid*, June 30, 1950; John William Rogers, *The Lusty Texans of Dallas* (New York, 1951), pp. 322-23.

4. *Dallas Morning News*, December 1, 1950.

5. *Ibid*.

6. Selma Robinson, "Texas Tells 'Em," *Collier's*, CIV (September 16, 1939), 18-19.

7. *Ibid.; Dallas Morning News*, February 6, 1951.

8. *Dallas Morning News*, January 5, 1951.

9. *Ibid.*, January 19, 1951.

10. *Ibid.*, November 27, 1951.

11. *Ibid.*, December 14, 1951.

12. George Sessions Perry, "Dallas and Fort Worth," *Saturday Evening Post*, CCXVIII (March 30, 1946), 43; *Dallas Morning News*, July 3, 1951.

13. "Texas Store: Neiman-Marcus is a Fashion Center," *Life*, XIX (September 3, 1945), 84.

14. *Dallas Morning News*, December 28, 1951.

15. Letter from Marihelen McDuff to Peter H. Wyden, July 14, 1950, Neiman-Marcus files.

16. Stanley Marcus, "Fashion is my Business," *Atlantic Monthly*, CLXXXII (December, 1948), 47.

17. *Ibid.*, pp. 43-44, 47.

18. Green Peyton, *America's Heartland: The Southwest* (Norman, Oklahoma, 1948), p. 196.

19. Letter from Marihelen McDuff to Peter H. Wyden, July 14, 1950, Neiman-Marcus files.

ORLAN L. SAWEY

# Origins of Uvalde County Cattle Brands

THE POPULAR INTEREST in cattle brands has led to a considerable literature on the subject, with stress being placed upon two points: one, all brands have stories behind them, and two, the most important consideration in designing a brand was to make alteration difficult. An investigation of the actual records of one Texas county indicates that both points have been overemphasized.

The brand registration books of the various counties are, however, a potential source of much information concerning the cattle industry. They contain the brands and earmarks registered by individual ranchers with the dates of registration, information that can be used to determine the periods of greatest development of the cattle industry, the periods of inflation, and the periods of depression. From the brand registrations can be traced the rise, and sometimes the fall, of certain cattle companies and individuals. From them it is also possible to trace the origins of brands, even without additional information.

The brand registration books of Uvalde County, upon which this study is based, are in the Archives Collection of the University of Texas. They are large, ledger-type books, bound in leather. One book contains the actual registration, in chronological order, of the brands recorded in Uvalde County from 1858 to 1875, as well as an index by names of the owners. The form of registration is as follows:

THE STATE OF TEXAS
COUNTY OF UVALDE

Be it remembered that_____

_____ of the County of Uvalde Brands and Marks as follows to wit  Brands thus_____  Ear marks thus_____.

Recorded on the_____day of_____A.D._____.

C.D.C.U.Co.

The second book contains an index of the first as well as an index of the brands registered between 1875 and 1886, records of cattle sales, and reports of brand and hide inspections. The index catalogues the brands according to the first letters, according to figures, and according to designs. All brands in each group are listed chronologically.

It was the practice for ranchers to register their brands in surrounding counties as well as in their own counties, for twenty-five counties are represented in the Uvalde County brand books. In this study, however, only Uvalde County brands registered from 1858 to 1875 are considered.

Much has been written about the origins of cattle brands, but most of the material is very general or deals with only a few famous brands. This study is an effort to analyze a large number in order to determine the factors involved in the choice of brands.

Of the total of 783 brands examined, 662 began with letters, 81 began with numbers, and 40 began with designs. Of the brands that were dominantly letters, 640 consisted of letters only, 17 of letters and numbers and 3 of letters and designs. Of the brands that were dominantly numbers, 53 were made up of numbers alone, 26 of numbers and letters, and 2 of numbers and designs. Of the design brands, 6 contained letters also, and one contained a number.

A widely-held theory that most brands consisted of curved letters, rather than sharp-cornered ones, because of the tendency of sharp-cornered brands to blot, is not borne out by this group of brands. For example, those beginning with J numbered 94; with H, 55;

with T, 51; with O, 39; with A, 37; with L, 33; with P, 32. It does not seem that the curved or angular shape of the brand had much influence on its choice. Most brands were too large for shape to make any difference. However, in the case of Y, the rounded lower case letter (in script) was almost invariably used.

In the numerous folk tales concerning the choice of brands, design brands have been emphasized. Yet of the brands registered in Uvalde County, only 45 out of the 783 were designs; there were only 10 before 1870.

Most of the brands registered in the 1850's consisted of single letters. B. A. Pulliam registered the brand A in October, 1858; J. E. Brown registered the brand B in September, 1856; J. W. Cummings, the brand C in August, 1857; J. G. Daugherty, the brand D in May, 1856. Each letter of the alphabet was chosen early. Since both A and B had been registered in January, 1867, A. Blackmon registered the AB Connected. Antonio Barrera, in January, 1867, found the AB already in use; so he used the Quarter Circle, Open A, B Connected. (Plate I.)

Perry Aiken, in February, 1871, found A, P, and PA in use; so he branded AK Connected, giving the phonetic representation of the first syllable of his name. After several hundred brands had been registered, it became difficult for a rancher to design a brand containing his initials, and, as a result, the use of designs and nicknames developed. Thus the transition was from single initials, to multiple initials, to designs and nicknames. Of course, there were exceptions to this general rule, but the pattern can be definitely traced.

Some ranchers were determined to use single or double initials, despite the fact that their initials were already registered, and so variants were registered. Some variants of A were Quarter Circle A and Open A (an inverted V). Variants of B were Lazy B and Quarter Circle B. Variants of other letters were obtained by placing a straight line (bar) either above or below the letter, placing the letter in a circle, doubling the letter, branding the letter in script, branding the letter backward, or making the letter "fly," "walk," or "run." (See Plate I.) In brands consisting of more than one letter it was the general practice to print the letters separately, rather than connected, especially the curved letters. One exception

174  FOLK TRAVELERS

1.         2.         3.         4.

      ℰ
5.         6.         7.         8.

  W
9.         10.        11.        12.

    SAE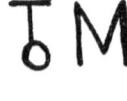
13.        14.        15.        16.

PLATE I

Examples of variants of single letter and combination letter brands

1. Quarter Circle Open AB Connected.
2. Quarter Circle A
3. Open A
4. Lazy B
5. Bar A
6. A Bar
7. Double A Connected
8. E (in script)
9. Backward B
10. Flying W
11. Running M
12. Walking M
13. Backward CMC Connected
14. JPR Connected
15. SHANE Connected
16. TO Connected M (Tom)

to this practice, the AG Connected registered by A. J. Garretson in October, 1872, so confused the clerk that he listed it as PG. The connected brands were more frequent in script. The clerk who catalogued the Backward CMC Connected, registered by Catherine McCarthy in December, 1858, listed it under the M's, thinking it was merely a fancy M. (Plate I.)

Some ranchers registered both the round and square printing of their initials, and some brands were a combination of printing and script. In the JPR Connected used by J. P. Rhiner, the back of the J was the back of the P, and the R was designated by using the P and separating the leg of the R from the P. (Plate I.) Other connected brands are the TJ used by J. H. Tucker, TJH used by T. J. Holcomb, TET used by T. E. Taylor, Bar TFL (with the F backward) used by T. F. Leakey, AC (with the C connected at the apex of the A) used by Nathan Cox, and the HC used by Hugh Cox.

Out of the total of 662 letter brands, 211 were obviously derived from the initials of the owner or owners; 43 were probably derived from the initials of the owner or his parents; 82 were obviously from the name of the owner; 213 were of undetermined origin. A group of 113 brands were derived from names of miscellaneous persons, objects, places and current events.

The brands which were obviously derived from the initials of the owner usually consisted of one, two, or three initials, depending on the time the brand was registered. Brands of cattle companies sometimes included the first letter of the last name of each member of the company. Often the brand consisted of the double of the initial of the first or last name of the owner; Angel Toveas thus branded AA Connected. Sometimes the initials were reversed; Hugh Cox branded CH, as well as H C Connected. Many times the rancher branded with his last two initials; B. W. Taylor branded BT. Sometimes the first two initials were reversed; A. J. Dillard branded JAD. Some ranchers used several arrangements of their initials; John Leakey branded Backward JL Connected, JL, JL on the hip and UV (Uvalde) on the side, L Backward J, Bar JL, JL Bar, and LJ. Some initials were used upside down; J. W. Patterson branded JMP Connected. Some ranchers used either two or three initials; L. D. Dobbs registered LD and LDD. Some brands were used either straight or "lazy"; Maggie J. Dolan branded MJD and MJD with the whole brand "lazy."

The group of brands which were possibly derived from the initials of either the owner or his parents usually contained one or more initials of the owner of the brand and other apparently unrelated initials. In October, 1860, W. B. Lease branded AL Connected. Ben Cox, in February, 1870, branded CC; Hugh Cox, Jr., in July, 1874, branded CIC. The latter brand was obviously derived from the first. John Kennedy, in May, 1872, branded CK. Gideon Thompson branded CT. C. W. Kincheloe branded HK Connected. Since R. H. Kincheloe branded HK, it is likely that the HK stood for an ancestor of the two. Other brands in this relatively small group seem to have had similar origins.

Brands obviously derived from the name or nickname of the owner were varied in form. Alfred C. Watson branded AL Connected F, the brand being taken from the first three letters of his first name. BL was registered by William Pulliam and BIL by B. W. Patterson, both brands being shorter forms of "Bill." A. B. Blakely branded BLA, the first three letters of his last name. Robert Labruce branded BOB. Hugh Cox branded COX. David Cook branded COOK. James Dalrymple branded DAL. David B. Patterson branded DAV, and Maria E. Patterson branded PAT. J. C. Dodd branded DOD. Eva C. Bowels branded EVA, while Mary Cortez branded MAR. Eliza C. McKinney branded EZ, the letters being taken from the first and fourth letters of her first name. Similarly, George Griffin branded GE and Henry Ramsey branded HE. Thomas Hannahan branded Hh Connected, the letters being taken from the first and sixth letters of his last name. W. H. Hill was able to include all the letters of his last name by drawing a line between two L's, so that the tops of the L's formed the sides of the H. John Holland branded HOL. Other name brands were IDA, IRA, JAC (Jacob), JAK (Jack), JIM, JOB, JOY, MON (Monroe), NA (Nathan), NOX (Knox), TIN Connected (Tinsley), PO (Poe), RU (Ruben), SHANE Connected, T Open A Y (Taylor), Th Connected (Thomas), TOM in several forms (Tom), WAR (Ware), WI (William), WIN (for Winia), WI, SH Connected (Wish) and WAL (Wall). (Plate I.)

Other combinations also were found. D. D. Pruitt branded IT,

ORIGINS OF UVALDE COUNTY CATTLE BRANDS 177

the last syllable of his name. John Birchfield branded J, HF Connected, and John Davenport branded J, NP Connected, the brands being taken from the first letter of the first name and a combination of letters from within the surname. In like manner, J. C. McGrew branded JRW. George Bellar branded LAR; J. W. Gilcrease branded LC Connected. Elijah (Lige) Daniels branded LDS. C. R. McPherson branded MC. W. C. Meacham branded MEM. E. T. Moore branded MO Connected, with the O between the sides of the M. J. S. Nixon branded NIX, R. N. McCarthy branded RMC. Pancho Garcia branded PC. Warren Cass branded SS. Telesforio Taris branded TRS Connected, with the S "lazy" and connected to the bottom of the T and R. Thomas Weymiller branded Wy.

In the group of miscellaneous brands, those taken from the name of the county were frequent. Among them were U, U Lazy H (registered by Cornelia Hammer), UA, UF, UIC, UI, UOV, ULX, and ULI. Other brands taken from the names of places were ALA (Alabama), OHO (Ohio), and SX (Essex). There were also several brands involving T and TX that probably referred to Texas. Brands taken from names and nicknames of people other than the owner were frequent. Examples are HAP, JIL, L Backward IZ, Bar LU and LUE, LUC, MOL, ANA and AN Connected, OLE, PET, ROP, SAL, SIS, SUE, TIL, and TIM. The brands involving figures were VII, Bar IV, IX, Quarter Circle IX, SIX, NIN, and TEN. The brands MIL (million?), LOT and FEW could be classified as giving amounts.

Brands reflecting the events of the times were AOL (absent without leave; registered in June, 1873), KKK (registered in August, 1871), KIL (registered in June, 1871), LED (registered in June, 1872) and MOB (registered in October, 1874). Animals and birds were represented in the brands. Among them were DOE, ELK, OUL, OWL, KAT, and PUP. As usual, variants of the OX brands were used. One person branded OX, and, several years later, OXL (after variants had been registered). Another person registered Bar OX and IOX (one ox). Another variant was OXI. The plural of the word was registered as OXS and OXN.

Representing the trouble ranchers had were TIX (ticks) and RUN. One rancher hoped his cattle would be FAT. Two words familiar on the frontier were brands registered by B. A. Bates—HOW and HOY (Spanish for *today*). Possible difference in opinion was expressed by IN and OUT. The weather was commented upon by HOT and ICE. Hell in Texas was represented by two brands, HEL and HE Connected LL. Financial status was shown by PD. One person branded OK in five different positions, while another rancher used OK in another variant. Other interesting brands were LIT, LIV, TAX, SO, TH Connected O, MIX, LIX, TUT, TOT, TOO, NOT, URN, THE and THE Connected, TEL, TIE, ALL, OUR, OIL, HED, HOP, FIT, LVE (love?) and LI, TE Connected.

Of the 213 brands the origin of which could not be determined, 159 were registered in the period between 1865 and 1875, when many brands were being bought and sold. The boom years were 1872 and 1873. In 1872 many brands were bought by individuals, apparently small ranchers. In 1873, which was a depression year, large companies, such as Adams and Company, Bates Brothers, and Birchfield Brothers bought a large number of brands. Many brands were purchased in counties other than Uvalde County and then registered in Uvalde County. A search through the brand books of other counties would probably reveal the origin of some of the brands.

Some of the brands were variants of an original, differentiating symbols being used to denote herds or ownership by different members of a family. Adams and Company registered several brands consisting of a diamond, with various letters inside, probably to designate different herds. One rancher branded HX in 1868 and HXE in 1870. One company branded ID, IDD and IDA. The last brand was bought from one woman named Ida and later sold to another with the same name. One rancher branded HOT, HUL and HUT. Another branded HIX, HOX, HOW and HOY, while his brother branded HOK.

Origins of few of the brands which were mostly numbers could be determined. The origin of the brand 1874 (with the 74 connected), registered in 1874 by J. M. Sanchez, is obvious. 7U, registered in December, 1867, probably stood for '67 in Uvalde. 20T may have meant "too hot." Initials of the owner were often represented in the brands containing numbers and letters. Typical are

# ORIGINS OF UVALDE COUNTY CATTLE BRANDS

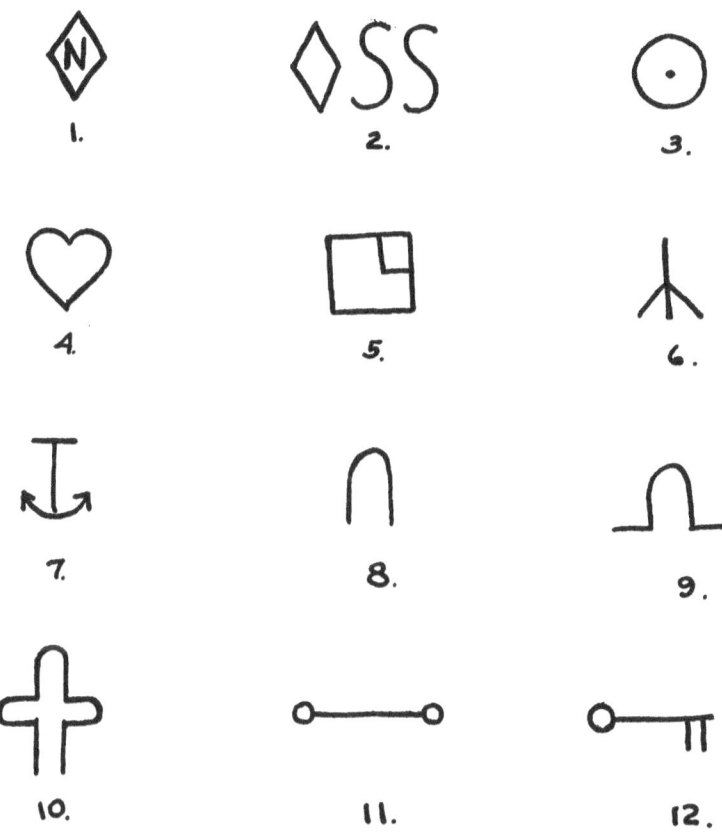

PLATE II

1. Diamond N
2. Diamond SS
3. Circle Dot
4. Heart
5. Flag
6. Turkey Track
7. T. Anchor
8. Horse Shoe
9. Hat
10. Club
11. Bridle Bit
12. Key

2W, registered by Silas Webster; 7HL Connected, registered by H. H. Levering; 7R, registered by J. P. Rheiner; and 7T, registered by W. S. Thompson.

Some of the design brands, also, included initials of the owners. Typical are the Diamond N (with the N inside the diamond) of M. Nussle and the Diamond SS of M. Spears. Few design brands gave indication of their origins. Some were evidently used because of their simplicity. For examples of design brands see Plate II.

Relatively few brands were registered by Mexicans in Uvalde County. Most of the brands contained the initials of the owners, either in print or in script; the Mexicans used script more frequently than did the Anglo-Americans. Pedro Villaneuva apparently did not know how to spell his name. He registered the brand PB, and it was entered in one place in the brand book as belonging to one "Pedro Buineva," and in another place it was registered under the proper spelling. Evidently, when Pedro went to the courthouse to register a brand he was undecided as to what brand he should use. The clerk suggested initials, giving him PB, and sent him away. Some Spanish brands, a few of which are reproduced in Plate III, have no apparent meaning.

Family brands and records of their transfer sometimes give interesting information. The brand AD was registered in 1856 by A. B., A. G., and Joseph Dillard, with varying ear marks. In January, 1867, A. G. Dillard registered the brand to be branded on the right side; Sophronia Dillard, on the left side, N. E. Dillard, on the left shoulder; and S. J. Dillard, on the left thigh. All cattle carried the same ear mark. In February, 1872, A. B. Dillard registered the same brand, with all ear marks. In August, 1857, J. W. Cummings registered C; in October, 1849, Mary Cummings registered Quarter Circle C. In November, 1871, J. E. Hewett, who had evidently bought both brands, registered them. In the brand book the word "died" is marked after his name; in March, 1872 each brand was registered by its original owner.

Sometimes the brands tell interesting stories, especially if they are examined with an eye toward how easily one brand can be worked over another. Situations similar to the fictitious one related below sometimes existed. Mr. A, in Medina County (a neighboring county), registered BEI. Mr. B, in Uvalde County, registered

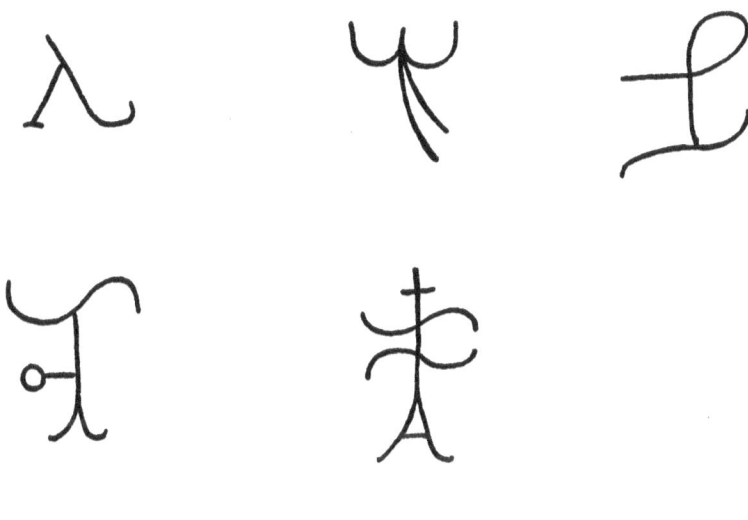

PLATE III

Examples of Spanish brands

BEL. Mr. A, in Medina County, registered BEE, and to make it safer, registered BEB in Uvalde County. One man, who was determined to forestall any potential brand blotting, registered AIL; AIL Connected; AH Connected L; A, HL Connected; AIE; and A2. Often cattle companies or individuals bought out brands which were similar to those which they owned. In August, 1871, Mr. A registered XV; in January, 1872, Mr. X registered XVL. Both brands were sold to the A and B Cattle Company (the original Mr. A was half owner) in July, 1872. Then, in December, 1872, Mr. B, the second member of the firm, registered XVE.

Sometimes the brand registration of certain cattle companies resembled the writing of names on law firms' doors. In February,

1873, Cox, Kelso, and Company registered the brand CK Bar H. When the brand for Kelso and Holbrook (the H of the first brand) was registered in May, 1874, the bar was removed, the brand reading CKH. Mr. Holbrook was evidently gaining influence, because on the same date the brand CHK was registered. However, beside the latter brand someone had written, evidently several years later, the word "discontinued." In March, 1872, Melverda Bates and Mary Blakeny registered TOX and TOX with a rail (long line) over it, respectively, with the same ear mark. Later, Melverda Bates re-registered Mary Blakeny's brand, having evidently acquired it from her.

Only a few general statements can be made as to the origin of cattle brands. Probably the ranchers were not as imaginative in choosing their brands as we have been led to believe, since the elaborately designed brands are in the minority. Most brands were created from the initials or the names of their owners. Even the complicated brands derived from initials or names were the result of the fact that the simpler brands had already been registered. The early ranchers registered simple initials. As the number of brands grew, it became necessary to choose more complicated brands, and some of the design and number brands were probably chosen because the initials of the owner had already been registered.

WILSON M. HUDSON

# I Want My Golden Arm

ONCE THERE WAS A MAN who had a golden arm. He died and the golden arm was buried with him. In the middle of the night a robber went to the graveyard and dug him up and took the golden arm. Before the robber got out of the graveyard he heard something behind him—clomp, clomp, clomp, clomp. Then he heard a voice, "I want my golden arm! Who's got my golden arm?" The robber was scared but he kept on going. He could hear clomp, clomp, clomp, clomp getting closer and the voice getting louder, "I want my golden arm! Who's got my golden arm?" He ran and hid in some bushes. But the clomp, clomp, clomp, clomp came on closer and closer and the voice was louder and louder, "I want my golden arm! Who's got my golden arm? CLOMP, CLOMP, CLOMP, CLOMP. "I WANT MY GOLDEN ARM! WHO'S GOT MY GOLDEN ARM? — *YOU'VE GOT IT!*"

This story used to be told to me by my older sister when I was a child. No matter how many times she told it, I never failed to feel the hair rising on my head and I never failed to jump out of my skin at that last loud "You've got it!" It was my favorite ghost story, and it still is.

Many years later — in fact, only recently — I decided to see what I could learn about the story. I looked in Thompson's *Motif-Index of Folk-Literature* under "golden arm" and found this motif identification: "E.235.4.1. Return from dead to punish theft of golden arm from grave." In the Aarne-Thompson classification of folk tales, "I Want My Golden Arm" belongs to type 366, in which a corpse returns to punish the theft of part of its body or an article of clothing. Thompson's *Motif-Index* cited several studies and notes on type 366, and I knew of the extensive comparative notes in

Mr. A. M. Espinosa's *Cuentos populares españoles,* published after Thompson's *Motif-Index.* Thus provided with a working bibliography, to which I added as I went along, I proceeded to read as many of the variants of 366 as I could lay my hands on.

Let me speak first of those versions in which the part stolen from the corpse is a golden arm or leg or a silver toe.

Mark Twain used to tell the story of the golden arm on the lecture platform.[1] He called it a Negro ghost story and he spoke in Negro dialect; he also imitated the wailing of the wind and shook to indicate fear and cold. A man who has lived alone with his wife buries her out on the prairie. At midnight he goes out into a snowstorm and digs her up and takes her golden arm. He hears a voice behind him crying, "Who got my golden arm? Who got my golden arm?" He reaches home, rushes upstairs, and hides in bed. Outside he hears the voice crying, "Who got my golden arm?" Then it is inside, right by his bed. "Who got my golden arm? — You've got it!" As he told it, Mark Twain could make people on the back row jump with fright. The pause before the last explosion, he said, was very necessary for the effect.

Mark Twain's story is fuller than my sister's. The one who steals the golden arm is married to the dead person, and the thief is pursued all of the way back home and into the house itself. The snowstorm is either a peculiarity of Mark Twain's story or an addition of his own, for it is not met with in other versions. The points of strong similarity are that the pursuit begins immediately after the theft and the end comes with the startling, shouted accusation, "You've got it!" My sister learned her story from our paternal grandmother, who was born in Texas of Southern stock, and it is likely that Mark Twain heard the Negroes tell about the golden arm during his young days in Missouri.

In an English version of the golden arm published first in 1866[2] and republished by Joseph Jacobs in 1890,[3] the thief and the dead person are married, but the pursuit does not begin at the burial place and a series of questions and answers leads up to the shouted accusation.

A man marries a woman with a golden arm. At last she dies and is buried. He gets up in the middle of the night, digs her up, and cuts off the golden arm. The next night he goes to bed with the arm under his pillow. The wife's ghost stalks into the room and pulls aside the bed curtain. Pretending not to be afraid, he asks,

"What hast thou done with thy cheeks so red?"

"All withered and wasted away."

"What hast thou done with thy red rosy lips?"

"All withered and wasted away."

"What hast thou done with thy golden hair?"

"All withered and wasted away."

"What hast thou done with thy golden arm?"

*"THOU HAST IT!"*

Other variants of tale type 366 in which a golden arm is taken from a corpse have been recorded in Friesland[4] and Tuscany,[5] but I have not seen them. The stolen part is a golden leg in some versions from Germany, Schleswig-Holstein, and France.

In their notes to *Kinder- und Hausmärchen,* Bolte and Polívka printed a version left in the hand of Wilhelm Grimm:[6]

There was once a general's wife who had a child, and that child had two kinds of legs when it came into the world, one of gold and one of diamond, and it died on the third day. She thought, why should the child take the legs along into the grave? She took them off and put them in a box. On the following night the child came and said that it wanted to have its legs of gold and diamond back again. So it came three nights one after another. On the third night the general's wife said at last, "I must give it back the legs; otherwise it will have no rest in the grave." She took the box and gave the legs to the child. The child took them and did not appear again.

Here it is a mother who takes part of her child's body. Without the immediate pursuit, the series of questions and answers, and the explosive accusation, this story does not have the dramatic form and effect of the versions which I have already summarized.

The variant from Schleswig-Holstein was recorded in Dithmarschen.[7] In this story a mother takes the golden leg from her son in the graveyard; the son later comes for it and accuses, not his mother, but the cook. The story runs this way:

There was once a man and wife who had a son. The son had such strong gout in his leg that finally the leg fell off; then no doctor could do anything about that. So now they had a golden leg made. But the gout became so deep in him that he could no longer last, so he died and they had to carry him to the graveyard. The wife thought that it would be a shame if the golden leg were to lie in the ground. So she went and got the golden leg for herself.

Then in the evening something began to make a noise in the peat shed and throw the peat all around, so that there was a terrible racket, and afterwards somebody started to howl, "My leg! My leg! My leg!" Thus the howling and knocking kept up all night long. The cook asked the woman what that was; the woman answered her that she [the cook] should ask him [the ghost], she did not know. But the cook did not have the courage to.

The next evening the same thing broke loose again, throwing the peat around and knocking so that no one could stand it, and always howling besides, "My leg! My leg! My leg!" The cook asked the woman again, but the woman would not tell her.

The third night the thing and the noise and the knocking and the howling were still louder than before. The cook had to go get some peat, but she did not have the courage. She said to the woman that if she would go with her she would question him [the ghost]; so the woman went with her and opened the peat shed. Then he began to howl and say again, "My leg! My leg! My leg!"

"Who has your leg?" said the cook.

Then the dead man said, "You have my leg!"

The editor adds a note saying that this last should be called out in a loud voice. This story has the same explosive accusation as the American and English versions related above. But why is the cook instead of the real thief accused? A possible answer to this question will be suggested later.

A French version from Gascony contains a great deal of repeated dialogue.[8] It begins with an explanation of how the golden leg is acquired. In going down a stairway one night without a candle a beautiful woman breaks her leg so badly that it has to be cut off. Her husband has a jeweler make her another of gold. Seven years later she dies and is buried with the golden leg. In the night a manservant steals the leg from the grave. Hardly has he returned to bed when a voice is heard crying in the graveyard, "Gold! Gold! Give me back my leg of gold!" In the morning the gravedigger comes to the husband and tells him that his wife does nothing but cry, "Gold! Gold! Give me back my leg of gold!" The husband goes to the graveyard and tries to find out what his wife wants, but she merely repeats her cry, "Gold! Gold! Give me back my leg of gold!" He tells her she is unreasonable and returns home, promising to have masses said for her. On the second day the gravedigger comes again and the husband sends a maid to the graveyard, but all she can get out of the wife is the same cry, "Gold! Gold! Give me back my leg of gold!" On the third day the gravedigger comes again and the husband sends the manservant who has stolen the golden leg. Afraid but forced to go, the servant asks, "What do you want, Madame?"

"It's you that I want!" And she comes out of the grave, carries him under ground, and eats him up.

This Gascony version has the familiar ending that makes the hearer jump, but it goes further and leaves no doubt at all about what happened to the thief. With its accounting for the acquisition of the golden leg and the final fate of the thief, it contains more "reasoned" exposition than any of the other versions considered so far.

In a folk tale from Texas a silver toe is found by an old woman while digging potatoes with her husband. She puts it under her pillow. In the night something knocks at the door and calls out, "Give me my silver toe. Give me my silver toe. Give me my silver toe." Twice the woman says, "I've got no silver toe for you," but at last she opens the door a little and sees something very strange outside. Then follows a series of questions and answers.

"What's them great long ears for?"
"To hear with."
"What's that great long hair for?"
"To sweep my grandmother's hall."
"What's that great long nose for?"
"To smell with."
"What's them great long nails for?"
"To scratch my grandmother's pots."
"What's them great big eyes for?"
"To see with."
"What's them great big teeth for?"
"To bite you, to bite you, to bite you!"

This story is one that Mrs. Emeline B. Russell used to tell her children. She lived in Goliad until she moved to Helena, Texas, in 1853. (By the way, my grandmother who used to tell the golden arm story lived for a while in Helena just after the Civil War.) Mrs. Bertha McKee Dobie edited Mrs. Russell's tales and rhymes for the Texas Folklore Society in 1927.[9] In her headnote to "The Silver Toe" Mrs. Dobie mentions another version with a silver toe from Arkansas and also calls attention to the parallels with the stories of Jacobs and Mark Twain and with the "Teeny-Tiny" of Jacobs, which I shall speak of later.

The golden arms and legs and the silver toes that we have been talking about—are they to be thought of as artificial, removable parts like ordinary wooden legs?

The same answer cannot be given for all of our stories. In Jacobs' English story there is no accounting for the acquisition of the golden arm (was the woman born with it as the child in Grimm was born with a golden leg?), and the husband is definitely said to "cut off" his wife's arm. In the Gascony story the golden leg is a replacement for an amputated leg. Perhaps we could theorize like this: the primitive mind would view the added or unnatural part as one with the flesh, like Pelops' ivory shoulder; the more sophisticated mind, reworking the same story, would rationalize the added or unnatural part as a prosthetic appliance. Then on the assumption that the primitive precedes the sophisticated in the order of development we might argue that the English version represents an earlier form than the French version. But let us not press the point; this line of reasoning leads to ambiguity, because "earlier in development" easily becomes confused with "earlier in historical time." It also leads to a search for "primitive" archetypes by a reconstruction from "later" forms, a process no longer recommended by reputable folklorists. Often we cannot determine what is primitive and what is sophisticated.

In stories in which a golden arm or leg or a silver toe is stolen the implied or explicit motive for the theft is avarice. In many stories that follow the same pattern a shroud or some article of clothing is stolen from the corpse. In numerous other stories of the same family a real part of a corpse is stolen and the purpose is cannibalism. For all of these the Aarne-Thompson classification sets up a single folk-tale type, 366, accompanied by the descriptive phrase "The Man from the Gallows." In their notes to *Kinder- und Haus-*

*märchen,* Bolte and Polívka seem to recognize two subtypes, one for avarice and one for cannibalism, as indicated by a twofold division in their comparative and bibliographical commentary. They publish and annotate a brief version of the Man from the Gallows left by the Brothers Grimm.[10]

Late in the evening guests come to an old woman. She has nothing left to eat and does not know what to cook for them. She goes to the gallows, where a dead man is hanging and cuts out his liver. She cooks it for the strangers, who eat it up. At midnight something knocks on the hut, and the woman opens the door. There is a dead man with bald head, without eyes, and with a wound in his body.
"Where is your hair?"
"The wind has blown it away."
"Where are your eyes?"
"The ravens have pecked them out."
"Where is your liver?"
"You have eaten it up!"

Numerous cannibalistic stories like this exist. In a variant from Gascony[11] parents take a leg from a corpse in a cemetery home to their gluttonous daughter, who eats it. The corpse comes and chants, "Give me back my leg. Give me back my leg." Later the corpse returns when the parents are in the field and orders the girl to heat water. When she has done so, it orders her to wash its right leg and she obeys. Then it orders her to wash the left leg too. She asks who has taken it. The corpse shouts, "You have!" and seizes and eats her.

A folk tale collected among the Mexican population in Austin, Texas, by Miss Soledad Pérez and published in the Texas Folklore Society Publication for 1951 is a variant of type 366 and involves cannibalism.[12] A poor woman kills her husband and makes a stew for guests that he has insisted on inviting. One night months later she sees a light in the distance and hears the tinkle of a bell. On successive nights the light draws nearer and the bell rings louder until the woman hears her husband's voice saying, "I have come for my entrails!" At last the light, the bell, and the voice come into the woman's room. Right by the bed, the husband shouts, "I have caught you!" and the woman dies of fright.

In Hispanic versions it is usually the *asadura* (entrails) that is taken from the corpse and eaten.[13] Sixteen out of nineteen Hispanic variants analyzed by Mr. A. M. Espinosa involve cannibalism and none the theft of a golden arm or leg. Mr. Espinosa regards the versions which he examined as containing traces of barbaric cannibalism suppressed by the Christian culture of the West. Cannibalism survives symbolically, it might be added, in the Christian rite of Communion.

It is tempting to interpret the golden arm or leg as a substitution for a real arm or leg and hence as a disguise for cannibalism. We should then have no difficulty in explaining why, in the golden leg story from Schleswig-Holstein, the cook is accused of having the leg instead of the mother, who earlier stole it from her son's grave: the cook had cooked and served the leg. The fact that the mother or husband sometimes steals the golden arm or leg could be explained as vestigial evidence of a form of cannibalism practiced by relatives to assuage grief. Cannibalism to prevent grief is well known outside of Europe.

This kind of reasoning has a certain plausibility, but why would cannibalism be disguised in some versions and open in others current among the same people at the same time? Such is the situation in Germany, France, and Italy. In England the story of Teeny-Tiny, which is as popular as the story of the golden arm, borders on cannibalism but stops just short of it.[14]

A teeny-tiny woman — the adjective is attached to every noun all of the way through — goes into a graveyard and picks up a bone. She takes it home to make soup and lays it in the cupboard. She lies down to sleep and is awakened three times by a voice saying, "Give me my bone!" At last she calls out, "Take it!" In another version,[15] without the *teeny-tiny,* a poor family is boiling a bone stolen from the graveyard; a voice calls three times, louder each time, "Give me my bone!" Then the narrator shouts, "Take it!" In America there is at least one variant of type 366 that points to cannibalism.[16] In a story from North Carolina an old man discovers what seems to be a human toe among some potatoes that he is roasting. He leaves it until the last but eats it too because he is still hungry. Then he hears a voice outside asking, "Where's my big toe?" He finds a strange creature called a wampus on his roof and questions it about its eyes, claws, tail, and teeth. With the last answer, "To chew your bones!" the wampus jumps down on the old man. The wampus seems to be kin to the Taily-Po that comes to a man's cabin for its tail, which has been cut off by the man and eaten or burnt, and chants a rhyme, "You know and I know/ That I want my Taily-Po!"[17] (Joel Chandler Harris tells a Taily-Po story in *Uncle Remus Returns*.) The big toe story from North Carolina is almost identical with the silver toe story from Texas told by Mrs. Russell, in which the silver toe is found by an old woman while digging potatoes. If we asked why it is discovered in the ground, the answer might be because that is where people are buried. Here the silver toe may be a substitution for an earlier real toe, or perhaps it is only an analogy to a silver arm.

Much less violent offenses than cannibalism are enough to call back the dead to punish the offender. Any form of grave breaking or grave robbing will arouse the dead to vengeance. No one would suggest that the taking of clothing or jewels from the dead is cannibalism in disguise. Many variants of folk tale 366 turn on such theft and often result in the death of the thief.

A story from Sicily relates that a crazy girl named Saddaedda steals the clothes from the body of a rich lady lying in church.[18] Saddaedda unintentionally pulls off the second leg along with the stocking and takes it home. At night the dead lady knocks and says, "Give me back my leg and stocking!" On the fifth night the corpse breaks in, strangles the girl, and carries off the leg and stocking to the grave. I have summarized this story because it involves the theft of both clothing and part of the corpse. In like versions from Tuscany and Venice three poor sisters take the clothing from their mother in the grave.[19] The youngest accidentally removes a leg with a stocking. The dead mother knocks on the door at night and strangles her. Need and close family relationship do not mitigate the mother's vengeance.

In the great collection of Russian folk tales by Afanasyev there is a story about a lazy girl who has the other village girls visit her and do her spinning.[20] One night when Lazybones boasts that she is afraid of nothing, the others tell her she must prove how brave she is by going to the church past the graveyard and bringing back the icon from the gate. She does so. At midnight she returns the icon. On the way back she sees a corpse in a white shroud sitting on a grave. She tears off the shroud and takes it to show the girls. After they have gone to bed the corpse knocks at the window and calls out, "Give me back my shroud! Give me back my shroud!" The other girls are terribly frightened, but Lazybones takes the shroud to the window and offers it to the corpse, who refuses, saying she must take it back where she got it. Suddenly the cocks crow and the corpse disappears. The next night the corpse comes again. Lazybones' father and mother try to hand it the shroud, but the corpse says again that she must take it back where she got it. Again the cocks crow. They send for the priest, who says it might be good for Lazybones to come to mass the next day. At mass a big whirlwind comes up and everyone falls to the ground. Lazybones disappears, leaving only her braids behind.

This story has a Russian setting but it is clearly a good example of type 366. The refusal of the corpse to accept the shroud at the thief's house and the insistence that it be returned to the graveyard is not a unique Russian characteristic.

We have looked at only a handful of a great number of stories like my grandmother's story of the golden arm. As incomplete and sketchy as my study has been, the story has been illuminated for me. I have not even raised the question of when and where the story originated and how it spread, for an answer could be hazarded only after each version had been assigned a date and place. Of one thing I am more convinced than ever — distance and language are no barriers to the movement of folk tales, which can travel freely from country to country without a visa and make themselves at home.

---

1. The story, together with directions for telling it, appears at the end of Mark Twain's essay entitled "How to Tell a Story." The story which E. P. Pabody heard Mark Twain relate has to do with the theft of coppers from the eyes of a dead wife. See E. P. Pabody, "Mark Twain's Ghost Story," *Minnesota History,* XVIII (March, 1937), 28-35.

2. In an appendix by S. Baring-Gould on household stories (No. 14), added to William Henderson's *Notes on the Folk Lore of the Northern Counties of England and the Borders* (London, 1866).

3. *English Fairy Tales* (London, 1890), pp. 138-39.

4. W. Dykstra, *Uit Frieslands Volksleven* (Leeuwarden, 1894), II, 31.

5. Referred to by T. F. Crane, *Italian Popular Tales* (New York, 1885), p. 370, n. 32. G. Pitrè had mentioned this tale in *Novelline popolari toscane* (Palermo, 1878), p. 12.

6. *Anmerkungen zu den Kinder- und Hausmächen der Brüder Grimm* (Leipzig), III (1918), 480.

7. Karl Müllenhoff, *Sagen, Märchen und Lieder der Herzogtümer Schleswig, Holstein und Lauenburg* (Kiel, 1845), p. 465.

8. Jean-François Bladé, *Contes populaires de la Gascogne* (Paris, 1886), II, 324-27.

9. "Tales and Rhymes of a Texas Household," ed. Bertha McKee Dobie, in *Texas and Southwestern Lore* (Austin, Texas, 1927; Texas Folklore Society Publication VI), pp. 41-42.

10. Bolte and Polívka, *op. cit.*, III, 478.

11. Bladé, *op. cit.*, 328-31. This story is called "La Goulue."

12. "The Return of the Gardener," in *The Healer of Los Olmos and Other Mexican Lore* (Dallas, 1951; Texas Folklore Society Publication XXIV), pp. 77-78.

13. *Cuentos populares españoles* (Madrid), III (1947), 116-21.

14. Joseph Jacobs, *English Fairy Tales*, pp. 57-58.

15. A. G. Gilchrist, "The Bone," *Folk-Lore*, L (1939), 378-79.

16. Ralph Steele Boggs, "North Carolina White Folktales and Riddles," *Journal of American Folklore*, XLVII (1934), 296.

17. For a version of the Taily-Po story, see John H. Cox, "Negro Tales from West Virginia," *Journal of American Folklore*, XLVII (1934), 341-42.

18. Crane, *op. cit.*, p. 238.

19. Bolte and Polívka, *op. cit.*, III, 481.

20. Tr. as "The Lazy Maiden" by Norbert Guterman in *Russian Fairy Tales* (New York, 1945), pp. 423-25. Another fine Russian version is the one published by E. A. Chudinsky in *Russkiya Narodnya Skazki* (Moskva, 1864), pp. 94-96. Since the story is not available in English, I shall summarize it from an oral translation which Mr. R. C. Stephenson kindly made for me. A rich lady takes her poor niece to live with her. When the lady's leg begins to pain her and draw up, she has a golden leg molded like the other. She becomes ill and dies, leaving the niece everything except the golden leg, which is buried with her. The lady's relatives go to law and take everything from the niece, who now wishes for the golden leg. On a dark night in a torrent of rain she digs into the grave and takes the golden leg — the aunt is not there. As the niece is leaving the cemetery the aunt appears and asks, "How do you happen to be here?"

The niece replies, "I was just going to your grave."
"Why?"
"To make my bows."
"At such a time of night and in such weather?"
"Yes."

Then the aunt seizes her by the shoulder and says in a terrible voice right in her ear, "Where is my golden leg?"

The aunt carries the leg back into the grave, and the next day the niece is found dead. The narrator concludes, "That's what it means to disturb the dead."

GABRIEL CÓRDOVA

# Black and White Magic on the Texas-Mexican Border

ALONG THE TEXAS-MEXICAN BORDER the practice of magic and witchcraft is still alive, the forms and rites for the most part going back to medieval times. Two specific instances, one of black and the other of white magic, will be presented here, together with a few generalizations.

The word *bruja,* witch, although almost always applied to a woman, may, with perfect correctness, be applied to a man, *brujo.* According to the belief prevalent along the Texas-Mexican Border, a *brujo* or *bruja* in order to practice the black art, must do two things: first, join in a contract with the devil; second, at the devil's instigation, with the proper horrid imprecations and blasphemies, abjure the Catholic faith, withdrawing the obedience due God. These two steps are known the world over and from the earliest times have been the basic requirements of all aspirants to witchcraft. The Christian churches are well aware of this fact. St. Jerome explains that a contract with Satan is spoken of by the prophet Isaiah in verse 15 of the twenty-eighth chapter: "We have made a covenant with death, and with hell are we at agreement."

St. Augustine also discusses such compacts at length. These formal contracts are still made today, and many *grimoires,* such as *Le Petit Dragon Rouge,* set out in explicit terms the precise formulas to be most efficaciously employed. All along the Border and northward as far as the Mexican population extends, books in Spanish on witchcraft and counterwitchcraft are sold in number. These books are printed in Mexico and cost little: for instance, *Embrujamiento* by "Dr. Papus" can be bought for seventy-five cents in Corpus Christi or San Antonio.

The Border *brujas* or *brujos* employ certain techniques which vary little, or not at all, from those used elsewhere in the world. The witch does not need to encounter her victim personally. She must merely obtain a bit of the victim's clothing, or better, some personal item such as hair, nail cuttings, offal, or urine. For this reason, many Indians bury their stools in secret places. In his study of witchcraft among the Navahos, Clyde Kluckhohn relates that these Indians are extremely afraid of having any of their bodily traces come into the possession of sorcerers.[1] This is also true of the Apaches and the Tarahumares of northern Chihuahua. After the *bruja* has obtained something closely associated with her victim's body, a certain formula must then be practiced. The material obtained from the victim may be buried, burned, or destroyed; this is accompanied by the recital of a spell which often fixes the number of days after which the enchantment will take effect. This incantation may be recited as is a prayer or a chant, or a combination of both. The saying of the Lord's Prayer or the Ave Maria backwards is also very frequently employed.

The "doll technique" is very well known in the El Paso area. An effigy is usually made from clay, and only rarely from wax or wood. I once asked Don Nicolás Favela, a Border *curandero*, or herb doctor, why this was so. He gave an answer which I had not heard before, but which makes good sense. Don Nicolás said:

> The reason why *brujas* do not make *muñecos* [dolls] of wood or wax is because this kind of *muñeco* can be burned. When this happens the spell is reversed and the *bruja* suffers. As you know, the one sure way to destroy a *bruja* is by fire. On the other hand, the clay *muñecos* are not affected by fire; on the contrary, the little dolls are hardened and made more perfect. In this way the enchantment against the victim is made stronger.

*Brujerías,* or sorceries, are carried out for a multiplicity of reasons. The most common are hate, revenge, envy, passion, money, power, knowledge, and very frequently the desire to do harm to a relative. These sorceries are directed against the victim or his family, against his place of business, his crops, his animals, and even against his automobile. Kluckhohn states that cars are often bewitched among the Navahos.[2]

While I was working as court translator in the El Paso municipal courts, I was fortunate enough to witness a case involving a witched automobile. Two men were arrested for fighting and arraigned before the court. When their case was called for trial and Judge R. P. Langford read the charges and asked for the testimony, the defendant refused to answer. The complaining witness, however, accused the defendant of trafficking with a witch and further stated that his new Ford had been hexed. Court cases involving witches are common in the El Paso courts, so common, in fact, that none of the court officials were unduly surprised. Since the El Paso Corporation Court is not a court of records, the following story told by the complaining witness is as accurate as Judge Dick Langford, City Attorney George Rodriguez and I can recall:

Well, *Juez,* I bought my Ford car brand new. A few days after I got it I got a flat. I did not think nothing of it, everybody gets flats. So I took the tire off, but I could not find nothing wrong with the tube or the valve. Then I thought to myself that maybe some neighborhood kid let the air out, so I said to my wife, "From now on I'm going to put that car in the garage every night and I'm going to lock that garage." *Juez,* that was about three weeks ago and since then every morning when I get ready to go to work my car has a flat. Not only that, the extra is always flat too. I have taken this car to about three or four garages and nobody can find nothing wrong with the tires. Now, the boss don't believe me no more that I have a flat every day and I think that maybe he is going to fire me. So this man and me are enemies and I know that he had something done to my car by a witch because he is that kind of a guy. So when I walked into the Barrel House Bar on Second Street and he was there I told him. So he told me a bad word about my mother so then we started to fight. And, *Juez,* I swear by my mother and the Virgin that what I say is true and that is the reason why we fight.

We tried to find the real cause behind their animosity, but both men refused to answer except to repeat that they were enemies. Later we found that their bellicosity stemmed from an infatuation both had for a waitress. The two men were asked to bring the witch to court, but both refused. Not even a contempt charge and a fine would make them reveal the witch's identity. This is not unusual; witches are seldom brought to court. People along the Border are extremely afraid of them — sometimes not without cause.

On the Border benignant witches exist as well as evil ones.

I have seen more than one instance in which some ailing person has been satisfactorily cured, and without doubt there are hundreds of other such cases. In November of 1952, through the aid of some very close friends who dabble in the occult, I was permitted to attend a *curación,* a healing session. A nine-year-old boy was to be unhexed.

The mother of the afflicted child did not at first know what was causing the suffering of her son. The boy had come home from school one day complaining of a stomach-ache and saying his head felt heavy. That night the boy went into a coma. A physician was called. The doctor, a reputable M.D., recommended that the child be sent at once to a hospital. The youth was then taken to the El Paso General Hospital, where he regained consciousness, but this happy state did not last long. The boy fell into a coma and continued to revive for short intervals. Needless to say, this caused some consternation among the attending as well as the resident physicians. The child continued in an unchanged state for several weeks, and at last it was suggested to the mother that to keep the boy in the hospital was not necessary since nothing could be done. What the medical diagnosis was I do not know as the mother had not understood the doctors. All she could tell me was that consulting a native healer or *curandera,* she had been advised that the boy was hexed. The mother had then made further inquiries and had found that her husband had a common-law wife in Juarez, Mexico. This other woman wanted the father of the boy to marry her but was unable to convince him since the man doted on his son and was unwilling to give him up. His legal wife had told the man that if he divorced her she would keep the boy. The common-law wife, seeking means of effecting a separation, had finally consulted a witch, who had in turn hexed the boy.

Everything was now ready for the healing. The boy was placed on a cot. Two women took hold of the lad's arms while another placed her hands with fingers interlocked across his forehead. A fourth then placed a hand around each of the boy's ankles and the stage was set. The *curandera* then brought out seven candles set in crystal holders and placed three of them at the head of the cot behind the woman holding the lad's head. These candles were in a line parallel with the boy's body. A candle was placed at the extremity of each arm, and two more were placed opposite the candle nearest the head. This pattern made a double cross with the boy's body lying on the beam and his arms extended along the lower crossarm. A small charcoal brazier was brought out and a fire started. The *curandera* then began to burn a handful of herbs in the brazier. She then arose and circled the boy three times, muttering words which I could not make out. Soon the boy's breath quickened; whereupon she brought out an ordinary paper sack on which a cross had been painted. The paint used was a bluish-green and radiating from the cross were several rays — five, I think. By this time I was becoming conscious of a disagreeable odor coming from somewhere in the room. Soon I perceived that the foul smell was coming from the child. The paper sack was then placed, open end down, upon the lad's face. In a matter of minutes the sack was removed and burned in the brazier. By this time the smell in the room was so bad that I thought I would faint. Luckily, however, the *curandera* ordered that the child's limbs be released and a window opened. We all kept our eyes on the child. Soon he began to moan and after a few minutes he regained consciousness, completely recovered. The boy is today as healthy as he ever was.

What the purpose of the various rites was, I have been unable to ascertain. That they had a significance, an important significance, is clear and I hope that some day I will find the answer.

1. *Navaho Witchcraft* (Cambridge, Mass., 1944; *Papers of the Peabody Museum of American Archaeology and Ethnology,* Vol. XXII, no. 2), p. 18.
2. *Ibid.,* p. 19.

EVERETT A. GILLIS

# Weather Talk from the Cap Rock

*Whether it's cold, or whether it's hot,
There's gonna be weather, whether or not.*

So THEY SAY in West Texas. And talk about weather in that portion of West Texas bordering on the rugged escarpment known as the Cap Rock is about as common as the weather itself. Passing the time of day in Lamesa, Lubbock, or Plainview usually means swapping ideas about rain prospects, growing seasons, or wind velocity.

And speaking of wind velocity, most of the talk about wind — and there is a God's plenty on the High Plains — reveals a characteristic folk wit, a tongue-in-cheek attitude. Cap Rock folk are a hardy breed, it is said, impervious to dust, drouth, dry winds, blue northers, and rambunctious critters. They have to be: between Amarillo and the North Pole there's only a barbed wire fence with a single strand . . . and that's down! That same fence persists in losing its barbs. The wind's so strong it keeps untwisting them. After a strong blow you can pick them up anywhere. They come in handy as staples. One farmer in Cochran County had a different sort of trouble with his fence. The wind kept blowing the barbs on his fence down to the corner posts; and in the spring when he should have been plowing he spent half his time just redistributing them. As in most windy parts of the country, Cap Rock communities make use of a handy device for measuring wind. They just hang up a log chain: at a forty-five degree angle, you have a fair breeze. When the chain stretches straight out and starts snapping off links, well, you can say it's beginning to blow a bit.

Such tall winds frequently blow themselves into tall tales on Cap Rock. It seems a newcomer to the Cap Rock country, in the midst of a forty-mile breeze, sought temporary shelter on the veranda of a farmhouse where an old man was sitting. "Pretty bad wind," pants the stranger, "does it blow like this much?" "Yep, you might say that it does," was the reply. "Fact is, it blows like this for weeks at a stretch. The rest of the time it blows like hell." Another newcomer, green to Cap Rock wind conditions, expressed his concern to an old-timer about the possible destructive qualities of the wind, with the question: "Do you ever have cyclones in West Texas?" The old man looked at him speculatively a moment and replied, without blinking an eye: "Can't say that we do, but the reason's plain, mighty plain: this straight wind we have out here blows so blamed hard that before a cyclone can even get started, it blows the stuffin' out of it."

West Texans are equally vocal on milder forms of weather, too. With perfect aplomb they brush aside the famous dictum commonly attributed to Mark Twain, "Everybody talks about the weather, but nobody ever does anything about it." They do! Or at least, they predict it. And this despite the familiar folk saying that only fools and newcomers predict weather in Texas. Since they are *neither*, they offer their neighbors infallible weather signs and listen to theirs. Of course, there are always a few tight-lipped philosophers who are too cagey to stick their necks out too far. Witness one old-timer. All he ever says on the subject of weather is: "I'm over sixty years old and I've noticed that this time of year we always have some kind of weather." Or another, a local citizen who remarked laconically to a stranger who was complaining of the weather: "If you don't like our weather, Mister, why just wait a minute!" One sure sign of a sandstorm, says another cautious weather prophet — the only one he knows of — is to look to see whether the sun goes down in the west. If it does — you'll have a sandstorm.

Yet predicting weather is a thriving business in the folk areas of the Cap Rock territory, if we are to judge from the multiplicity and popularity of weather signs quoted — especially with reference to rain. Many of the following may represent wishful thinking, but they are sworn by.

If the sun goes down behind a cloud on Wednesday, it will rain before Sunday night.

If it rains when the sun is shining it will rain again the next day.

If the sun goes behind a cloud bank, it will rain within three days.

If the wind blows out of the northwest for three days, it will rain.

If it rains on Easter Sunday, it will rain for the next seven Sundays.

If it rains on Monday, there will be rain three days of that week.

If it is red in the west on Sunday evening, it will rain before Wednesday.

If you hear a rain crow, there will be rain in the near future.

Some prophets take to rhyme:

> If a rooster goes to roost a-crowing,
> He'll have a wet head in the morning!

> If it thunders before seven,
> It will rain before eleven.

> If it rains Sunday before mess (dinner)
> It will rain all the week, more or less.

> Evening gray and morning red
> Will bring down rain upon your head,
> Evening red and morning gray
> Will send the traveler on his way.

Other signs are equally promising for rain:
> a terrapin crawling from low ground to high
> flies swarming on a screen or around cattle
> a hen basking and stretching in the sun
> a dry spring that begins to run
> wind out of the east for three days
> a tarantula crossing a lane or highway
> a ring around the moon (stars within the ring indicate number of days)
> a new moon with crescent tipped (water will run out)

a newly killed snake hung on a fence (the higher the snake is hung, the more rain will fall)

One elaborate way of predicting moisture is to set up a rain calendar, which is done in the following manner: on New Year's Eve a large onion is cut into quarters and the small cups of onion slices are removed without destroying the skin inside each cup. Twelve of these, to represent the months of the year, are set around the edge of a container and the starting cup indicated as the month of January. An equal teaspoon of table salt is poured into each onion cup. Next morning the cups will indicate by their individual condition dry months, little-moisture months, and ample-rainfall months for the whole year.

Drouth, bad weather, snow, hail, and frost are equally predictable if the right signs are known: a ring around the moon, a coyote howling between sundown and dark, a "sun-dog" in the west all indicate bad weather; a bushed-up horsetail, an electric storm; a whirlwind, a new moon seen during the afternoon, or lightning in the north mean dry weather; cattle bunched together against a fence, cold weather. Running horses indicate an approaching storm. Sheet lightning is usually a sign of wind. Cattle will run and play and sniff the air when a norther is coming. Thunder in February assures a frost or a freeze in April. When smoke settles to the ground, it is a sign of falling weather. A hard winter may be predicted by certain natural facts: a thicker bark on the north side of a tree; thick shucks on corn, thicker fur on the coyote. One of the best natural weather prophets of all for weather business is the mesquite. A big crop of mesquite tree beans is a sure indication of a coming dry year. If the winter is going to be hard, its bark will be thick in the fall. And when it leafs out in the spring, you can know that winter is definitely over. This last is an infallible sign.

Of course, all these weather signs may be thrown out the window if you realize that the weather for an entire year may be predicted simply by observing the climate during the first twelve days of January. But you must be sure to note accurately the amount and direction of the wind, the temperature, and the time of day that changes occur if you expect your foresight to be accurate.

Invariably on the Cap Rock, whether about wind, sandstorms,

or rain, weather talk is seasoned with folk wit and the salty tongue. The folk like their weather with a little humor. "We had a fourteen inch rain today," says one weather reporter — "fourteen inches between drops." "The fall of temperature in the Panhandle," says another, "is as fast as a Texas ranger reaching for his gun." And there is the old catch phrase: "Never make any kind of a trip without taking an umbrella, a fan, a slicker, and an overcoat." But the one that most vividly divides folk wisdom about weather and folk laughter is the following:

Rain early in the morning is like an old woman's dance — it won't last long!

ELTON R. MILES

# The Devil in the Big Bend

IN THE FOLKLORE of Western civilization probably no single figure is better known or more generally accepted than the devil. In the Anglo-American tradition he early became a comic character, though something of his terrifying nature survives in place names such as the Devil's Elbow for a sharp bend in a rushing river, the Devil's Sinkhole for a deep cavern, or the Devil's Kitchen for steaming, bubbling mud springs. Names like these are common in America, particularly in the Spanish Southwest. A glance at the map of Texas from Del Rio to El Paso shows a Devil's River with a Devil's Lake, a Devil's Backbone, a Devil's Ridge, a Sierra Diablo, a Diablo Plateau, and a Cerro Diablo. The devil is taken seriously by the Border Mexicans, who sometimes think of him as actually present in the neighborhood of places bearing his name. About halfway between Del Rio and El Paso, where the Rio Conchos joins the Rio Grande, the people of the Border tell and believe a strongly localized legend about the doings of the devil.

The story begins over 350 years ago, when the padres came with the Spanish adventurers up to the old Chihuahua Trail to La Junta, devotedly bearing their holy crosses on foot in advance of the procession of mounted explorers and iron-helmeted soldiers. La Junta, or the junction, was the settlement now known as Ojinaga and Presidio, where the Conchos River flows out of the Mexico desert to join the winding Rio Grande in the western edge of the Big Bend. The padres found there thousands of simple, agricultural Indians living in earthen houses and irrigating their corn and beans on the banks of the two rivers. By using simple diversion ditches or by simply working the subirrigated bottoms, where the river waters seep under the banks to feed the stalks of corn at the roots, these primitive Indians coaxed their living from the sandy soil.

205

Though the Rio Grande is now an international boundary with a separate nationality represented on either shore, the Rio Grande now has, as it did then, a single basic culture on either side. This culture has its roots in the river; its speech and folk heritage are Spanish; its ultimate origin is Indian. To this day the binational community of Ojinaga and Presidio are one, because the reason for the existence of the two towns is that the Conchos there adds its waters to the Rio Grande and helps to form a green oasis in a great wasteland.

It is said that at La Junta there was a *cura,* or pastor, left behind with a small church to administer to the souls of the Indians. This priest is commonly identified as *Cura Urbán,* though sometimes he is called Gómez, Pedro, or Urbano. This *cura* was confronted with one of the most difficult problems a man ever faced, for his parish was overrun with evil-doing touched off by the devil himself. To his horror he came to learn that the dwelling place of his Satanic eminence was a cave, high on the face of the north cliff of a jagged limestone mountain not five miles south of the building in which he preached. From his cave on the cliff the devil surveyed the entire valley, up and down the two rivers and across to the distant Chinati Mountains.

The devil even made personal appearances to terrorize the people and to destroy the crops and irrigation ditches. Sometimes he would leap from the depths of the mountain to the mouth of his cave with a gigantic lariat in his hand. He would twirl and arch his loop across the dry valley of cactus and scrubby creosote for twenty-five miles to Chinati Peak, and pull it tight. Up and down this rope the devil would dance, prance, and grimace at the horrified Indians, simple farmers working their land for a meager living for their families. As terrifying as his hellish rope dances were his occasional gallops up and down the valley bouncing a great, pear-shaped iron ball, smashing and destroying everything and everybody that came in his path. And with his fiery breath he would wither the crops, stop the rain, and dry up the rivers which were essential to life.

Worse still, he corrupted the morals of the community or caused bodily injury and death. He would creep down the mountain at night, an evil figure dressed in black, to whisper evil suggestions into the ears and hearts of Cura Urbán's parishioners. It was Satan who was responsible for the terrible wave of infidelity in the family and home, the rebellion of children against their parents, and the rash of open murder that seemed to be the rule on the three shores at La Junta.

One evening he came into La Junta seeking a night's diversion. That same evening, in defiance of her parents who ordered her to stay at home, a young and beautiful *señorita* stole out of her little adobe house in a grove of willows and cottonwoods near the river, slipped through the field of sheltering corn, and joined the dancers at a neighbor's house, where the candlelight was shining and the guitars were strumming.

There was an unusual, foreboding atmosphere at the dance. While the dancing, drinking, and noisemaking went on, a most unusual guest was present, a handsome stranger in black who seemed to preside over the entertainment. With horror freezing her soul, the young woman saw the man in black approaching her, walking not on human legs, but strutting on scaly, spurred legs like those of a rooster. She knew immediately that this strange, half-human suitor was the devil himself.

The devil courteously offered his arm, and in defiance of her family and church and in fear of her strange partner, she madly whirled with him among the fearful young dancers to the lively thumping guitars. As the candles dripped low at the approach of morning, the dance was over and the horrified guests saw the beautiful *señorita*, her head defiantly high, leaving with her hand upon the arm of her demon lover, who stalked beside her out the door on his taloned feet.

Anxiously, the people in the valley of La Junta waited for dawn. In tears, the girl's parents set out at sunrise to find their missing daughter. In a dry irrigation ditch, splashed with blood in the dust, they found her mangled body, clawed and scratched from face to foot by the talons of her satanic partner.

Thus, Cura Urbán found his parish, sunk in sin, desperate with ruined crops in the fields, and terrorized with fear of pain and death. Only one step forward had been made. With a few loyal parishioners, Urbán had directed the sawing out and nailing together of a wooden cross, and he had dedicated that cross to the task of driving the devil from La Junta. If there is any charm that will drive away an evil spirit, it is a cross.

Despondent at his empty church, Cura Urbán left his little room one day and went for a walk southeast of town toward the rearing, jagged parapet of rocky mountain. The good padre strolled in deep meditation through the straggling creosote, trying to think what he might do to save his poor parishioners. At length he reached the base of the mountain, having thought of nothing that would help. He looked up the steep incline, blanketed with jagged stones, cactus, and thorns, to the deeply notched crest. Along this route he knew the devil's cave to be, overlooking the valley below. Upon pretext to himself that he needed the exercise, he began to climb, pushing on without thought toward the devil's own domain.

After about fifteen minutes of climbing over the sharp and gouging rocks and through the *lechuguilla,* growing like clumps of vicious knife blades, he was about half way to the base of the crevice. On the brink of the cliff, hundreds of feet above the valley floor, he became suddenly aware of a dark stranger dressed entirely in black, leering at him with dagger-point eyes.

"Where are you going, Cura Urbán?" asked the stranger. "And why do you look so melancholy?"

Desperate to confide his troubles to somebody, Cura Urbán said, "I am Cura Urbán, placed here at La Junta to administer to these wilful people. I am in deep despair because they drink, gamble, philander, steal, and break God's law in every way they can think of. To make it worse, the devil himself seems to be at work in the fields and hearts of La Junta to destroy my feeble attempts to redeem these poor Indians."

Seeming to sympathize, the dark stranger recounted episodes of infidelity, murder, and robbery, naming names and giving details. To the good padre, this talk began to sound curious, for the stranger was telling things of which only Cura Urbán could know, as they had been revealed to him in the strictest confidence of confession.

Suspiciously, the padre inquired, "Who are you?" He was gripped with horror at the stranger's reply.

"I am the devil. In heaven I was not satisfied with my low rank, so I tried to grab the reins of power from God. I was soundly defeated and was bodily thrown out of heaven with my rebellious companions.

"As I fell through the sky toward the planet earth, I knew I was an exile forever from the heavens, so I tried to think of a place where I should like to live. As the approaching mountains and valleys of the earth came more clearly into view, I could see far below my feet a tall and pointed peak, which I named 'La Mitra.' When I landed on top of the peak, I saw a most beautiful valley lying below. I knew I could not be happy here for in its beauty it would be too sharp a reminder of the heaven to which I can never return.

"So I spread my wings and took flight once more, heading south. When I found this desolate and tortuous mountain, I took my abode here in this cave overlooking the valley, and here I have lived ever since. My mission is to corrupt the hearts of men and women alike, and to sow wickedness wherever I can. When night falls, I take advantage of the dark shadows, go into the town and the houses and whisper into the ears and hearts of your parishioners and advise them to do wrong, and not to pay any attention to you, Cura Urbán."

With a leer, the devil concluded, "I am succeeding in your town, Cura Urbán, for I can see it in the way you cast your eyes in melancholy to the ground."

The padre lifted his eyes quickly. Rage and fury suddenly burst in his soul. Without a word, he leaped upon the devil with flying fists. Taken by surprise and in sudden pain, the howling devil sought escape by leaping up to his rope stretched between the mountain tops and across the valley. Holding before him the wooden cross his faithful few had made, the priest advanced upon the devil. The white magic worked, the cable broke, and the devil fell screaming to the valley floor. Not yet vanquished, the devil scrambled up the mountain, broke off great chunks from the crags and cliffs, and hurled them at Cura Urbán, who was safe behind the holy cross. As a last resort, Satan attacked with his great iron ball, bouncing it about upon the shaking earth to crush the brave padre under its tremendous force. Somehow, Urbán stretched the end of the broken rope from the cave to the valley floor. When he staunchly advanced again with his cross, the devil dropped the ball with a howl and disappeared up the rope, across the valley, and into his cavern on the face of the mountain cliff.

From the dark safety of the depths within the mountain, Satan continued to yell and wail with alarm and spite. To complete the holy spell, Cura Urbán scrambled up the mountain and rammed the cross into the rocky ground near the mouth of the cave, so that the devil might be forever sealed away for the safety of the people and the land at La Junta.

Wearily, the victorious Cura Urbán trudged back down the steep incline; but his work was not yet done. He quickly gathered the few faithful ones in his parish and warned them, "Though I have whipped the devil and have driven him into his cave, we must make sure that he always remains there."

The grateful and willing parishioners closely followed Cura Urbán's directions. They followed their leader up the rocky mountainside, and on the pinnacle above the cave they took up the rocks on the hillside and piled them up without mortar to build a stone shrine, about ten by fourteen feet, with an entrance opening upon the valley. From the valley they brought up four-inch cottonwood logs for rafters and willow sticks to lay across the rafters as a support for the white earthen roof. Then, after levelling the floor by filling in white limestone flour, they placed the cross in the rear of the shrine, that it might stand forever as a charm to keep the devil in his cave directly under the foot of the shrine. The mountain was then named *El Cerrito de la Santa Cruz*, the little hill of the holy cross, and the cave is known to this day as La Cueva del Diablo.

Even yet, however, they were not through. To make sure that La Junta would be safe from the evil one, the good padre and his followers built a long and sturdy fence across the valley between mountains to keep the destructive spirit away from the settlement.[2]

Peace and religious devotion now reigned at La Junta on the three banks formed by the Rio Grande and the Conchos. The people confessed their sins, gave themselves to Christ, and did penance at the shrine on El Cerrito de la Santa Cruz. Sin and misconduct almost entirely disappeared and the people came to church regularly, even though they might have only a long shirt to cover themselves in the Lord's house.

The victory of Cura Urbán over the devil was so greatly appreciated that an annual ritual grew from it. Once a year on the third of May, Holy Cross Day, the holy cross used to be taken from the shrine of "The Devil's Grotto," as it is sometimes called, and brought into the valley to bless the crops on all sides of the rivers where the devil had once laid them waste.

But while the cross was removed from the mouth of the devil's prison, other measures were taken to see that the evil one did not escape to resume his terrible habits. A day or two before Holy Cross Day the men and boys gathered brush and firewood, grubbed creosote roots, and then brought the fuel on their backs and on burros and built bonfires along the trail to the mountain cave. When the brush piles were ready, lined from the mouth of the cave down the steep path, across the valley of young crops to the river, the priest went up the trail, making the sign of the cross and sprinkling holy water on the brush piles and consecrating them to their holy magic of keeping down the devil. On the night before Holy Cross Day the fires were lighted, and to strengthen the spell, the people about the cave would fire their guns, beat on tin pans, yell, and make a great riot to frighten the devil so that he would not dare make an appearance above ground. Sometimes the brush would be placed so that the fire would take the form of a great burning cross on the rearing slope.

On Holy Cross Day a procession of devotees removed the cross from the shrine, brought it down the rugged trail to the valley floor, where the priest, followed by the procession, carried the cross about the fields blessing the crops and praying for a fruitful yield of cotton, corn, beans, and melons and for plenty of water in the river. At the end of the day, the procession filed back up the mountain, and restored the cross to the shrine, where it continued to serve as a charm against evil.

In the town, while the fires were burning at night, women and young people used to walk in groups about the street, singing in high nasal tones songs in which one could distinguish the phrases *"el diablo"* and *"la Santa Cruz."*

A milder form of this annual celebration is now current, and there are now three crosses in the chapel instead of only one. Not in several years have the fires burned for Holy Cross Day, but each May 3 the crosses are removed from the chapel by devotees at four in the morning and carried down the mountain and across the field to the house of a Señora Samaniego. The crosses are kept there until May 17, upon which day they are restored to the shrine. As for the fires, they are still burned on Hallowe'en to forestall a witches' orgy in the region of La Cueva del Diablo.

The shrine serves the year round as a place of worship, as in many another Southwestern community with a mountain shrine nearby. In earlier times, penitents used to walk barefoot up the mountain to atone for sin. Several elderly residents of Ojinaga and Presidio have made sure of their atonement by walking with bleeding feet through thorns and cactus to the cross to pray for forgiveness. A woman in Alpine proudly says, "My grandmother is one who left blood upon the mountain." Twenty-eight years ago an observer noticed spots of blood all along the trail as he climbed to the shrine. Today, there is no such evidence; instead, worshipers dressed in their Sunday finest climb the mountain to pray and to enjoy a holiday outing.

The little stone shrine, ten by fourteen, still stands and still shelters the wooden cross, now neatly covered with green cloth, presumably the same one used by Cura Urbán in the past to drive the devil from La Junta. The green cross extends about six feet from floor to ceiling, and is adorned with a white veil and a necklace of paper flowers. On each side stand two smaller wooden crosses, adorned also with veils. All three crosses are decorated with sacrifices and emblems which people have left — mirrors, necklaces, rosaries, paper flowers, and letters scrawled to patron saints. Other letters hang from the rafters, their dates showing the shrine to have been in constant use. Twenty-eight years ago boxes with burning candles set in bottles were placed before one cross. The candles now burn in tumblers, where they are less likely to be put out by strong mountain-top winds blowing through the entrance. Each devotee was once obligated to bring at least one candle so that there would always be candles in the chapel. Nowadays, an old broom stands in a corner, so that a visitor may sweep out the orange peels or candy wrappers left by a less tidy predecessor. On the south wall, opposite the door, a bench is formed by a six-by-six timber about five feet long laid across two stones, as a cool and quiet place for rest and meditation.

Though the devil is now imprisoned in his cave with its entrance dynamited, he still appears occasionally — they say — in the shape of strangely malformed animals. Once a group of playing children saw a burro without a tail. When they called to their parents to look at the funny burro, the animal disappeared into thin air. Sometimes a jack rabbit is seen dancing upon his hind legs, as Satan used to dance upon his rope. Once an old woman, more curious than cautious, observed that this dancing rabbit had no forepaws. When she reached out to take the strange animal, it disappeared, causing her to stick a painful *lechuguilla* thorn into her hand. Sometimes the devil appears as a sow with the face of a beautiful woman followed by little pigs, all of which have the same face. In the form of the siren sow especially, he falls in behind those who have drunk too much *tequila* as they cross a dry river bed. The sow and her pigs follow and make the poor drunkard fight, break windows, and do evil things he would not otherwise have done.

At least twice the devil slipped through, in grotesque human form, the barriers erected by prayer, burning fires, and charms, and one of these occasions was on Holy Cross Day itself. Once on May 3 he assumed the form of an impish little hunchback and fell in with the procession trailing behind the good priest as he went from field to field blessing the crops. As the priest chanted and the people tried to act sober and devout, the little hunchback devil created havoc, leading ladies into mud puddles, making dogs howl, pushing men and boys into the river, and breaking people's garters. It was a mad Holy Cross Day.

On another occasion — and many Big Bend families carry this tradition to this good day as a terrifying experience of their grandmothers — a group of little girls were playing grown-up in the dusty streets of Ojinaga. Under the beaming sun they dressed in their mothers' old hoop skirts and danced in a ring they formed by joining hands and sang an evil song about the effects of marijuana. They should have known better, for the utterance of evil words surely brings on evil itself. They sang of how marijuana makes the smoker lurch in his walk and makes him talk funny and makes his eyes wobble in a peculiar way. Suddenly, as if springing from the ground in the center of the ring, there appeared a terrible, toothless old hag, clothed in dirty flowing rags of black, her fiery eyes flashing crimson rays upon all about her. The children screamed, scattered, and ran — and to this day, the red eyes of the black old hag are vividly remembered.

It appears, as Mody C. Boatright has said, that this legend and ritual grew out of two principal sources: one, the Indian's elemental fear of supernatural influence over human welfare and his desire to appease that power; two, the early missionary's attempt "to phrase the message of the Church in terms which the Indian could comprehend."[3] Certainly the legend points to Spanish missionaries among naked Indians of two and three hundred years ago, who came to worship in nightshirts that they might be decently covered.

Beneath the superstructure of Catholic legend, perhaps there lies an Indian legend of far more ancient origin. Sometimes in this story the Christians' Satan assumes the role of a prank-loving evil spirit, a type not uncommon among American Indians. Satan's fall from the sky is Hebraic-Christian in origin, but many other details seem indigenous.

The legend is appropriate to the climate of the country between El Cerrito de la Santa Cruz and Chinati Peak, where the ghost town of Shafter now stands. That area, where Presidio lies, has the reputation of being the hottest in Texas,[4] while north of Shafter the cool Texas highlands begin, extending for over a hundred miles through the Green Valley region and the Davis Mountains. In the legend, it is the Mitre Peak area between Fort Davis and Alpine, which reminds the devil of heaven. When this legend had its origin, the Green Valley country was waist deep in waving green grama grass, the valleys were dotted with sparkling pocket lakes, and the spring-fed draws ran brisk with crystal water. Small wonder that the devil moved to the torrid desert that begins at the southern foot of the Chinati Range!

The story might even point to Indian attempts to explain volcanic action in the Big Bend. Satan's howling and yelling in the cave might be a primitive explanation of subterranean disturbances, attributed at first to a spirit within the mountain, later to the Chrisian devil. Volcanic eruption is suggested by the fact that Satan was believed to have hurled great chunks of mountain and rock and bounced his iron ball through the valley of La Junta. Though the limestone hill on which the Devil's Cave is located is of sedimentary origin, it is littered with volcanic particles that fell in the remote past. One may guess that ancient Indians, irrigating the valley, were suddenly beset by falling volcanic fire that slew their members and ruined their crops, and that they attributed their misfortune to an evil spirit in the mountain.

Whatever its ultimate origin, the legend persists. It is said that even the stone foundations of the international bridge at Presidio were laid one dark and moonless night by the devil himself. Also, an iron ball is on public display at Ojinaga today, in Saragosa Street,[5] purported to be the very same iron ball and the same place it was dropped by Satan upon his flight before the holy cross up his rope to his hole in El Cerrito de la Santa Cruz. And there he lies in patient waiting, looking for a chance to sneak back into the valley and work his evil again.

---

1. Informants for this paper are Ralph Sigala, Del Rio, who unearthed in Alpine a typewritten manuscript in Spanish, entitled "Un Paseo a la Montaña de la Cruz," signed by C. Bowles, Past., and dated December 10, 1925; Mrs. Ethel Nail, Mrs. Kathryn Walker, Mrs. B. F. Berkely, Mrs. Berta Lassiter, Miss Isabel Lafarelle, Miss Grace Segura, Mr. Sam García, Mr. Milton Smith, Mr. V. J. Smith, and Lillian, my wife, who learned much from Mrs. Carmen Lafarelle, all of Alpine; and Señor Jesus Rohana and Señor Nieves Samaniego, of Ojinaga, Mexico. New material has been combined with that in an essay by Mody C. Boatright, "The Devil's Grotto," *Texas and Southwestern Lore* (Texas Folklore Society Publication VI), Austin, 1927, pp. 102-6.

2. In later years a counterlegend developed to explain the superstition that the devil lives in a cave on El Cerrito de la Santa Cruz. It is said that a priest in Ojinaga, before the devil myth developed, knew of a rich cache of gold that lay hidden in the cavern. Finding two men who seemed trustworthy, the padre sent them up the mountain to bring the gold to him so that it could be spent in building a new church. The men proved unreliable, however, and skipped across the Rio Grande, gold and all, to the States. To save the rest of the gold, the priest then invented a legend to the effect that the devil lives in the cave and holds under his power that area between the shrine and the mouth of the cave. With such a belief prevalent, thieves are discouraged from entering the cave to steal the rest of the gold. So there the gold remains, an eternal temptation to Coronado's children.

3. Boatright, "The Devil's Grotto," *Texas and Southwestern Lore,* p. 106.

4. In all fairness to Presidio, it must be pointed out that it is not the hottest town in Texas. There are many towns in Texas with

recorded temperatures every year much higher than any Presidio has ever experienced. It is true, however, that this border town is the hottest in Texas on more days in the year than is any other town. This is to Presidio's credit in the winter.

5. Another legend says that this iron ball was a prized possession of Malinchi, the mistress and guide of Cortez, the conquistador. The ball is cast iron and the lower side tapers and extends into a shaft that is buried in the ground. It is said that it is humanly impossible to dig it out; it has been tried. A good guess by Mr. V. J. Smith as to the nature of this object is that it probably is a pestle formerly used in the Shafter works to crush the ore for the smelters.

PEGGY HENDRICKS

# Wham, Jam, Jenny-Mo-Wham

ONCE UPON A TIME there were a little boy and girl whose grandmother was called a witch. People said this old witch had a magic ball that she used in hunting children. The little boy and his sister wondered if these scary tales could be true. They were so curious to find out what their grandmother was like that they begged their mother to let them go visit her. When the mother heard that the children wanted to spend the night with the old grandmother, she became worried and told them, "No, my dear children, you cannot go, because no child has ever returned that spent the night there."

When the little boy and girl began to cry, the mother finally consented to let them go if they would be very careful. Before they left, the mother kissed them good-bye; and the boy told his mother not to worry. He said that he would put his twelve dogs in their pen and that, if something happened to him and his sister, he would give his special whistle that only the dogs could hear. He told his mother that if they barked for a long time she should let them out to come to the rescue.

It was about two in the afternoon when they started out for their grandmother's house, and before long they saw her working in her yard. When she saw the children, she clapped her hands together and seemed very pleased to see them. She asked them to come inside and see her own two small children. Together they went inside

*This story used to be told me by my great-aunt, Mrs. Betty Shamburger Atwood of Tyler, Texas, who says she heard it sixty years ago from Hattie, the family's nurse and cook. About Hattie, Mrs. Atwood writes, "She died a few years ago. I think she had Indian blood mixed with Negro. Her mother did. But where did she hear those stories? Were they her own and if they were, how wonderful!"*

and met the other children, a boy and a girl about the same age and size as they were. The little boy and girl thought their grandmother's children were somehow strange and queer.

A while later the little boy saw his grandmother behind the house sharpening a knife she had taken out of her belt. He walked up to the grindstone, and the grandmother let him turn the handle for her while she sharpened the knife.

"What are you going to do with this knife?" asked the little boy.

She answered, "I am going to kill a wild hog."

Then she built a large fire beneath an iron kettle and filled it with water. Soon the water was boiling and boiling. By this time the sun had set, and the old lady told the children to eat the corn pone on the table and go upstairs and get ready for bed. She followed them and showed them which pallet to sleep on. To her own children she gave a dark sheet, and to the little boy and girl she gave a white sheet to cover with. Pretty soon her children were asleep and the little girl finally dozed off, too; but the little boy was afraid to go to sleep.

The old witch told him to go to sleep, but he replied, "No, Grandmother, when I am at home and cannot sleep, my mother gives me a harp to play."

Down the stairs she went and returned with a harp which he played and played. Again the old witch told him to go to sleep; but he said, "No, Grandmother, my mother gives me a fiddle to play when I'm not sleepy."

So she got a fiddle and brought it to him. Then she sat down on the stairway and waited with her long knife hidden under her apron. At last the little boy could hear her snoring and knew she was asleep. Quietly he awoke his sister. Then he spread the white sheet that the witch had put on them over the other children, who were still asleep. The boy and his sister tiptoed toward home. Pretty soon the witch woke up and went to the white sheet and killed the children. When she lighted the candle, she found she had killed her own children and was very angry.

Immediately she went to the closet and got down her round glass ball. She flew out the door and down to the road. She rolled the magic ball down one road, and soon it came back, so she knew they had not gone that way. Next, she rolled it down another road. When the ball did not return, she knew that this was the direction the children had taken. The children heard the rumble of the magic ball and figured the witch was coming, so they climbed a catalpa tree. At the top the boy gave his whistle for his dogs. Back in the pen the dogs heard the whistle and began to bark and bark until the mother came and turned them out.

Soon the witch came with her ax and began chopping down the tree. While she chopped, she sang out, "Wham, Jam, Jenny-Mo-Wham," in a loud voice.

And every time she sang this the little boy would say, "Catalpa, catalpa, grow big at the bottom, little at the top."

Every time a chip fell out, another one grew back. But the witch kept on chopping and singing, "Wham, Jam, Jenny-Mo-Wham!" It wasn't long before the twelve dogs came running toward the witch. They yelped and jumped and tried to bite her, but her long knife killed all except one last dog. He jumped at her throat and sank his teeth in and killed her. After the witch was dead, the children came down and cut out the witch's heart and rubbed it on the noses of the dead dogs, and they all came back to life.

# Richard's Tales

RECORDED BY JOHN LANG SINCLAIR
TRANSCRIBED BY STELLA A. SINCLAIR

## Mr. Rabbit in Partners

ONCT UPON A TIME they was a bear, a fox, a rabbit and a coon and a wolf. They all got together one time and they decided to buy 'em a large—buy 'em a big piece of land. So they went ahead and they bought the land and then after they bought it then they seed that it needed claring up; course they couldn't get anybody to clare it up for 'em; they tried and tried to get grubbers to grub it up, but they couldn't get anybody; and so they wanted to get it ready so they could cultivate it, plant it; and so they said one day to each one another, they said, "Well, the only way that we can do this, I reckon — get that land all fixed and ready in time is for us to do it ourself." So they said, "Well I reckon so, can't get anybody to do it for us."

So they went to work then, bought up a whole lot of groceries and things like that; got 'em over to they homes, and they set the morning when they all would staat to work; and so the morning come when they, they went ahead then before they left the house and made 'em a big fire and put on a great big pot of peas and got 'em staated to cooking in order for the peas to be done at dinner time so they could all go home then and have they dinner and rest awhile and then they would come back to they work and so they did; they got the peas started; they all walked on out then — Mr. Rabbit, Mr. Fox, Mr. Wolf and Mr. Bear, they all came on down to the field walking and talking. When they got down there they all staated to work grubbing, and cutting, talking and everything and they worked good for a good while; and 'long after while why Mr. Rabbit hollered, "Hey!" Someone say, "What's the matter with you, Mr. Rabbit; you gone crazy?"

"No; I jest thought I heard my wife hollering a while ago."

"Oh, man, go on to work; they ain't nobody a-calling you; what you hollering about?"

"Well, all right." And Mr. Rabbit went ahead then and they all worked and worked and worked and worked. Drectly Mr. Rabbit hollered, "Ho!"

Say, "Now, Mr. Rabbit," say, "what's the matter?"

Says, "Man, my wife called me." Say, "That woman jest worries me to death"; say, "I guess I better run on up and see what is the trouble with her."

So he struck out then, runned very fast and he got to the house and why he run right on in to the kitchen whar the peas was a-cooking at. And he seen the peas was a-getting along pretty good and he got him some and staated to eat. So he eat all the peas he wanted; and he got all he wanted; then he come on back then walking along and got down there and —.

Said, "Mr. Rabbit, you got back!"

"Oh, yeah, I got back."

"Well, what was wrong? What was matter with your wife?"

"Oh, man I got prettiest newborn baby up there you've ever seen in your life. My wife jest hollering for me to come up there and name it."

"Did you name it?"

"Oh, yeah, I name it."

"What did you name it?"

"I've-Jest-Begun!"

And he went ahead then and he worked and worked a while and went ahead going on with his work and went, "A-HEY!"

"Mr. Rabbit, now you'se crazy; now what's the matter with you? Why don't you cut that out, go to work?"

"Well, I thought I heard my wife calling me; well, I ain't going to pay no attention to her this time; jest let her holler."

And so he went ahead and worked, you know, and worked awhile.

Drectly, "HEY!" again.

"Mr. Rabbit is you crazy? What's the matter with you? You ain't heerd nobody calling you?"

"Oh, yes, they is." Says, "My wife called me again." Says, "That woman run me wild; I better go on up there again." Say, "I'm going to go this time, but I sure ain't going no more; I tell you that."

He went on up there and run right in to the pot of peas, staat eating; got there, you know, and eat and eat— eat all he wanted and he turn around and he come on back; got back down to the boys whar they was working.

Say, "Mr. Rabbit, what was the trouble this time?"

"Well, my wife had another pretty little old baby there and she wanted me to name it."

"Well, did you name it?"

"Sure, I named it this time."

"What did you name it this time?"

"Half-Gone."

He went on to work then; he worked and worked a while and they talked, you know, and laughed and having fun working.

Drectly Mr. Rabbit hollered out again, "Ho!"

"Oh, Mr. Rabbit, what do you keep on acting that-a-way for? Why don't you cut that out and go to work? We don't hear nobody holler."

Say, "My wife, well, I know my wife called me again; man, she calling and worrying me; I said I wasn't going no more, but I'm going this time; I know I ain't going no more this time." Say, "Next time she call I jest ain't going."

He pulled out then and he went on; got up there he went right straight on to the kitchen then; he went to the pot of peas see how it was getting on; course peas was getting on further about being cooked done; he staat to eat; he eat and eat and eat; he jest cleaned 'em all up. Jest scraped them all out; didn't leave any. Got through when he come on back, then walking very slowly, he was tired and didn't move much. Got down there.

"Oh, my wife had another little old pretty baby over there;
    Say, "Mr. Rabbit, how'd you get along this time? What was wrong?"

she jest can't name none of those babies; she has to have me name every one of them. I don't know why she can't name a baby."

"Well, did you name it?"

"Yes, I named it."

"What did you name it this time?"

"Well, I named it Scrap-Bottom."

So they went ahead then and they worked and worked and worked; dinner time, close to dinner time then. And worked on a while and so dinner time come; so they begun to get hungry, and they felt like eating something. They talked all the morning about that pot of peas they had and how they was going to eat those peas and they was going to lay off and get the peas and rest a while after they got full from nice peas. So they decided, "Well, we better go on and eat then and come back after a while after we rest a while." So they pulled out then, and went on up there, got up there and they all reshed right on into the pot of peas see how the peas was getting along. When they got there they looked and all the peas was gone. No peas, no nothing. Everything's gone. Well, they all looked upon another, say, "Well, what's wrong? What's become of the peas? Why, somebody's been here and eat up all the peas."

Well, it come up on.

Say, "Why, Mr. Bear, you, what about it, you been here?"

"No, man, you know we've all been down there working."

"Mr. Rabbit, you know anything about this?"

"No, I don't know a thing about this."

"Well, now, you been to the house, two three times now, and you bound to know."

"No; I don't know a thing about it; I don't know nothing about 'em. I ain't had time to fool with no peas this morning. I had to tend to my wife, name the babies and everything; I ain't even been around the pot."

"Well, now, Mr. Rabbit, somebody knows something about this."

So then they all got together.

"Well, now something's got to be done about — now what we going to do about it — all this?"

Then they all got together and then they decided on what they was going to do. Say, "Well, I tell you, the way we'll do now will be to dig a great big old deep pit and we'll put bresh and logs in the bottom of it and we'll dig it so wide and each one of us will run and jump it; and the one that falls in it, that's the one that eat the peas up; and them that jumps it clare, course, they all right; they won't have to be responsible for it."

So they dug the pit; spent the rest of the day, I guess, digging the pit jest like they want it. And then when they got it all fixed why then they said, "Well, who's going to be the first one to jump?"

Well, Mr. Rabbit, he decided he want to jump first. So Mr. Rabbit backed off a good ways and come a-taring as hard as he could chase. He made his jump so fur over it why he jumped 'bout five or six foot further than the width of the ditch was in the clare. And next to come, Mr. Wolf. He jumped. Next come Mr. Fox, he jumped over. Next come Mr. Coon; he went over. Poor Mr. Bear, he come along jest a-toddling. He went to jump and he got about half way and away he went down in it.

And said, "Oh, yes." Mr. Rabbit said, "I told you I didn't eat those peas. You see Mr. Bear eat those peas up."

So Mr. Bear, he was burned up as a punishment for eating all the peas.

### Mr. Rabbit in the Pea Patch

Onct upon a time they was a wolf an' a rabbit and they decided they would go in partners and plant 'em a pea patch. And everybody knows that a rabbit really loves peas, of course, and so they worked at it then and they got the land ready and they bought the seed for the peas they were planting and everything, and then they went ahead and oh the peas come up pretty; they got a good staat; the peas and everything like that; and of course, after the peas come up, then cultivating time, why then they went to work and they cultivated the peas and they got 'em to growing and it rained 'pon 'em and everything, and oh the peas jest growed right on out fine.

Well, ole rabbit and ole wolf went by one day and looked at the peas after they become growing size, and they staated putting on their blooms and everything nice, and oh they just look good, wonderful. Well, the ole wolf said to the rabbit, says, "Well, now, Mr. Rabbit," says, "ain't going to be long now and we going to have lots of peas to eat."

Mr. Rabbit say, "Oh, yes, sure man, we going to have all kinds of peas out here. We're going to have dried peas, we're going to have snap peas; we're jest going to have everything that we want. We're jest going to live good."

Ole wolf say, "Sure, Mr. Rabbit, that's right; that's jest the way we oughta feel now; we have a cut it ease[?]." Ole rabbit said, "Yes, sir." And it wasn't too long till the peas staated, then got, got in eating size. And the old rabbit he staated slipping down then taking them — eating off the peas; he eat so many of 'em until it jest become as a general destruction, jest look like they wasn't going to be any peas left. And so Mr. Wolf would go down there and he looked at the peas, and the peas was jest disappearing so fast that he couldn't tell what was going on. Tied 'em up. Eat some more. So he went back.

Say, "Mr. Rabbit, you been down to the pea patch today?"

Say, "No, I haven't been down there because I haven't had much time."

Say, "Well, Mr. Rabbit, they's something wrong with those peas; you oughta go down there and look at 'em."

"Well, I'll go down there and look at 'em some time."

Say, "I'm jest telling you now that something has to be done about those peas."

Mr. Rabbit wasn't very much interested in 'em anyway; he didn't go to see about it. And after while Mr. Wolf went back again; every time Mr. Wolf would go back, peas would look worse; something was gone with 'em all the time.

Got back to Mr. Rabbit, "Mr. Rabbit, is you been over there since I seen you?"

Say, "No, I haven't been over there; yeah, I'll go over there and look at it."

"Now, Mr. Rabbit, they's jest something oughta be done 'bout those peas."

Mr. Rabbit wouldn't be interested 'bout 'em and ever time Mr.

Wolf explains something to him 'bout 'em, why he didn't know nothing 'bout it and he didn't have time to fool with 'im, or nothing like that.

So Mr. Wolf said, "Now, Mr. Rabbit, you won't do nothing 'bout those peas; now I'm going to put something in there; doggone it, I ain't going jest lose all the peas; I worked so hard to———."

"Doggone it, if Mr. Rabbit won't do nothin' 'bout it; he won't get interested 'bout it or nothing."

So Mr. Wolf went to work then and brought him out a good big old tar baby and he put the tar baby out in there, you know, and fixed it some kind of way, I don't know how; he fixed it so —. And so the first day that he put it in there in the evening that night Mr. Rabbit decide to get him a big ole mess of peas; so Mr. Rabbit went on down to the pea patch; got right on the row whar the tar baby was exactly —. And walking on down there, I suppose kinda singin' as he went along, knowed what kind of a mess — what kinda of a dinner he was going to have the next day — good old pea dinner. And he walked along, directly he run upon this here tar baby sitting in the road and he was very much surprised; course he didn't know what it was. Looked at him; went up close to it.

Say, "Heh! what are you doing here?" And the tar baby didn't say nothing.

"Heh, you!" And the tar baby didn't say anything.

"What's your name?" And the tar baby didn't say a word.

"Why, can't you talk?" Didn't say a thing.

Say, "Now I know one thing; you better talk; if you don't, now by the goodness, I'm going to jest shore give you a sock." Tar baby didn't say nothing.

"Well, talk! You better talk quick. Or I'll shore give you a sock now." Didn't say nothing.

He hauled off, boy, and he really socked the tar baby with the right hand; jest as hard as he could ram it there; he jest socked it; tar baby jest sit there; he was satisfied.

"Here, now do you think you done something smaat? You better turn my hand loose; I know one thing; I've got another one here; you think I ain't got another one; I got one here powerfully bad and if I give you a pop with that, by the goodness, you'll be gone under." He jest talk to him and talk to him.

Say, "Now you better turn it aloose!" He wouldn't turn it aloose and he give it a sock. But that time Mr. Rabbit *didn't* know what to do; he had both his hands; got a kind of getting a little bit worried then about that.

Mr. Rabbit says, "Hey! My goodness you better turn my hand aloose now. Think you done something smaat now. "TURN it aloose!!" He wouldn't turn it aloose.

"You think you done — I got a foot here; if you don't turn my hand aloose —. You better turn it aloose or I'm going to give you a kick and if I do why I'll go clare through you!"

Wouldn't say anything. "Ain't you going to turn me loose?" Ain't turned loose. He up and hauled off and gave him a sock with his foot — oh, gave him a powerful kick. Didn't turn it aloose and didn't say nothin'.

Mr. Rabbit began to get so worried; oh, he began to feel like —.

"Hey! turn me aloose now. TURN ME ALOOSE! You better turn me aloose, think that the last foot I got? I got another foot here; boy, it's jest, jest, jest too bad; if I kick you with this foot I'll kick you all to pieces. TURN LOOSE!" Didn't turn him aloose.

Oh, he hauled off and give it a pop jest as hard as he could kick the doggone thing.

"Oh, boy," say "you don't know nothing; I'm liable — I'm going to come over here with my head drectly and I'm going to give you a butt with that head. BOY! it's jest going to knock you out. Turn me loose now! If I butt you with this head I bet you that'll wake you up." He wouldn't turn him aloose, and oh he hauled off with his head an' give it a pop and that head stuck and all foh feet and his head stuck in. He sat up there and he studied and he said, "Oh," he said, "please turn me aloose." Say, "They's a — TURN ME LOOSE! I'll tell you." Say, "Now listen," he say, "if you turns me aloose then I never will be caught back here again." Said, "If you jest turn me aloose I won't come back no more. Turn me aloose, will you?" Say, "Now I got a date in with my girl for tomorrow night to dance and gotta be a big wedding tomorrow night and I-I-I-I gotta a date to dance with my girl; I shore don't want to disappoint her." And said, "Couldn't you turn me aloose and let me go? I-I- want to go." Said, "I jest don't want to miss that wedding tomorrow night." And the tar baby wouldn't say a word.

And there did he beg the tar baby to turn him aloose 'cause he shore didn't want to miss going to the wedding the next Sunday night because his girl was shore depending on him and he didn't want to disappoint her. Of course, he loved his girl; couldn't blame him much for that. And he begged all night long until the breaking of the day of the next morning. The ole wolf came out at dawn; of course the ole wolf was walking along — and drectly he walks up on the old tar baby and thar was Mr. Rabbit hung on to Mr. Tar Baby hard and fast; couldn't get aloose. After the ole wolf looked over and he seed Mr. Rabbit hanging to the tar baby.

"Oh, yeah! Aha! Thought you was smaat; you been getting the peas all the time, wouldn't say a word about it. Now, tried to get you interested in the destruction of the peas and you wouldn't get interested. And now I got you."

"Oh, now, Mr. Wolf, don't staat that!" Say, "You know I— I ain't been down here; first time I come down here; told you the other day I was so busy I couldn't come. I come down here to look at the peas to see what could be done about it and I got to monkeying around with this here old tar baby or whatever you got here — or what you call it — got to fooling 'round with it, see what it was and I got caught on it and I couldn't get aloose. That's how you caught me here."

"Oh, Mr. Rabbit, that ain't it; you jest been getting the peas. Why don't you jest tell the truth 'bout it?"

"Oh, now, Mr. Wolf, I ain't telling no lie."

"Well, I'm going to take you in anyway."

So Mr. Wolf cut him aloose from the tar baby; went on to the house. And Mr. Rabbit begged him all the way to the house, tried to confidence him that he wasn't getting the peas; but he couldn't do a thing with Mr. Wolf. Mr. Wolf took him on in and he put him in a some kind of a little old building, you know, pretty nice little old place he put him in. Mr. Wolf went on then about his business. Of course Mr. Wolf liked chicken and of course I guess he was raising chickens, and he went about his chicken feed and then he milked his milking cow and feeding his hogs and everything like that. So after a while he was out there feeding and doing up his work, he heard Mr. Rabbit around in the little place where he had 'im in the run-around — you could say he had him in jail for one thing. Mr. Rabbit staated singing:

"Hurrah! Hurrah! I wished I was in the pea patch,
 Hurrah! Hurrah! I wished I was in the pea patch."

Mr. Wolf say, "My goodness alive, Mr. Rabbit! I didn't know you could sing; man, you can sing good; I like that song you singing."

Of course, Mr. Wolf liked it so well because he done caught Mr. Rabbit in the pea patch.

"That sure is a nice song, man; that sounds good. Sing that song again, Mr. Rabbit."

"Oh —. I can't get no air out here; you oughta put a feller where he could get a little air out."

"Oh, Mr. Rabbit, sing it again, will you?"

Mr. Rabbit:

"Hurrah! Hurrah! I wished I was in the pea patch,
 Hurrah! Hurrah! I wisht I wuz in the pea patch."

"Oh," say, "Mr. Rabbit, I didn't know you could sing that good. My goodness alive, man!"

He came walking on around where Mr. Rabbit was then. Say, "Sing it again, Mr. Rabbit." Said, "You jest sing it another time, I won't ask you to sing it no more."

"Well, Mr. Wolf, I jest tell you this — if you want to hear me sing it good to you I think you should get a little oxygen in — open the doh a little bit; you know I ain't going out; 'spect a feller to sing in all this here tight place; no breeze, no nothing; can't get my breath good; if you put me where I can get my breath I'll sing it good for you."

Mr. Wolf was so interested over the song, knowing he had caught Mr. Rabbit he thought he was doing something pretty smaat anyway and Mr. Rabbit's song 'bout the pea patch; so he open the doh then and Mr. Rabbit kind of stuck his head out say, "Now a feller can kinda sing; get a little air now." Say, "I'll sing it for you now."

Mr. Rabbit opened up again,

"Hurrah! Hurrah! I wisht I wuz in the pea patch,

Hurrah! Hurrah! I wisht I wuz in the pea patch!"

And 'bout that time, boy, you'd oughta seen Mr. Rabbit right down the road with his little steps, right down the road.

And wide open the wolf was down the road to grab Mr. Rabbit in the front of Mr. Wolf; and I wisht you could have jest seen the dusty breeze that they did kick up all down the road; you jest couldn't see nothing. You'd looked behind 'em to see which way they went, couldn't a seen which way they wuz going on account of the —— [?] and the dust — just a regular dusty breeze.

Mr. Rabbit run down the road — he know jest exactly 'bout how he could get a ole —— [?] prickly pears and briars and he struck out at 'em; course everybody know a dog and a wolf ain't got no business in there.

After while Mr. Rabbit went right in that and, boy, did he get away from Mr. Wolf! And he went straight on in the house and he cleaned up; took him a good bath and put a fine suit of clothes on.

And, boy, he didn't say nothing to his girl that night.

## Mr. Wolf Plays Dead to Ketch Mr. Rabbit

Onct upon a time they was a wolf and a rabbit and, of course, the wolf — they was friends all right, but the wolf was more friend to the rabbit more so because he wanted to get a chance to eat the rabbit up, but the rabbit was watchable, and the rabbit thought that that was what he wanted, but he always watched Mr. Wolf and Mr. Wolf he jest tried every way he could to make friends with Mr. Rabbit so Mr. Rabbit would trust him, you know, but Mr. Rabbit never would trust him 'cause he jest always felt that that was what Mr. Wolf wanted to do to him, so he put Mr. Wolf to scheming, you know, and he wanted to scheme a way, you know, so he could get a chance to eat 'im up, but he found Mr. Rabbit was smart and Mr. Wolf couldn't even get a chance to do that. So Mr. Wolf told some of his other friends, "Now, I surely would like to get hold of Mr. Rabbit; I want to see if I can't eat him up; now I want to work out some kind of way that I can catch him." And he said, "Do you all know any way I can work out to catch Mr. Rabbit?"

They say, "No."

Say, "Well, I'll tell you what I'll do." Says, "I'm gonna, if you hep me, I might work a way out to get 'im."

And here's what he intend. Say, "Well, I'll tell you what I'll do." Say, "I'll go home and I'll go to bed and get desperately sick. I think Mr. Rabbit's a pretty good friend."

Of course, Mr. Wolf didn't know Mr. Rabbit was watching.

So say, "I'll get desperately sick and go to bed and I'll send a ronner over there to tell Mr. Rabbit that I'm in mighty bad shape and for him to come over for his suggests at."

So Mr. Wolf, he goes along and ondresses, and he goes to bed and he tells somebody to go running quick to send for Mr. Rabbit.

So they run on over there and told Mr. Rabbit Mr. Wolf was awful bad; he better come on over, because he was jest about to die.

Mr. Rabbit say, "Well, what's wrong with Mr. Wolf?"

Say, "Well, I don't know; he just got sick all at once; say for you to come; he shore wants to see you."

So Mr. Rabbit say, "Well, tell 'im, tell 'im I'll be over there; I'm so busy now, I can't go right, right away; jest tell 'im I'll be over."

So they went on back and told Mr. Wolf.

Mr. Wolf say, "Well, that's a mighty poor way for a feller to be a friend." Say, "He oughta come on over to see me; I want to see him."

So he didn't go, Mr. Rabbit; and he sent for him again.

Got over there, Mr. Rabbit say — they says to Mr. Rabbit, "Mr. Rabbit, Mr. Wolf shorely want to see you; say he ain't expecting to live; and that he's gonna shore die; say he shore want to see you before he die."

Say, "Well, tell Mr. Wolf I'll be right on over; I is certainly sorry; but I'll be over there jest as quick as I can get there. I jest, jest have to see Mr. Wolf. I feels sorry for him too."

So they goes on back and tells Mr. Wolf that Mr. Rabbit said he shore feels sorry, but he'd be right on over jest as soon as he could get over there. Sure was sorry; hoped he'd get all right.

Mr. Rabbit jest monkey around that-a-way, you know ontil the news that Mr. Wolf had made — Mr. Wolf makes another, another decision in his mind deciding on what he could do to scheme up a way to catch Mr. Rabbit. So Mr. Wolf, he seen that that wasn't going to work out so well; so he thought up another scheme then to work on Mr. Rabbit.

Say, "Well, I'll tell you what I'll do." Say, "You all run over there then and tell Mr. Rabbit that I would like for him to see the last of the body anyway." Say, "Have him to come over there jest to see the remains and tell 'im I'm dead."

So they went on over there and told him, "Well, Mr. Wolf's passed away; he's gone now and you won't see him alive any more; he's dead." Say, "You better come on." Said, "But he said in his dying minute, the last minute, as he was dying, that he should would love to have got to see you before he die, but said to tell you to be shore and come over to see the remains. Said to be shore to be over."

And so Mr. Rabbit say, "Is he dead?"

He said, "Yeah, he's gone now and said fer you to be shore and come."

Say, "Well, I'll be right on over."

Of course, they was fixing Mr. Wolf up and laid 'im out on his cooling board — dead then. That's what they told Mr. Rabbit, "I expects he'll be on his cooling board when you gets there."

Said, "I'll be right on over then."

And so, shore enough, the ronner went on back and told 'im what Mr. Rabbit said; and so they had Mr. Wolf laying out on his cooling board; he was absolutely dead. And Mr. Rabbit went on over and he was very careful 'bout the way he is when he got there. And so he walked up to the doh very quietly and he spoke to everybody and they spoke and says, "Well, I heard poor Mr. Wolf passed away."

So they said, "Well, yes, he's gone now and you didn't get to see him and he want to see you awful bad before he died; he jest sent word for you to come over and see the remainders was here."

"I'm here," he say. "I'm mighty glad to see it."
Said, "You shore he's dead?"
Said, "Well, shore he's dead."
Say, "Well," says, "now it's mighty funny; it's queer the way he's acting; he's laying too still."
"But, well, he's dead though."
Say, "Well, I went to see a lots of dead people; I've never seen nobody acts that-a-way."
Say, "Well, how do people act when you go to see 'em when they're dead?"
"Well, when I — the last dead person that I went to see when I walked in, they kicked they legs way up yonder and says, "Baaa—baaa."
And jest about that time Mr. Wolf kicked his legs out. Says, "Baaaa — baaaa."
Mr. Rabbit said, "That's the funniest ghost I ever seen; I ain't never seen a ghost yet pick up his legs and say, 'Baaa — baa!'"
And he runned home.

## Mr. Wolf Goes A-Fishing

Onct upon a time they was a wolf and a rabbit. Times got pretty porely with them. They couldn't find anything to eat. And they would go out over the country hunting fur something to eat. They jest hunted everywhere they knowed to hunt; they jest couldn't find a thing; and they studied and studied what would be the best thing for them to do to get something to eat, but they couldn't think upon nothing. They come on back home and Mr. Wolf told Mr. Rabbit, say, "Now Mr. Rabbit," said, "what can we do fur something; can't find nothing nowhere; what you reckon we should do?"

Mr. Rabbit say, "Well, I don't know what we can do; jest can't find nothing."

Mr. Wolf said, "Well, I'll tell you what I'm going to do, Mr. Rabbit." Say, "How about going a-fishing? Ketching some fish — we could do that."

Mr. Rabbit said, "Oh, I ain't a-going fishing 'tall."

Say, "Well," say, "if you ain't going," say, "I believe I'll go along." But says, "You better come on and go because get something, so we can see if we find, get us something to eat. We'll staave to death, man!"

Ole rabbit say, "No! I ain't going fishing 'tall."

"S'all right," says, "well, I'm going fishing." Said, "If I go fishing and ketch any fish," says, "I'm gonna eat 'em myself. I'm not going to give you none."

"S'all right, if you going fishing, I'll eat jest as many as you will."

And old Wolf say, "I'll be doggone if you will; you get none of my fish if I ketch any."

Old rabbit say, "All right; you go ahead on."

Say, "Well, I'm going on."

So the old wolf went on. Got all his things together, all hooks, fishing rods; he struck out to the creek; he got over there, baited his hook; threw his hook out in the water; he didn't have it out there anytime 'till a big nice fish dropped it. Take that fish out; bait his hook again; threw it out and another fish grabbed it. Jest as fas as he could get his hook baited and get it out in the water why the fish would bite and he'd ketch 'em. He had powerful good luck; jest stayed there and fished and fished; he jest caught the nicest string of fish you ever seen in your life; oh, he jest caught him a nice mess of fish. He — jest's the late of the evening come, why he thought that he'd better quit fishing 'cause—. Of course, he'd throw his hook out in the water; and the more he fish the more he wanted to fish. And so when he staated to think that he would quit and go home —.

He pulled his line up; got his little bottle of fish, struck out for home down a little trail he always traveled to the river. Got a way on the way and he come to a little mound of prickly pear stuff there, walking along thinking 'bout what a nice supper he was gonna have; he walked right up on a dead rabbit laying in the road. He said, "Gracious alive, here's a dead rabbit laying here; I wonder if that's Mr. Rabbit that I jest left at the house this evening; wonder if he's done staaved to death; I told 'im he's gonna staave to death; certainly do look like him." Said, "I oughta take him home with me; have this mess of fish and the rabbit too — it's something to eat. 'Nough to last me a good while." Said, "Well,

I'll go on and leave him anyway; I gotta get on to the house, clean my fish, cook up my supper."

So he left the rabbit lay there and he went on and soon as he got out of sight Mr. Rabbit come alive, straighten himself up and acrost the woods he went, made a circle through the brush and turned on around to the same trail where Mr. Wolf was going along. He lay down, stretch hissef out for dead. Mr. Wolf walked up on him.

"Here's another dead rabbit. Aha, the rabbits is shore dying; I know now Mr. Rabbit done staaved to death. There he lays there. Shore looks like him. Now if I had a got that other dead rabbit I seen back there, get this one and then my mess of fish I'd have enough food to last a long time. Oh, you know, I blieve I'll lay my fish down by this one and go back get that one; it wouldn't take me long. And if I do why, my goodness, I'll be success."

So he laid his nice little stack of fish down by that rabbit, went back to get the other one and soon as he staated back, why Mr. Rabbit arised and grabbed his fish and away he went. So when he got back to that other rabbit what he thought was back there, why this rabbit was gone. So he said, "Well, I'll go on back; I know I have one rabbit and a string of fish." And he went on back there whar he left his fish and that other dead rabbit and when he got back there the rabbit had done got his fish and was gone. And Mr. Wolf didn't have any fish and no rabbit either. So he jest had to go to bed hongry and he was awful disappointed.

## Bear Misses Rabbit

Onct upon a time they was a ole bear. The food got very scarce in his home and the ole bear got very hongry and he did not know what to do and then he studied and studied what he would do fur something to eat. Well, he made it up into his mind then that he could go out and hunt into the wilderness round over the woods, see what he could find.

And then he staated out; he looked and hunted, hunted, but he couldn't find anything, but still he wouldn't give up because he was hongry; but still he continued to look and then he found a little rabbit — he jumped him, a little rabbit, and he ran him and ran him and the little rabbit got very tired and still he kept a-running and the bear was very hongry and he wouldn't give up. He ran the little rabbit and ran it and so the little rabbit run until he found a down tree a-lying on the ground and the little rabbit run into the hollow of the tree and the ole bear run to the tree and looked into the hollow and he could see the little rabbit in the hollow tree. So he studied and thought of how he could get it out but he could not get the little rabbit out. He picked up the ole log and he rolled it and stomped and rolled but the little rabbit still clang therein because he was afraid; and the ole bear picked up the log and he stood it up on the end and he bounded it against the ground bam! bam! bam! but the little rabbit clang therein because he was afraid. And he throwed the ole log down to the ground and he rolled it and the little rabbit still clang therein because he was afraid. He changed end and he took the ole log and he bammed it to the ground on the other end bam! bam! bam! but the little rabbit clang therein because he was afraid. The ole bear throwed the log down and the little rabbit still clang therein. Then the ole bear had to study what he could do because he could not get the little rabbit out excepting he go home and he get his ax. Still he knew if he ran home to get his ax the little rabbit would be gone when he come back. And he did not know what to do; he would look in the log and would see the little rabbit, but he was afraid to leave it; then he made it up in his mind that he would run home right quick and come back. And he was so worried and oneasy, for he knew the little rabbit would be gone when he come back.

And he would start home jest as fast as he could go, but he would think right quick what would happen if he left; he was turning on back to the ole log because he knowed the little rabbit would be gone; an he would go back to the log and he would look up into the log; he could see the little rabbit, but he was so hongry that he could not give up the idea of not getting the little rabbit out, and he staat home again and he would get off a piece and he would get afraid, and he would run back to the log; and he kept a-doing so until he started and he come back to the log.

And then at that time Mr. Frog walked up and Mr. Bear said to Mr. Frog, "Mr. Frog, will you do me a favor?"

Mr. Frog said, "Why shore I'll do you a favor."

Said, "I've got a THING in this log and I cannot get it out. I've got to go home and get my ax to cut that THING out. Would you keep that THING in there till I go home and gotten my ax?"

Mr. Frog said, "Shore I'll keep it in there."

Mr. Bear say, "Well, if that THING staats out, all you got to do is say, 'Shush! Shush!' "

And the little rabbit heard him and onderstood every word of it. And so the bear staated then running jest as hard as he could to go home and get his ax. Time he got jest about half way home the little rabbit stuck his head out; he had heard everything Mr. Bear had said.

And the little rabbit said, "Mr. Frog, will you please sir do me a favor?"

And Mr. Frog said, "Shore I'll do you a favor."

"Would you please let me out because Mr. Bear is trying to get me out of here and if he get me out I know he will eat me up. Please let me out!"

Mr. Frog say, "Shore I'll let you out." Say, "Now don't let that THING out. Scare that THING back up there."

So Mr. Rabbit say, "Shush! Shush! Shush!"

And down the hill he went jest as hard as he could tear out, and jest 'bout the time that Mr. Rabbit got away and out of sight, up come Mr. Bear with his ax on his shoulder. And he ask Mr. Frog did the THING come out.

Mr. Frog say, "No, Mr. Bear, the THING didn't come out!"

"Well," he said, "thank you, Mr. Frog, I'll see you. You can go on to church."

Mr. Frog went on his way to a great big meeting. Mr. Frog went on then to his church meeting. Mr. Bear, he proceeded then in cutting little chips out of the log, and he cut one little chip out of the log and he looked in and he couldn't see Mr. Rabbit; slugged another chip out and look in and he couldn't see Mr. Rabbit; then all the way up and down the log he slugged out chips peeping in for Mr. Rabbit, but he couldn't see him. Then after he didn't see Mr. Rabbit he got on one end of the log with his ax and he gash down on the log and he split the log wide open into two parts, but he didn't see Mr. Rabbit; still he wasn't satisfied 'cause he was shore that Mr. Rabbit should have been inside. Then he taken one half and he slugged his ax down in that half of the log, but he couldn't see Mr. Rabbit; and he slugged his ax down into the other half of the log and he poke forward but he couldn't see Mr. Rabbit. Then he wondered what could be the trouble or where did Mr. Rabbit go, but still he couldn't be satisfied because he was hongry. He taken his ax and then he split and made chips out the ole log. Still he couldn't find Mr. Rabbit. Well, he decided he would go on over to the big meeting where Mr. Frog was; hunt Mr. Frog then; see if the THING come outa the log. He walked on over there to a big crowd of folks and said, "Have you all seen Mr. Frog here anywheres?"

Say, "Yes, he was here jest a minute ago. He was jest a-standing up here a-talking to the people, jest a little bit ago."

He walked to another crowd of folks, asked them, "Has you seen Mr. Frog round here?"

Say, "Yes, he was round here jest a little bit ago."

He could hardly find Mr. Frog in a big crowd of people. He walked to another crowd and he looked for Mr. Frog, and finally he found Mr. Frog. Walked up to Mr. Frog, say, "Mr. Frog, I want to see you a minute."

Mr. Frog say, "All right."

Say, "Mr. Frog, what come outa that log when I left? Did that THING come outa that when I left, Mr. Frog? Did *anything* come outa there?"

"Well," Mr. Frog say, "didn't nothing come outa there but a rabbit!"

Say, "Why, you fool you; that was the THING!"

### The Bear and the Baby

In the days of old where the old settlers staated to settling the country they had a very hard time settling. They had to get work wherever they could get it and they had to go a long ways from home, and the bears was bad; the wild animals was very bad. The cattle ranged just wherever they could in the wild woods. They was a family in the woods that lived into the woods, and sometimes the men of the home had to go a long ways from home to get work; they had a little baby in the home and at night the baby would cry a lot. And it usual so that a bear will take up with a baby; they likes little babies.

They would come round the homes after everyone had gone to bed to pick up the table crumbs offa the yard, and it would hear the baby cry at night, and so this ole bear, he would come regul'r every night, and the little baby wouldn't be feeling so good and it would cry a lot at night. And at last one morning the mother had to go to the springs where they got water — was a ole well and they had to dig a hole in the deep sand and the water would seep in and they could get a bucket of water for the house. So at last one morning the ole bear laid around and the mother left the house to get water and the ole bear slipped into the house and stole the baby.

And the baby was gone all day, and the father came in late that evening and the baby was not yet located. Well, they went around from home to home and they notified all the peoples they could clost to the settlement, but the settlement was very fur apart. No knowing where they could get help, so they got the people together and they started looking for the ole bear, but they could not find it. And they look and they hunt for it days and days, but they couldn't find it; and they finally give the baby up and they couldn't ever find it, but the bear kept the baby and he raised it.

He carried it down into the bear cave where bears usually stay and the bear fed it on such as it could get by with, and it did raise it and it kept the baby for years and years until it become a very large child. And so when the bear go out to hunt food, why it would roll a huge rock over the cave while the little baby could not come out. But the baby would come to the top of the cave and it would peep out through the little window hole so it could peep out to see the traffic and the cowboys which would pass by and stop, and it would hear the cowboys yelling at they cattle that was passing. In those days it was wild and lots of wild stock and baby would jest sit there, and at last it was one day the cowboys pass and running over the rock and a-herding of the cattle, and they heard a little tone of a voice which they thought it sound like human beings and it went like this, "Yoo-o-o." And so they stopped and listened, but they was in a very big rush to get round and keep the cattle in the foregoing, and the little boy would yell and try to 'tract them. And finally they stopped and they got very 'tractive, and they went round to the rocks and all round the rock caves and the bear caves and sure enough they found the little boy, but still they had to get a-plenty of help. And after they got the help they begun to roll the stone from the cave and the ole bear come after them and, boy, did they have a fight. It was nothing fur them to do but murder the ole bear so's they could get the child; but they got the child and they carried it home, but it was never like it was before when human being made.

### The Ox and the Mule

Onct upon a time there was an old brace of ox and an old brace of mule, and they was very faithful work animals on the farm and they worked and worked and worked. And so one day they got tired; it got hot on them and the old ox he's very perter anyway when he gets hot. So they got together one day and they got to talking.

And he says, "Is the old guy what drives you pretty hard when he drives you?"

Says, "Oh, yes, he drives me vary hard; how does he drive — how does they drive you?"

Say, "Oh, awful hard. Don't you get awful tired?"

Say, "I shore do get tired."

Say, "Well, spose we quit work."

"All right."

"Let's us don't work; let's don't do anything; let's jest — let's jest don't work for 'em."

Say, "Don't care how they beat us and what they do to us, how they use pitch forks on us and all."

Say, "Let's jest stand right up to it and don't work."

Say, "All right."

So they got together on that. They stood pretty pat on it. And so the last day they took 'em out to work; and they took the old mule out and hollered, "Get up there!" But he didn't want to go and he didn't go. So they rattled the chains around and give him several raps over the head and progged him on and so the old mule quit again; he didn't want to go; he wouldn't work. So they had to take him out and bring him to the house.

So they had the old ox took out and staat to work him, but he laid down on 'em; he jest wouldn't go. So they come in that day and they got together say, "What did you all do? Why what did you do?"

"Didn't do nothing; what did you do?"

"I didn't do nothing."

"Work for 'em?"

"No; I didn't work."

Say, "Well, let's don't work; we ain't gonna work."

So they took 'em out again. They beat the old mule so bad that he jest had, till he jest had to go; course a mule he pretty easy to work if you whip him enough; so they whipped the old mule right on up there and, of course, the old ox he was tired of it, why he didn't want to work; he didn't work. So his Marster said, "Well, if he didn't work, why of course I'll have to sell 'im to the butcher."

And of course the old ox he didn't want that; and so they brought him in one day and the old mule asked him, say, "Did you work?"

He said, "No, I didn't work."

Say, "Well, what'd you do?"

Said, "I jest didn't do nothing; you hear them say anything about me?"

"No, not a word; but," said, "I seen old Marster and the butcher standing down there talking a mighty long time, said, 'Shall I take the old ox back?'"

That evening the old ox work mighty good.

## Dead Colt Come to Life

Onct upon a time there was a wolf and a rabbit and the times was pretty porely and they thought that they would get out and hunt them something to eat. And they hunted everywhere they know, but couldn't find anything. And they come back home. They hunted everywhere; they hunted upon the mountains and they hunted in the valleys they hunted in the wilderness. They hunted everywhere and they couldn't find nothing. And then they decided to walk on the hillside to see could they find something up there. And so they did and they goes up there and they finds an old mare and a little colt and the little colt was laying down in the sun; it was fast asleep; it was sunning itself; and the mother was there on the hillside grazing on grass, hunting something to eat fur herself. And the rabbit and the wolf, they thought the little colt was dead, but it was not. And they 'cided to get it settled what they could do to get it home.

So the rabbit told the wolf to turn hissef around in order that they may tie his tail to the colt's tail, being his tail was short and wouldn't tie. So the wolf says, "All right!"

And then the wolf turned around and the rabbit comes up and ties his tail and he ties it in a knot so that it is impossible for it to get aloose. And jest time he got it tied real good the colt waked up; jumped up, staat to run. Rabbit go so 'cited, hollered to Mr. Wolf, "Hold! Mr. Wolf," he said, "Hold! Mr. Wolf, don't let 'im get away! Hold. Don't let him get away." And the rabbit got so 'cited he didn't know, — he didn't know what to do anyway. Kep a hollering to the wolf, "Hold! Hold!"

And the wolf replied, back to him, "How in the hell can I hold him with nary foot teching the ground?"

### Couple Gets Burned Stealing Sheep

Old Marster had an ole colored man and an ole colored lady on his plantation. He thought they was very, very honest people, good old feller, honest Negro, and he had a very good bunch of sheep. And sometimes the sheep would bear down by this old colored feller's house and on, and he told this old man and his wife to kinda watch those sheep and to take care of 'em and all and see to 'em. And so once in a while this ole man and his wife would slip out on the Marster and they would butcher one; he didn't know it. They'd take it back into the house, dress it, clean it and hide it; eat it.

So, at last one day they taken the notion that they was going to kill 'em another sheep. And the bunch of sheep was looking pretty and they were laying out white and snowy as sheep generally be. And out into the bunch of sheep where they were playing, why it was a great big pile of new-takened-out fresh ashes, white as the sheeps was laying out, and somebody had done taken a half a barrel of live coals out with the hot ashes and throw 'em out and of course there I reckon they lay all 'round them hot ashes come cool night in the winter.

And so the old gentleman he grabbed up his knife right good and said, "Well, I blieve I'll go out and butcher sheep." And everybody sound asleep; nobody around. Say, "You're up; I'm gonna catch one and I'm going to jump on 'im; look like I can't handle it, why you run up and help me."

Old lady say, "All right, I shore will."

All right, he runs out and he gets pretty clost to the batch of sheep. Some of the sheep, they got up, stirred; some they lay pretty still. And that which lay pretty still perhaps these pile of ashes; it was a big pile and it stay white as the sheep; and this old gentleman thought he'd jump on the gentlest sheep, and he jest made him a flounce and jumped on that big pile of ashes. It got all those live coals in there and then his wife got organized for her to come and help him, and she seen him kicking and he was on the pile of ashes and it was so hot he couldn't get off of it, laying over there a-kicking. And she a-running then and jumped on the sheeps with 'im to help him with the sheep, and it was a pile of ashes there and it was burning so bad she couldn't get off.

So they both lay there a-hollering and a-kicking and they waked up everybody on the place. Old Marster, his son run down; they want to know what was the trouble with 'em, what they hollering, what is they doing there. So they told 'im some of the sheep was in the fire and they was trying to get the sheep out of the fire and they got in the fire theyselves and was burning. They taken them on out; they taken them out of the fire; taken them to the house, put 'em to bed and the next day, why, they killed a sheep and give 'em one.

## Sheep-Head Dumplings

In olden days, the way the old-timers would fix they dinner, they would fix they dinner and go on to church; fix dinner kinda and come back and it would be 'bout ready. Well, in them days they killed beeves maybe under a big tree; didn't have any fancy butcher markets like they do these days; they jest butchered and if anyone wanted to buy meat, why they would jest cut them off a slug while they butchering it, kinda weight it kinda commonly; anybody want to buy a head, you know, or any part of a piece of meat, a sheep or anything, they would sell it to them for 'bout a dime, or fifteen or twenty cents, or something like that. The old-timers would boil a beef head, and that would feed a host of people; lots of meat morely on a head, moren a person think; would jest boil all the meat and then take the bone out; bone would be very near bleached; it would after it dried.

And so this lady was going off a church — a ole colored woman. They didn't have no church house, jest a arbor — a brush arbor — white people had it also; had good service — better'n they do now. They had the brush arbor and then this woman cooked the head — put it on early that morning and jest before she went to church she dropped the dumplings in there, and tole the girl after she come back from Sunny school, tole her, "Now you take care of this; don't let it burn or boil over. When it cook so long take it offa the stove."

And the ole girl went out to play somewhere like the girls do now, and the ole woman went off to church. She sitting on outer edge of the arbor, you know, kinda where her boy could see her. And them old-timers was more watchfully, you know, and she kept watching you know, and they'd watch they skillet fire and so she would watch back and look. So the ole girl come in, and when she did think of the head, why she come in and, boy, the head was jest a-kicking; that old head was jest a-heating, and steam had it jest a-turning over and over and all down side of the pot — drop — dumplings had done kicked out, you know, and dropped down on the side of the pot on the stove — one of the worst looking wrecks you'd ever seen. Ole dumplings had done fell out, you know.

Then the boy come running in behind the girl and jest tore out to the church house jest as hard as he could, running; jest before he got there his momma seen him. She started waving her hand and beckoning for him to slow down and wait 'till she come to him, you know. He jest kept a-running and when he got closter, she jest start winking her eye at him and tole him to stop.

He say, "Oh, don't be a-winking and a-blinking, momma; come on home quick." Say, "That ole sheep's done butted all those dumplings outa the pot!"

## The Travelers

Onct upon a time they was two men traveling and in them days they wasn't any railroads; they hadn't even seen a railroad track; some people had. These folks was traveling; they got tired and they thought they would lay down for a rest, but they didn't know they had laid down clost by a railroad track at all. They lay down and it was the early part of the night, but they both dropped off to sleep they was so tired. They just slept and slept and slept. Train came along 'bout twelve or one o'clock. One of them woked up and he seen the train pass and he didn't know what it was. Them lights all lighted up and that great big bull eye on the front throwed the light way down on the track, you know; he didn't know what to make of it; but he didn't even wake his partner up; jest let it go by. But it wasn't long till another train come by; it jest blow and blow, "Hooo-o-o! Hoooo-o-o! Hoo-hoo-hoo-hoo."

Other one had done passed and gone on and this one come jest a-blowing; so man jest shook his partner, said, "Wake up; looka here what's going on here. Wake up quick and look." Said, "What do you know 'bout this? Hell done moved one load and it's going to move the other one."

## Slave Hears God and the Devil Counting Souls

In the days of old — well, you could call it slavery times. On one plantation they was a Marster, he had a boy they called him Sambo. Well, he choose this boy rather than all the others. Marster happened to be a cripple; he was onable to walk. And he had this boy to carry him, everywhere, carry him in his rolling cart, and he 'tend to his horse, hitch his horse up and drive his horse to the town fur him; he rode him around from business place to business place in town. They was many other plantations clost by where the old-timey colored people would have they Saturday night's dance for a good time and that's all they could get outa life in them days. They didn't have any transportation only to go by foot and that was enough for them.

Well, Sambo ast his Marster one Saturday as he went along to town, "Marster," he said, "I'd like to go to the dance tonight if I could get off."

Marster said, "Yeah, you can get off when your work's all done tonight; why you go right ahead."

Well, he finished his work; got it all done and tole his Marster he believed he'd go then. He had to go by a cemetry; he was walking along between sundown and dark; it was clost to dark. As he got clost to the cemetry he heard a voice and he stopped and listened and it was some parties that taken some roasting ears outa somebody's plantation and they was a-counting the roasting ears. The olden days the way of counting, they didn't count like peoples do now that's up in larning and teaching. They counted, "One for me and one for you. One for me and one for you." And they had two sacks for roasting ears, and as they went through the gate they dropped two down there at the gate and they knew they dropped them, but they were a-getting away and didn't want to stop. And Sambo heard and he rushed back to the house jest as hard as he could run and calls to his Marster when he got there.

Said, "Marster! Marster!"

"What do you want, Sambo?"

Says, "I was passing by the cemetry while ago and I heard somebody talking down there and it's God and the devil; they's a-counting souls down there in the cemetry."

Marster tole him, "Now, Sambo, that ain't true."

Sambo say, "Yes, sir, Marster, it's so!"

Say, "You take me down there; you roll the car out and take me down there and if it ain't so I'm going to give you a thousand lashings."

Say, "I don't care, Marster; you can give me as many lashings as you wants; it's true!"

So he put his Marster in the rolling chair and started out and got down the road and heard the same voice, "One for me and one for you. One for me and one for you."

Marster say, "Yeah, I hears it; I hears it now, but roll me up a little bit closter."

So he rolled him on a little bit closter, but Sambo was awful scared; he didn't want to go any further; could still hear him counting, "One for me and one for you. One for me and one for you."

"Roll me on up to the gate."

Sambo say, "Marster, now that's God and the devil counting souls; you're getting mighty clost; you jest shouldn't go up there."

"That's all right; roll me on up to the gate!" He roll him on up to the gate and time he got to the gate he heard him still counting; he was jest bout through.

He said, "One for me and one for you. One for me and one for you." Say, "You know them two down at the gate — you take one and I'll take the other."

And ole Marster rolled outa the cart — he never walk a step in his life before, and he beat the little nigger to the house. Jest outrun him and was there sitting at the house when he got there.

## The Hanted House

In the olden days peoples used to travel without any transportation and mostly they walked — no cars, no trains and very few horses for people to ride then. People usually didn't have horseback riding anywhere they wanted to go and at any time, so they walked. And so it was a walking traveler; he had jest walked and walked for days till he had walked hisself down, and he was tired and he walked to a town. It was lots of people and in those days the peoples didn't mind letting a person stay all night; you could mostly walk up to anybody's house and ask could you stay all night and they would welcome you in. Course, days like it is now, nobody trusts peoples and they would not welcome them in to stay all night 'cause they find them too tricky.

And this ole boy went to a home and hollered, "Hello!"

Someone come out. "Could I stay all night?"

"No, we's all crowded; we don't have a place for anybody

tonight; go down to the next neighbor down there and perhaps he'll let you stay."

He walked down to the other neighbor and walked in. Said, "Hello!"

They come to the door. "Can I stay all night?"

That was the rules in them days; they'd ask to stay all night and they'd take them in. But he said, "No, I'm sorry but I'm crowded out; but it's a ole house down the road; it's a farmhouse and it's a mansion; it's the most beautiful house in this town; it's jest a very pretty house; nice big building and it's plenty in there; you won't have to worry 'bout food; you won't have to worry 'bout bed clothing; you won't have to worry 'bout nothing. All you got to do is to go in there and take over, but I don't believe you can stay."

"Well, why? All I want is a permit to stay and I'm shore I'll shore stay because I'm tired."

Say, "Well, you welcome to go on and stay and take over and have everything like you want; it's a fine place but nobody's ever been able to stay there."

"Well, all I want is permission to stay."

So he walked on down there; it was about two miles and he walked and walked; he made it there. Doh was not locked; all he had to do was to take over; he walked in and looked around and it was jest beautiful inside; was so nice; oh, Lord, it was pretty. Well, the first thing he done then he preparing himself something to eat. He went into the kitchen and he started to cooking and getting things fixed, you know, and he fix him a fine supper; sat down; eat his supper; and usually after peoples eat they rolls themsefs a cigarette; and in those days it was no ready rolls; peoples jest rolled they cigarettes like the old-timers used to do; roll them and light them; so he rolls his and light it, and he was sitting there a-smoking. Great big yellow cat come and walked on through the house; he didn't pay no 'tention to it, but say, "Well, good gracious that's a big cat! Guess he jest a cat in this house." Cat didn't pay no 'tention to the man and man didn't pay no 'tention to the cat. Cat walk through into another room; then after a little while the man was still smoking his cigarette, directly the cat come walking back; sit way up; great big tall cat sitting up there and drectly the cat spoke.

"Boy, it's lonesome here tonight; ain't nobody here but me and you, is they?"

And the fellow said, "No, dogone it; they ain't going to be nobody here but you!"

And he jest busted the floors a-going home. He got out and he jest ran and ran and ran through the woods jest a-killing hisself getting away, and he run so he thought he was out of the way of the cat and he sit down and say, "Well I'm going to rest a little bit now; I'm not going back there." So he a-sitting there a-resting and a-talking to hisself and he seen something and a great big cat walked up again.

Say, "Oh boy, we really had a race; I didn't know you could run that-a-way."

And he said, "You ain't seen me run yet; the race ain't taken place!"

And he jest run off and left the old cat.

## The Scrawny Calf

In olden days when they was settling up the country well the ranchers had big ranches and the ranches was well stocked off. And they had, some of them, lots and lots of cattle, and on one ranch they had acres and acres of land and thousands of head of cattle and they had lota cowboys in there a-working all the time and they would take out their lunch and they would take the doctoring materials, ropes, and doctor for worms and different stuff. Why they would ride up on the stock upon the range that needed doctoring and when they got through that, why later on in the spring when the boss man thought that all of his stock was ready to go to market he would have the boys to round up, to drive them in to corrals to pen them for market; of course they would have them branded and marked; working hard all the time with they stock.

But one year they rode up on a little scrawny calf and the boss man told them to leave it alone because it wouldn't do to go to market; to let it grow and get full developed more so. And they let it go by and the next year they rode up on the little calf in the cut-back, — bringing out, branding, roping and riding — they rode up on it again and it wasn't no bigger than it was the first year they rode up on it. It was hongry; it was poor; it was appetity and grazing hard and the boss told them to leave it alone, not to bring it because it was too little and wouldn't do.

And so the year go by, and they went out to cut back and brand, and they rode up on it again in the same condition, and the boss tole them to let it alone and the next year if it wasn't no better, why they would jest shoot it because it was jest eating up the grass and wasn't no good and wasn't developing. And so the next year *did* come and they was cutting back, riding, roping and branding, and they ran up on it again, and it was little and appetity and hongry and had not gathered any flesh and so the boss demanded them jest to kill it — shoot it. At the same time the boss had been missing the stock; cattle had been disappearing; fences had been cut and everything, and they did not know what had happened.

So they shot this little ole calf, and they found it was a Indian disguised wrapped up in calfskin, jest a-grazing, and as soon as the privilege and the time came ripe, well it drove the cattle out. And when they killed it, they never missed any more cattle because it was a disguised Indian.

## Turkey and Wild Indians

The country was trying to get settled up; the old settlers was moving in slow and the Indians was here. Plenty of them — the Indians; they was all kind of wild Indians then in this olden days, and the old settlers was very fond of hunting wild turkeys, but the Indians had those little old Indian caves under the ground. And the old-timers whenever they taken a notion to go out on a wild turkey hunt, they would get they guns and start out early in the morning, 'bout the time the wild turkeys begin their gobbling at the saying of daylight in the morning; could hear the wild turkeys from up in the trees; they would be agoing, "Gooly, gooly, gooly!" The old-timey hunters would answer them back; they would holler, "Gooly, gooly, gooly!" And they would follow those wild turkeys sometimes and maybe sometimes they would get a chance to shoot one, but the most of the time the Indians, they larned to trap those; they would stay under the ground and the old-timers could never tell where they was. And sometimes they would call the turkeys, "Gooly, gooly, gooly!" And the Indians they would answer them back and they would think it was a wild turkey, and they would advance and advance, thinking it was a wild turkey, and they would keep a-talking to the turkey, and every time they hollered the old Indian would say, "Gooly, gooly, gooly!" They would answer back. Of course it would continue on that way and so when they got clost enough to the Indian harbor, the Indian would usually shoot the turkey hunter, and the turkey hunter would never get back home again, and the people would never know what happened to him.

So at last one day another turkey hunter went out and he was talking to the turkeys and the turkey would gobble back, and so he walked up one morning a-hollering, "Gooly, gooly, gooly!" And he heard an onusual voice, "Gooly, gooly, gooly!" And he went ahead and kep walking; drectly he discovered one of those Indians with a big feather on his cap under the ground, and he stuck his head out of the hole and he said, "Gooly, gooly, gooly!" And so the hunter answered him back and jest as the Indian raised his head to holler, the hunter shot him and killed him, and that was the last of the wild Indians.

## Possums Turns to Pigs

In the olden slavery days, old Marster had a slave on his place, and he forgot to tell him what he wanted him to do before he left the house, and he want him to come real early the next morning and do something around the place that he wanted him to do and he didn't tell 'im. He thought he would walk down to the house that night after supper and tell 'im, but he saw 'im come up early that morning. This fellow was a great hunter; he hunted all the time and he caught coons and he caught possums, different things like that, and he eat 'em. He taken a notion one day he'd pick up a coupla of his Marster's pigs and take them home. He fix them as people use to do when they use to cook the little baby pigs, you know, and put red apples in they mouths and bake 'em. Well, he taken a coupla pigs along and dressed them, had 'em on the fire cooking, and about that time his Marster walked up, want to know what he had and he says, "Well," he says, "I put two possums in the kettle to cook and it's the funniest thing that you'd ever seen in your life. I've never seen that before in my life, that two possums could turn to a pair of pigs!"

## The Deer Hunters

Onct upon a time they was two colored people and they did not know what a deer was; they jest heard other peoples talk about deers, and they wanted to kill a deer; so they went out on a fellow's farm and ast him could they deer hunt on his place. He tole them, yes, they could go out.

So they had they guns all ready, and he said, "Wait a minute; I know where they's a great big one."

He say, "You can kill you one."

But neither one of them had ever seen one; didn't know what a deer was; didn't know what it look like.

Say, "I'll tell you; if you go off on down there, right straight down there until you get to that mound of bresh, and it's a deer in there all the time — a great big buck; it's easy to kill; it's right gentle; it ain't wild; and I know you can kill it."

So they walk on down there. One of them says, "Now listen," say, "now you go on that side of the brush and I stay round this way and watch, you know. I'll go in there and jest ease through that and it will walk out and then you shoot it."

So this fellow walked around on the opposite side of the bresh and this other fellow kept a-easing on through there; he was a-watching for the deer; and the one was on the off side kept a-looking and a-watching. And the wind was blowing; it blowed the smell of the other fellow off, and the one the wind didn't blow the odor to; why the deer came to him. And here come the deer jest a-walking along; the other fellow jest follow along through the bresh; jest look every minute; maybe he'd hear that fellow shoot because the deer was gentle, and drectly the deer came a-walking out, and the fellow seen it but he never knowed what a deer looked like, and he stood up there and looked at it real good, you know, and he was all the same time a-watching the bresh for the deer to come out; but he looking at that one walk by, and drectly the man walked through the bresh and look out.

Say, "Did you see the deer?"

Said, "No."

Say, "Didn't see nothing come out at all?"

"Oh, no, I never seen a thing come out at all, only a man come walking out here with a big rocking chair on his head."

# Contributors

JOHN Q. ANDERSON teaches English at Texas Agricultural and Mechanical College. He wrote a dissertation on Emerson under Floyd Stovall at the University of North Carolina.

ROY BEDICHEK is Director Emeritus of the Bureau of Public School Service. This official title may be unfamiliar, but everybody knows of Mr. Bedichek's part in organizing and maintaining the Texas Interscholastic League. In his travels about the state, Mr. Bedichek preferred to camp out rather than sleep in town, so that he could be close to and study wild life. *Adventures with a Texas Naturalist*, his first book, was published in 1947, and *Karánkaway Country*, his second, in 1950. Both are a rich combination of facts and philosophy brought together by a mind nourished on a wide variety of reading and observation. When Mr. Bedichek has finished writing his history of the Interscholastic League, he will no doubt return to the nature subjects that he knows and loves so well.

MODY C. BOATRIGHT followed J. Frank Dobie as editor for the Texas Folklore Society. He is professor and chairman of the English department at the University of Texas, where he teaches courses in the literature of the West and the Southwest. Besides a number of shorter articles in the field of folklore, he is the author of *Gib Morgan: Minstrel of the Oil Fields* (Texas Folklore Society Publication XX, 1945) and *Folk Laughter on the American Frontier* (Macmillan, 1949). He is now completing a book on the growth of the cowboy myth in America.

GABRIEL CÓRDOVA teaches at Bowie High School in El Paso. He has acted as interpreter for the El Paso municipal courts, where he learned of the first instance of witchcraft reported in his contribution. He has collected folklore of all sorts in the El Paso region and in Chihuahua. In 1952 he took third place in the competition for the Jo Stafford Prize in American Folklore.

J. FRANK DOBIE has been for years the strongest moving force behind the study and the creation of literature in the Southwest. His latest book is *The Mustangs,* published in 1952. "A Plot of Earth," which appeared in the Spring, 1953, issue of the *Southwest Review,* may be the beginning of an autobiography. It is hoped that Mr. Dobie will go on with the story.

EVERETT A. GILLIS is a teacher of English at Texas Technological College. In 1948 he received the doctor's degree at the University of Texas. He is a publishing poet as well as a teacher.

JOSEPH W. HENDREN teaches at Western Maryland College in Westminster. While on the faculty at Rice, he contributed an article on the sources of "The Trail to Mexico" to *Coyote Wisdom,* the Texas Folklore Society's publication for 1938. A student of Gerould's at Princeton, Mr. Hendren has published a number of articles on the ballad and also a book, *A Study of Ballad Rhythm* (Princeton, 1938). On the subject of rhythm and music in the ballad, Mr. Hendren is a leading scholar.

GEORGE D. HENDRICKS teaches at North Texas State College. He is the author of *The Bad Man of the West* (San Antonio: Naylor, 1941), now in its second edition. In 1951 he completed *Western Wild Animals,* a doctoral dissertation written at the University of Texas under Mody Boatright's supervision. At the spring 1953 meeting, Mr. Hendricks was elected President of the Texas Folklore Society for 1953-54.

PEGGY HENDRICKS comes from a family that helped establish Tyler as a rose-growing center. She is the wife of George D. Hendricks. She lives in Denton and has two children.

JAMES HOWARD has taught in both the history and the English departments at the University of Texas. He is now working on a history of Dallas since 1910, which he will present as his doctoral dissertation at Harvard.

WILSON M. HUDSON teaches English at the University of Texas. Among his courses is Life and Literature of the Southwest, which was originated by Mr. Dobie. He has contributed several Mexican folk tales to the publications of the Texas Folklore Society, and he edited *The Healer of Los Olmos* for the Society in 1951.

ELIZABETH HURLEY has worked as reporter and editor on several Texas daily papers. She taught journalism at the Texas State College for Women from 1951 to 1953, and now is teaching the same subject at Pampa High School. To collect material for her article she made a two-thousand-mile tour over the state in the summer of 1951.

ELTON R. MILES is professor of English and chairman of the department at Sul Ross State Teachers College. He took the doctor's degree at the University of Texas in 1952.

AMÉRICO PAREDES is from Brownsville. He has just completed "Ballads of the Lower Border," a master's thesis written under R. C. Stephenson and Mody Boatright at the University of Texas. Mr. Paredes, who is himself a *guitarrero* and singer, plans to continue studying the Texas-Mexican border ballads in the field.

E. J. RISSMANN is a business man in Austin, Texas. He tells something about his early life on Bear Creek in his article. In a letter to the editors he says, "In the back of my mind has been an ambition to write a book of some sort about the Bear Creek country."

ORLAN L. SAWEY teaches at Texas College of Arts and Industries. He has just completed "The Cowboy Autobiography," a doctor's dissertation written under Mody Boatright at the University of Texas. An essay of his, "Pipe-Line Diction," contributed to the Texas Folklore Society's annual for 1943, has been frequently referred to by students of the language of oil workers.

RICHARD SMITH lives at La Vernia, Texas. He has been working in dairies for a long time. As he says, "I got my dairy calling when I was about ten or eleven years old." He worked on the dairy farm of the Sinclair family for five years. Many years afterwards the late John Lang Sinclair, author of "The Eyes of Texas," invited his old friend to visit him in New York. Recognizing Richard's ability as a storyteller, Mr. Sinclair had Richard record a number of his stories on the office Dictaphone. Later, Mrs. Sinclair (Stella A. Sinclair) transcribed Richard's dictation. She has kindly permitted the Texas Folklore Society to make a selection from Richard's stories, all of which she intends to publish in a book of their own.

ROBERT C. STEPHENSON teaches English, Spanish, and comparative literature at the University of Texas. Among his courses is one in the European ballad. He has a wide linguistic range.

# INDEX

Afanasyev, 191-92
Alonso de Morales, 101
Alvírez, Rosita, 112-14
"Amantes de Teruel, Los," 94
Anderson, John Q.: "Emerson and the Language of the Folk," 152-59
Andrews, Roy Chapman, 35
Anecdotes, 1-17
Animals; see specific names of
Animals, grateful, 108
Animals, wild: names of, 40-46
Anthem, 9-10
Arbor, brush, 244

"Babylon; or, the Bonnie Banks o Fordie," 92
Bad news, breaking, 10-13
"Baffled Knight, The," 55
Ball, magic, 218-19
*Ballada*, the Russian, 86-96
Ballad types, Chernyshev's
C4, 94
C6, 89
C33-35, 90
C121, 93
C171, 93
C212, 93
C213, 94
C244, 93
C249, 92
C250, 92
C259, 92
C262, 93
C324, 93
C325, 94
C328, 94
C329, 93
C334, 93
Ballads, 47-74, 86-96, 97-109, 110-14; see ballad titles
"Barbara Allen," 47-74
Bat, vampire, 28-31
Bear, Mr., 220-24, 235-38
Bear steals baby, 238-40
Becero, 100, 102
Bedichek, Roy: "Folklore in Natural History," 18-39
Bent, A. C., 24
Big Bend, 205-16
Big Lake Field, 80-82, 83, 84

Bighorn, 40-41
Birds, hibernation of, 24-25
Bird's song, 21
Blair, W. Frank, 24
Boatright, Mody C.: "Aunt Cordie's Ax and Other Motifs in Oil," 75-85
Border ballads, 110-14
"Braes of Yarrow, The," 55
Breland, Osmond P., 24, 25
Buffalo hide, 16-17
Bullfrog, 23-24

Calf disguise, 249-50
Cannibalism, 190-91
Cat in haunted house, 248-49
Cattle brands, 171-82
Cats, Manx, 32-33
Colt comes to life, 241-42
Coon, Mr., 220-24
Córdova, Gabriel: "Black and White Magic on the Texas-Mexican Border," 195-99
*Corrido*, Mexican, 87, 100, 113
"Corrido de Rosita Alvírez, El," 113
Cougar, 41-42
Counting souls, 245-47
Coyote and heron, 8-9
Cries, street, 115-38
"Cruel Mother, The," 55, 93
*Curandero, curandera*, 196, 198-99

Dances, 143, 144-45, 207
Darwin, Charles, 30
*Decameron, The*, 17
Deer hunters, 252-53
Devil, 205-16, 245-47
Devil's Grotto, 211
Ditmars, R. L., 30
Dobie, Bertha McKee, 188
Dobie, J. Frank: "The Traveling Anecdote," 1-17
"Doncella guerra, La," 89
Dunn, John, 14-15
Dust, 8

Early, Gen. Jubal, 3-4
"Edward," 63
Emerson, Ralph Waldo, 152-59
Espinosa, A. M., 184, 190

259

## INDEX

"Fair Flower of Northumberland, The," 94
"Fair Margaret and Sweet William," 67, 92
Folk language, 152-59
Folk tales, 97-109; type 366, 183-94, 217-19, 220-53; see Tales
Folkways, 139-51
Fowler Farm Oil Company, 78
Fox, 35-36
Fox, Mr., 220-24
"Frankie and Albert," 99, 113
"Frankie and Johnny," 113
Frog, Mr., 236-37

"Gay Goshawk, The," 94
Gillett, Capt. James B., 8
Gillis, Everett A.: "Weather Talk from the Cap Rock," 200-204
Golden arm or leg, 183-94
Goodnight, Charlie, 4
Grant, Ulysses S., 5
"Guarinos," 87, 89
Guns, 6-7

Harris, Joel Chandler, 8, 191
Hartman, Carl G., 31
Haunted house, 247-49
Hawking cries, 115-38
Heart, witch's, 219
Hendren, Joseph W.: "Bonny Barbara Allen," 47-74
Hendricks, George D.: "The Names of Western Wild Animals," 40-46
Hendricks, Peggy: "Wham, Jam, Jenny-Mo-Wham," 217-19
*Heptameron, The*, 17
Heron and coyote, 8-9
Holy Cross Day, 211, 213
Houston, Sam, 1-2
Howard, James: "Tales of Neiman-Marcus," 160-70
Hurley, Elizabeth: "Come Buy, Come Buy," 115-38
Hudson, Wilson M.: "I Want My Golden Arm," 183-94

Indian: disguised as calf, 249-50; calling turkey, 250-51
Ivan the Fool, 104-8

Jackson, Governor, 12-13

La Fontaine, 107
Language of the folk, 152-59
Larsen, Henning, 16
"London Bridge Is Falling Down," 144
"Lord Randal," 63

Magic, black and white, 195-99
Magic ball, 218-19
"Man from the Gallows, The," 188-89
Margaret of Navarre, Queen, 17
Mark Twain, 11, 184, 201
Matthews, Brander, 15
McClesky, John and Cordie, 75-78, 84
McGinnis, John, 11
McNeil, Irving, 22-23
Miles, Elton R.: "The Devil in the Big Bend," 205-16
Motif, 15; the new ax, 75-78, 84; the lucky breakdown, 78-82, 84; the million-dollar drink, 82-84, 106; E. 235.4.1, 183-94
Mud, 7-8
Mule and ox, 240-41

Natural history in folklore, 18-39
Negroes, 242-43, 243-45, 245-47, 251-52, 252-53
Neiman-Marcus, 160-70

Oil, motifs in, 75-85
Ojinaga, Mexico, 205-16
Opossum, 28, 31-32, 42-44, 251-52
"Our Goodman," 90, 91
Owl, burrowing, 20
Owl and hen, 33-35
Ox and mule, 240-41

Panther, 16
Paredes, Américo: "The Love Tragedy in Texas-Mexican Balladry," 110-14
Pérez, Soledad, 189
Pickrell, Frank, 81, 82, 83
Pig, praying, 27-28
Place names, 205
Play parties, 143
Possums turned to pigs, 251-52
Prairie dog, 44-45
Preachers, 6
Presidio, Texas, 205-16
Pushkin, 91, 95-96 n. 10

"Queen of Elfan's Nourice, The," 99

Rabbit, Mr., 220-24, 224-30, 230-33, 233-35, 235-38, 241-42
"Ram of Darby, The," 102
Rat's tail, 26
Rattlesnakes, 148
Resuscitation, 219
Rissmann, E. J.: "Folkways on Bear Creek," 139-51
Robin Hood ballads, 60, 92, 96 n. 11, 100

# INDEX

*Romance*, Spanish, 88, 89, 90, 91, 98
Roosevelt, F. D., 5
Roosevelt, Teddy, 10
Russell, Emeline B., 187-88, 191
Rust, John, 76-77

Sawey, Orlan L.: "Origins of Uvalde County Cattle Brands," 171-82
Scott, Sir Walter, 95 n. 10
Sheep, stealing, 242-43
Sheep-head dumplings, 243-45
"Shoot the Buffalo," 144
Signature in ballads and folk tales, 97-109
Silence, breaking, 13-15
Silver toe, 188, 191; see Golden arm
Simmons, James R., 35
Sinclair, John Lang, 220, 256
Sinclair, Stella A., 220, 256
Singing, 143-44
"Sir Neil and Glengyle," 55
Smith, Richard: "Richard's Tales," 220-53
Snake swallowing young, 35, 36-37
Stephenson, R. C.: "The Western Ballad and the Russian *Ballada*," 86-96; "Signature in Ballad and Story," 97-109
Strahorn, Carrie Adell, 9
"Sugar Lump-O," 144
Sunflower, 18
"Sweet William's Ghost," 93

Taily-Po, 191
Tales, 160-70, 220-53; *see* Folk tales
Talk about weather, 200-204
Taylor, George C., 12
Teeny-Tiny, 190
Thomas, Gates, 1
"Thomas Rymer," 104
Ticks, 33
*Tragedias*, 112, 114
Train from hell, 245
"Twa Corbies, The," 91, 99
"Twa Sisters, The," 93, 102

*Uncle Remus Returns*, 191
Urbán, Cura, 205-16

Vance, Zeb, 2-4

"Walking on the Green Grass," 144
Wallace, Alfred Russell, 29-30
Wallace, Bigfoot, 4
Wardlaw, Frank, 3
Watterson, Col. Henry, 15
Weather, talk about, 200-204
Weaver, Joe, 77
Whaley, William G., 18
Whiskey, 15-16
"Who Killed Cock Robin?" 94
Witches and witchcraft, 195-99, 217-19
Woodpecker, pileated, 22-23
Wolf, Mr., 220-24, 224-30, 230-33, 233-35, 241-42

www.ingramcontent.com/pod-product-compliance
Lightning Source LLC
Chambersburg PA
CBHW030311080526
44584CB00012B/528